THE FINANCIAL PLANNER:
A New Professional

THE Financial Planner: A NEW PROFESSIONAL...

Yesterday-Today-Tomorrow

Loren Dunton

President, National Center for Financial Education

While a great deal of care has been taken to provide accurate and current information, the ideas, suggestions, general principles, and conclusions presented in this book are subject to local, state, and federal laws and regulations, court cases, and any revisions of same. The reader is thus urged to consult legal counsel regarding any points of law—this publication should not be used as a substitute for competent legal advice.

©1986 by Longman Group USA Inc.

Published by Longman Financial Services Publishing, Inc./Chicago a Longman Group USA company

All rights reserved. The text of this publication, or any part thereof, may not be reproduced in any manner whatsoever without written permission from the publisher.

Printed in the United States of America.

86 87 88 10 9 8 7 6 5 4 3 2 1

Library of Congress Cataloging-in-Publication Data

Dunton, Loren.
  The financial planner.

  1. Financial planners—United States. 2. Investment advisers—United States. 3. Investment analysis—United States. I. Title.
HG179.5.D85 1986   332.024'01   85-23821
ISBN 0-88462-544-3

Acquisitions Editor: Ivy Lester

Development Editor: Karen Berger

Cover/Internal Design: Cameron Poulter

Senior Production Coordinator: Vicki M. Weisberg

To my wife Marta, who has been willing to
help the NCFE in so many ways...

and

To my longtime friend, Christopher Hegarty, who not only helped create the financial planning profession all those years ago, but who was the first to do something for consumers by serving as board chairman of the National Center for Financial Education.

"Profession...
a calling requiring specialized knowledge and academic preparation."

"Professional...
one that engages in a pursuit or activity professionally."
Websters 'New Ideal' Dictionary

CONTENTS

Preface ix

Part One: The Need 1
Chapter 1 The Rich Get Richer 4
Chapter 2 Social Security: Yesterday and Today 9
Chapter 3 The Need for Financial Education and Planning 12
    An Interview with Bob Leary 17

Part Two: The Way It Was 21
Chapter 4 The Stock Broker and the Securities Industry 23
Chapter 5 The Insurance Agent and the Mutual Fund Rep 28
    An Interview with H.L. Jamieson 32
Chapter 6 The Banker 34
    An Interview with Donald R. Pitti 41

Part Three: The Influences of Change 47
Chapter 7 Financial Writers and Talkers 49
Chapter 8 The Society and Its Divisions 55
    An Interview with John Keeble 64

Part Four: Financial Counseling Today 67
Chapter 9 Financial Planning as an Add-on 68
Chapter 10 The Sales Approach 75
    An Interview with Edward W. Chin and Oliver M. Stafford 86

Part Five: The Step Beyond 91
Chapter 11 Financial Planning: Upper and Lower Case 92
Chapter 12 Financial Planning: Lower Case 99
Chapter 13 Financial Planning: Upper Case 104
    An Interview with Edwin P. Morrow 113

Part Six: Important Scenes in the Picture 117
Chapter 14 The Giants: A New Force 118
Chapter 15 The Computer and Its Roles 129
Chapter 16 The Academic World 138

Part Seven: Perspectives, Dangers and a Look Ahead 143
Chapter 17 An Analogy to Physical Health 145
Chapter 18 Regulation: Coming and Needed 150
Chapter 19 Chronicling a New Profession 156

Part Eight: Building on the Foundation 165
Chapter 20 Today's International Association
 for Financial Planning 167
Chapter 21 The College for Financial Planning............................173
Chapter 22 The Institute of Certified Financial Planners 177
Chapter 23 Networks, Services, and Other Associations 181

Part Nine: The Financial Planning Career 189
Chapter 24 The Career Counselor's Dilemma 191
Chapter 25 Is This Career for Me? 200
Chapter 26 Questions, Answers, Predictions and Warnings 210

Part Ten: Who's Who in Financial Planning............................219
Self-Profiles
  Alexandra Armstrong..224
  Ben Baldwin..226
  James A. Barry, Jr 229
  John T. Blankinship, Jr 222
  Graydon K. Calder 235
  Bill E. Carter 237
  Kenneth and Donna Carter 240
  Martin J. Cohen 242
  Stephen P. Donaldson...245
  P. Kemp Fain, Jr. 247
  Robert W. P. Holstrom..249
  Charles G. Hughes, Jr...251
  H.W. Kasey Jones..255
  David M. King..257
  Lawrence A. Krause 259
  Vincent A. Lazara...262
  James E. Moss..264
  Lee D. Pennington 266
  Gary Pittsford 270
  Robert Poage...273
  Andrew Michael Rich...275
  Gilman Robinson 277
  Morris G. Sahr 279
  Edward H. Savant..281
  Harry Scheyer 284
  Robert J. Underwood...287
  Venita Van Caspel 290
  Lewis J. Walker...294
  Lewis M. Wallensky 298
  Henry L. Whiffen...301
  Judith Zabalaoui..303
Some Special Notes..306

PREFACE

As with other professions, the role of the financial planner arose out of change and need. Changes following World War II had a tremendous impact on how Americans viewed and handled personal finances. During the postwar years, we observed the rise and delineation of the middle class, an increase in the number of college-bound students, the growth of the Baby Boom generation, and the greater number of a person's retirement years. Meanwhile, financial changes such as rising income taxes, inflation, more discretionary income, tax shelters, mutual funds and others influenced the lives of people in the 1940s, 1950s, and 1960s.

By the 1960s, the need for intelligent planning for our personal financial futures became apparent. But, it wasn't until the 1970s that concrete action plans began surfacing. Recognizing the need, more and more mutual fund sales representatives and insurance agents began taking on tasks that would eventually lead to the practice of financial planning, as we refer to it today.

Gradually, others in the financial industries recognized that the counseling posture was more effective than an attack on other segments' products. More financial industries noticed that while objective advice and counsel might defer or even cost an occasional sale, it frequently brought greater long-term dividends in the form of long-standing client relationships.

As more people in the 1960s and 1970s found themselves in higher tax brackets, willingness to seek and pay for financial advice developed naturally. In turn, the financial industry began watching the rise of an increasing number of fee-only financial planners.

This book offers an inside look at the way the financial planning profession evolved and the implications of that new breed of professionals to those practicing in the financial services industry, as well as to those who might want to choose financial planning as a career.

The emergence of a profession, of course, also depends on factors other than need. There must be at least a small body of practitioners informally filling that need, and eventually they must be recognized by people outside the discipline.

An association to which individuals can belong is also necessary. While not crucial, local chapters and regular meetings with other professionals contribute greatly to the growth necessary for the attainment of professional status. A code of ethics and its provisions are essential, so that some standards can be maintained by the professionals.

While we certainly can acquire expertise on our own, and frequently do, individual and collective professional recognition is often achieved by having a recognized academic institution and a course of study. As a requirement for certification, proctored examinations add more credence to the new profession. They also assist in public and professional acceptance of financial planners.

Finally, at least during the 20th century, in order for a new profession to emerge and gain recognition, it needs both its own publication and a national educational certification program.

While I did the research, conceptualized the necessary structure, and formed the organizations that could make the financial planning industry a profession, I merely provided the foundation. A founder owes far more to the thousands of people who help his or her dreams come true than those people owe the founder. Today, thanks to many such people, I see the financial planning service gain recognition as a profession and the financial planner as a new professional.

The Financial Planning Profession

To be more complete and of greater value to those interested in the profession, this book includes a number of interviews following many of the chapters. The people interviewed are some of the pioneers and developers of the financial planning profession.

I hope that the interviews will give readers—whether students, scholars, career counselors, history buffs, practitioners, or others involved in the financial services industry—a portrait of the financial planning profession of yesterday, today and tomorrow.

Coast-to-Coast Financial Planner Profiles

The financial planners profiled at the end of this book constitute a cross-section of the financial planning profession. They represent a wide variety in terms of age, sex, style of operation, and experience. However, these are only a sample; many of the finest and best known financial planners had to be left out. They know who they are and, in many cases, so do I.

Not everyone who claims to be a financial planner is, of course. But, for the most part, financial planners are sincere and conscientious practitioners who enjoy a real satisfaction from preparing individual plans (often with the help of a computer) to help people accumulate or conserve assets and achieve specific financial goals. Naturally, the *implementation* of those plans, not the plans themselves, makes for a better life.

The financial planner self-profiles in this book are not standardized. I want you to know them as they see themselves and as they view their profession. I admire them, along with the many others that space precluded me from including in this book. I think you will, also.

LOREN DUNTON
PRESIDENT,
NATIONAL CENTER FOR FINANCIAL EDUCATION

PART ONE

The Need

"If Your Free Enterprise System
Is So Good...."

"If your free enterprise system is so good, Mr. Dunton, then why do you have to turn to socialism to take care of your retired people?"

Twice I was challenged but unable to answer that question, while my wife and I were taking our two teen-age daughters on a year-long trip around the world. To make the trip, we cashed in our life insurance, sold our stocks, leased our home, and visited 25 countries. We made it an education, not a vacation.

Later, I learned that President Kennedy had delivered a speech to Congress in which he observed that 95 percent of the nation's people were dependent upon Social Security when they retired. Skeptics in my audiences, including people with communist or socialist sympathies, were referring to that speech to disparage the free enterprise system of the U.S.

Obviously, they reasoned, something *was* wrong with the concept on which this system was based. Even if the free enterprise system provided more material benefits, more freedom of choice, and more lifestyle options than any other government or society in the history of the world, it still resulted in a large percentage of people depending upon a social security system that was conceived mainly to prevent destitution in old age.

The inconsistency puzzled me, too. So, when I returned to the United States, I did some research. I found out that while we were doing an outstanding job in this country of getting people to *spend* their money, we weren't showing them how to put much aside for the future. The competitive relationship among different segments of the financial industry was contributing to a problem, rather than offering a solution.

"Internecine warfare" is what I called it. The insurance agents were criticizing securities, telling their clients that more insurance was the answer to almost every financial question. The mutual fund representatives were, in turn, ridiculing insurance and recommending their favorite fund instead, while the stock brokers often were promoting first one stock and then another, to keep turning over accounts for a little extra commission. Meanwhile, the neighborhood real estate broker was lauding properties as the answer to accumulating wealth, while the banker was insisting that the only safe place for money was in the bank.

Certainly, such blatant criticism of other segments of the financial industry to make one's particular segment look golden in comparison was one cause of damage. In addition, the government was giving free rein to companies and industries that encouraged people to spend freely today with little regard for tomorrow's consequences, while it simultaneously closely regulated and restricted companies that were trying to get people to put more of their personal finances aside for the future.

During that period, other forces also were at work. The development of Social Security was gradually lulling not only the potential poor but also the growing middle classes into a false sense of security about retirement income. The government encouraged the idea that it, not the individual, was responsible for our future well-being. The savings mentality instilled by frugal parents and grandparents was being eroded by a Congress that decided a good way to assure votes and loyalty was to provide greater Social Security benefits.

Given little incentive to save for the future, Americans were an easy target for Madison Avenue hucksters, desiring more and more of their discretionary dollars. It became common for consumers to spend their next paycheck before they even received it. Indeed, it wasn't long thereafter that the seductive influences of easier credit led consumers to spend not next month's but next *year's* income.

Even the government was taking the short view by measuring the health of the economy solely by how much we spent. The more we spent, the healthier our economy and, by inference, ourselves. It became almost patriotic to spend.

I began observing that the cliche, "The rich get richer and the poor get poorer," was ringing all too true. Wanting to do something about it, I initially thought to write a new book. However, as I learned more about bankers, stock brokers and insurance agents, I realized that it would take more than a book to bring about any real and necessary change. The rich who were getting richer were obviously benefiting from something unavailable to others.

That something was informed and objective advice as to how to accumulate money and make it grow. For those fortunate few, legal counsel, tax advice, and estate planning were contributors.

But while the rich had the luxury of considering these options, the lower-and middle-income groups in this country were frequently too busy to give their personal finances much thought. They were merely trying to make ends meet. And, if they even took the time to attempt to consider such options, they rarely could afford objective or knowledgeable advice.

Often, they were exposed to salespeople trying to sell them high-commission insurance. If they hadn't been taken or influenced unduly by the 1929 stock market crash, they frequently were victimized by a stock broker who was more committed to the next commission than to a client's future financial well-being.

The more cautious people who contacted a banker were usually advised to keep their money in the bank, often at a passbook savings rate that couldn't even keep pace with inflation. The more affluent, of course, got to deal with the trust department. However, even the trust departments, charged with "conservation of assets," did a good job of allowing those assets to be consumed by inflation. During the 1950s and 1960s the rich were seeing their money growing at exciting rates in mutual fund deposits, while those with money in bank trust departments were often observing their assets shrink. For many of us, even more frustrating than the internecine warfare amid the banking, securities and insurance industries was the shrinking volume of discretionary dollars earmarked for the future.

I admit, it was with more hope than reality that we began to conceive of a united financial services industry where different segments worked together as a team rather than as individuals, representing self-interests. Still, we undertook with vigor the job of developing a new profession whose members would place their clients first and their companies second.

Someday, maybe even now, these priorities are the norm for financial planning. For today, I wouldn't mind being asked, "If your free enterprise system is so good, Mr. Dunton, then why do you have to turn to socialism to take care of your retired people?" But, today, no one would be likely to ask that question, for it would lack much of its punch, as more people are embracing and implementing financial planning.

1 The Rich Get Richer

The free enterprise system and capitalism both incur criticism. But perhaps none rancors more than the cliche stating, "The rich get richer and the poor get poorer." As a strong proponent of free enterprise since my college days, I admit that statement still infuriates me. But, this observation changed my life:

> It seems like the only people who can get professional and objective financial advice are those who already have accumulated money.

Indeed, that statement used to be true, and not too many years ago either. We were faced with a ridiculous situation in this country of abundant opportunity. The people most needing solid financial advice in order to accumulate or retain money were finding it nearly impossible to obtain that advice. Even people with high incomes too often encountered biased salespeople of one financial product or another.

Worse than the subjective, one-sided pressure was the disparagement each segment insisted on inflicting on other segments of the financial industry. As a result, it's little wonder that as President Kennedy observed, "Less than five percent of the people in this, the richest country in the world, are able to retire without depending on government subsidy."

Fortunately, that statement was made more than 20 years ago. Today, thanks to many committed individuals, many average-income families can obtain objective counseling that will help them achieve long-range financial goals. Such counseling is not coming from someone skilled solely in insurance, mutual funds, securities, banking or real estate. Instead, it often originates from an individual trained in one of these fields, but also educated to consider living trusts, wills, tax shelters, mutual fund timing services, real estate investment trusts, collectibles, gold funds, interest-sensitive insurance, annuities, syndications and numerous other financial tools and approaches that can be specifically tailored to a personal financial plan.

Nor is this multi-product approach limited to the individual financial planner. Companies large and small are beginning to offer prospective and existing clients a myriad of financial products. Some credit larger companies' commitment to the client's best interests was the direction of Donald Regan during his tenure as president of Merrill Lynch. In the early 1970s, he suggested the concept of a department store of financial products.

Nevertheless, it was also noted that "A highly professional financial department store cannot be staffed with clerks or just salespeople, like today's dry goods stores. It will have to be manned by highly trained, qualified, knowledgeable and objective financial counselors."

While not everyone in the financial profession has yet achieved excellence, more are striving today than were even 20 years ago. Some financial planning companies still fall short of complete objectivity in every area. However, more are attempting to achieve that goal today, and the general consumer is benefiting from that commitment.

Licensing and Certification

Today the financial industry is characterized by a burgeoning development of multiple licenses. For example, each state licenses qualified individuals to sell insurance. An NASD (National Association of Securities Dealers) examination is necessary to sell securities, mutual funds and other equity products.

Recognizing the desirability of multiple licensing and greater professionalism within the financial industry, more than 100 companies joined together to support an educational, nonprofit organization—The Society for Financial Counselling, Inc.—between 1969 and 1975.

During the first two years of its inception, this society created two nonprofit organizations. One of them, the International Association of Financial Planners, now known as the International Association for Financial Planning, Inc. (IAFP), currently has more than 20,000 members. The other, the College for Financial Planning, Inc., currently conducts six courses and examinations leading to a professional designation as a CFP (Certified Financial Planner). Each spring and fall, the College conducts conferments for several hundred attendees.

Like the family doctor, the Certified Financial Planner is usually a "general practitioner." That is, he or she can handle 80 to 90 percent of the cases directly. However, like the family doctor, the financial planner may have to refer for specialized assistance. When special expertise is required, such as the services of an attorney, an accountant, a life underwriter, or a chartered financial analyst, today's trained financial planner is usually well-qualified to coordinate these additional services for the client's ultimate benefit.

Designed similarly to the Certified Public Accountant, Chartered Life Underwriter, and Chartered Financial Analyst programs, the program of conceptual financial planning subjects, which was primarily developed by

Jim Johnston and Lew Kearns, began this way:

Financial Planning I	Basic Financial Planning
Financial Planning II	Investments
Financial Planning III	Risk Management
Financial Planning IV	Professionally-Managed Investments
Financial Planning V	Counseling the Business and Professional Person

Later, Dr. William Anthes, president of the College since 1979, updated, toughened, and expanded the courses and examinations to six. Today, the CFP designation is as prestigious as the primary designations in most other professions.

Better Advice Becoming Available

Even more important than the professional designation is the growing recognition of the financial planner's availability not only to the wealthy, but also to most income groups.

In addition to the College for Financial Planning, Inc., nearly 100 other colleges and universities across the country are committed to teaching the financial planning courses conceived by the original college in Denver. (Chapter 21 discusses other collegiate offerings more thoroughly.)

This nationwide availability of academic knowledge and expertise is permitting more people to qualify themselves as financial planners, capable of helping other consumers to avoid financial mishaps. (Chapter 26 will look at this more thoroughly.) As Donald Simon, board chairman of the National Center for Financial Education, observed, "People considering a career helping others achieve long-range financial goals have an unusual satisfaction to look forward to. They can take pride in the fact that they are encouraging people to *save, invest, and protect* [their income] for the future, rather than *spend* so much so self-indulgently on today's short-lived pleasures."

The new army of conceptual financial planners, who are marketing an intelligent and balanced savings, investment and insurance program geared to the future, may soon be able to refute critics of our economic system. The work of those financial planning soldiers already is reducing the percentage of people that must turn to the government for help.

In fact, more financial education, along with a widespread acceptance of the need to begin financial planning early, could easily prove that the fault is not with the free enterprise system. The worst the critics may be able to argue is that, led by Madison Avenue, we merely concentrated too long on getting people to spend rather than save or invest.

Although the government traditionally has been unduly lenient toward companies trying to get people to spend money, while it has more closely regulated companies that were committed to helping people save and invest money, even that is changing. Thanks to Ralph Nader and active consumer groups, the government is now analyzing the actions of the first group more closely. Also, it appears that national attention has shifted to emphasize or at least recognize that people need and deserve special incentives for planning for the future. The Individual Retirement Account (IRA) is a good example of that governmental shift.

However, even without the plaudits, one of the most exciting careers as we approach the 21st century is that of the financial planner. If enough of them continue conscientiously helping people plan for a better financial future by solving money problems and working toward financial goals, the poor as well as the wealthy may be able to get richer. To paraphrase Tim Redman, CLU and Director of Training and Education for the Columbus (Ohio) Mutual Life Insurance Company, the new saying will go something like this: The enlightened get richer, while the ignorant remain poor.

The Need

Needs don't grow out of new professions; new professions grow out of needs. One of the misconceptions prevalent in the 1970s was that people turned to financial planners in growing numbers because a growing number of people were calling themselves financial planners. While that may be partially true, people actually started turning to financial planners because of the growing complexity of their financial lives. That complexity stimulated the growth of the financial planning profession.

During the 1960s, inflation, increased taxes, and salary increases often landed people in higher tax brackets. More importantly, double-digit inflation was making a mockery of the traditional, low-interest savings alternatives.

Professional planner Bill Park of North Carolina credits the growth to the "smorgasbord of new alternative savings and inflation vehicles." He points out that these myriad options helped intelligent people realize that a financial planner might be what they needed.

Other observers attribute the phenomenal growth of the financial planning profession to an increasing reliance on specialists for assistance. For example, in the 1940s and 1950s, many people were proud that they could prepare their own tax returns. During the 1970s and 1980s, however, it became not only a status symbol, but also often a wise and economically feasible alternative, to have a specialist prepare income tax returns. In fact, many industry mavens note that the tax preparer is another professional who wasn't visible or even available to the general population a few years ago.

Personally, I've observed for some time now yet another subtle reason that many people are deciding to work more closely with a financial planner. In the 1960s, while I was doing research for a book on how to have more self-discipline, I often heard people bemoan their lack of motivation. Now I hear them say something similar: "I know Frank and I should have enough self-discipline to live within a budget. But until we started going to Mr. Johnson, our financial planner, we could never even force ourselves to prepare a budget, much less live within it."

We might as well admit to a truism of human nature. Most of us need the influence of a third party, even to do the things we know we should do. We need the constant goading of a doctor to make sure we modify our dietary habits, the reminder of an exercise instructor to keep us in good physical shape, and the advise of a financial planner to control our spending and keep our monies on the asset side of the ledger. The ability of so many people during the 1960s and 1970s to afford such reinforcement certainly has sped up the growth of the financial planning profession and the use of financial planners by a broadening income segment.

Undoubtedly, criticism of the free enterprise system bothered post-World War II generations more than it has previous ones. As a result, in the 20 years after World War II, more people wanted to do things with their money that made their dollars grow, as the rich had done for years. "Put your money to work" became an often-voiced admonition.

More people wanted to accomplish this and looked for ways to do so. They began finding solutions with the advice and counsel of a trained, objective financial planner.

2 Social Security: Yesterday and Today

"Inflation, Social Security, income taxes, longer retirement, materialism, credit availability, and the growing self-indulgence of people."

That's the way I answer questions as to what made the climate in this country so receptive to the growth of the financial planning profession. Ironically, Social Security at first glance appears to be the one item that should have made it *less* necessary to do financial planning in the last 50 years. After all, Social Security was conceived as a government-monitored tax program for retirement that insisted on forced savings that employees and employers would pay. Wouldn't that enforced savings out of each paycheck get us into the habit of savings?

The answer, of course, is a resounding *No!*

The Social Security program wasn't designed to be a retirement program for most people in this country. More important, the withholding did not encourage those who weren't already putting money away for their retirement to start saving. In fact, it did just the opposite; it lulled many people into thinking their retirement was being assured by Social Security, when in reality that was not the case.

The Beginning

In 1936, Congress enacted legislation to create the Social Security program. The purpose of the program was to provide a financial floor that would protect senior citizens from poverty. As proposed, the Social Security program was to be another tribute to the free enterprise system. Proponents argued such a program would not only encourage people to save but would also protect those who didn't. Under the new system, the first payments to retirees were made in 1938. For several years, more than 30 people paid into the program for every recipient. The maximum contribution was one percent of the first $3,000 in wages, or merely $30 annually. The rate was increased to $45 in 1950, to $72 in 1954, and to $144 by 1960.

What Happened

Perhaps the following quote from a 1947 *Ladies Home Journal* article by Sylvia Porter, a well-regarded financial advisor, illustrates best what happened to the "collective unconscious" of the 30- and 40-year-olds then:

> Every month I buy a regular government bond—one of those $18.75 savings bonds that 85 million of us bought during the war and that tens of millions of us own right now. These bonds are the best, the safest bargain in the world. What's more, over their ten-year life, they pay interest of almost 3 percent: which means that a decade from now, my $18.75 bond will be redeemed at $25, my $3 investment will come back to me as $4....
>
> Because I have a job, I'm also under the federal Social Security system—along with 46 million other Americans, probably including your husband and perhaps yourself. Every week, a small sum is deducted from my paycheck to give me the benefits of Social Security when I'm old. These benefits range all the way from a minimum of $10 a month to a maximum of $84 a month, depending on how long any of us remains under the system and how much we earn. I figure I'll be receiving $10 to $15 a week from Social Security when I'm 65, and that plus my $102 a month (from savings bonds), should take care of me nicely.

Sylvia Porter was far from the only one deluded. Other enthusiasts started promoting Social Security as the wonderful answer to a financially comfortable retirement. One of the more active promoters was Congress itself, which began passing legislation to allow for early retirement. Then, not only did Congress increase Social Security benefits to those who had paid into the program, it also began distributing payments to millions of dependents, survivors, and others who hadn't contributed one cent to the program.

What started as a well-intentioned program that could have remained actuarially sound—with minor adjustments to take into account changes such as longer life spans—began unraveling.

Sure, 30 wage earners, which even the originators realized might drop to 20, could support one older recipient. However, Congress also became more generous with the benefits and eligibility for Social Security, while greatly increasing the withholding taxes future generations were to pay. By the 1950s, 15 wage earners were supporting one recipient. Still, Congress continued increasing benefits and taxes for Social Security. By the 1970s, there were only seven workers for each recipient.

By the 1980s, the picture got even worse. Now, there are only five Social Security taxpayers providing the benefits for each recipient. And, if the system isn't changed soon, the ratio of workers to recipients will be reduced to three to one.

That Isn't All

If you find those statistics unsettling, you will find the following appalling:

- In 1950, Social Security took one percent of the federal budget. By 1982, it required 26 percent; some interpreters suggest that it now requires 28 percent.
- As an average, merely one third of what people receive from Social Security can be considered their fair return (annuity plus interest). Two thirds of what they are receiving is simply welfare.
- The average recipient gets back everything he or she paid into Social Security (plus interest) in less than three years. However, most recipients will continue to collect benefits for 10 to 15 years after extracting every cent they originally paid into the program.

Now, that would be fine, if we really had a wealthy Uncle Sam who could afford to distribute such benefits. Unfortunately we don't, so our children and grandchildren are and will be paying for those retirements.

The first 23 years, when Social Security taxes rose fivefold between 1937 and 1960, were bad. However, the next 23 years were even more shocking. During that time, the maximum employee contribution rose from $144 to $2,391—16 times greater! By 1985 the maximum contribution rose again, to $2,792, an increase of almost 17 percent.

Social Insecurity

According to the results of a recent ABC-*Washington Post* poll, people over the age of 60 are not concerned about the status of the Social Security system. However, among those between 45 and 60, about one third felt the program would collapse before they retired.

People under the age of 45 were even more pessimistic. Among those 31 to 44, 56 percent said the program would not exist for them. And, among those 18 to 30, 74 percent thought they would never get old-age benefits. They expected to pay into the system and never collect a dime.

For concerned financial planners, that's actually good news. The consumer group from 18 to 60 no longer has a "Social Security will take care of me" attitude. They can and should be motivated to prepare a financial plan for themselves, as well as implement that plan immediately.

In addition, younger people are not banking on Social Security for their retirement. So, they too should be more receptive to planning and preparing for their personal financial futures.

According to Peter G. Peterson, former Secretary of Commerce, roughly 30 percent of Social Security payments have been going to 20 percent of the people who need them *least*; only 20 percent reach the 30 percent of those who need them most. This inequity and the size of the tax burden being passed to our children are what I object to, not the Social Security program itself.

3 The Need for Financial Education and Planning

"We're turning out of our schools a bunch of financial illiterates."

That's the opinion of Paul Richards, Director of Education for the National Center for Financial Education (NCFE). In a recent speech he noted the lack of financial education available not only in the secondary schools but also the colleges across our country.

To illustrate his point, let me confide a personal example. More than 40 years ago, I was a young assistant personnel director, recently out of college, and helping to construct one of the naval air bases in Kodiak, Alaska. In my desk drawer were 14 uncashed checks; there would have been more had the payroll department in Seattle not threatened to hold future checks if I didn't cash the ones I had stashed in that drawer. They were not even drawing interest!

How could a college-educated young man, supposedly intelligent, be so incredibly ignorant of the financial facts of life? I hate to admit it, but the extent of my financial education, or at least the only part that stuck with me after I left college, could be easily summed up as follows: "If you don't cash the checks, then you can't spend the money." During all those years in grade school, high school, and college I hadn't even learned about compound interest and investing.

Why? Then and still too frequently now we teach a lot about *economics* and little about *money*. It should be the other way around.

What Schools Should Teach

Students in this country are taught the basics of our society's economic system and how to compare that system to global markets. However, the schools often don't teach about the real monetary system in this country. I am not referring to the Federal Reserve Board; I'm referring to the fact that students need to learn how to *spend* their money intelligently. Also, in their daily lives, they can use information on different methods to *save* money—the value of interest, the magic of compound interest, the time value of money, and the "rule of 72," as well as ways to calculate which banks or other savings vehicles offer the best value in interest. They should be learning how mutual funds and other investments operate. A basic course in insurance should be far more prevalent than it is in our current curricula.

Money plays such a crucial function in our lives that it's nearly criminal not to devote more school time to it. Students need to learn about their money first, then our economic system. They are not the same.

Our schools would help us greatly if they started offering more courses covering how to:

1. *spend* your money effectively;
2. *save* money intelligently;
3. *insure* adequately against life's risks;
4. *invest* to stay ahead of inflation;
5. *plan* in order to achieve short- and long-term goals.

With this important information as a foundation, we might be able to reduce the number of people dependent upon governmental assistance.

The Educational Gap in Financial Matters

Personal Financing

The educational gap apparent in the 1940s and still prevalent today, coupled with the difficulty in getting objective advice concerning personal financial matters, led naturally to the need for a professional like today's financial planner.

Not many of today's high school graduates enter the adult world knowing much about the financial facts of life. They lack information about what I call the Big Financial Five—spending, saving, investing, insuring, and planning. Those graduating from college are in much the same situation.

"But they learn, as soon as they start drawing a paycheck!"

That was a typical response, when I began researching the topic in the 1960s. It was poppycock then; it remains poppycock today. Typically, people in their 20s still are not equipped with a fraction of the information about personal financing that they need to make their paychecks work. Until recently, there wasn't even a professional to whom they could turn, if they realized that they needed help.

Government Benefits

In 1984, the government released a study that Census Bureau Director John Keane described as detailing how government benefits are apportioned in the U.S. In its coverage of the study, the *New York Times* headlined the article "Census Bureau Study Reports Nearly Three out of Every Ten Get Benefits."

That's a thought-provoking observation. Undoubtedly, some people are shocked to realize how high that figure has risen, particularly in a country that prides itself on individual initiative and the power of the free enterprise system to provide for those living under it—without the need for governmental assistance.

Before this survey was released, I had conducted some informal research and found most people to whom I talked thought that the figure was one in ten. Even more disconcerting, however, was that the study noted that more than half of the 66 million people receiving benefits were not getting them from a Social Security program into which they had paid, but rather from other types of financial assistance. In other words, we are paying for socialistic programs, or welfare if you prefer, with our free enterprise tax dollars.

Financial Education and Capitol Hill

Financial education is crucial in the nation's schools; it is even more crucial in Washington, D.C. Congress soothed my generation of 60- and 70-year-olds with promises of extravagant Social Security benefits, compliments of our benevolent Uncle Sam. Except it isn't Uncle Sam who is paying the tab. Instead, we mortgaged the future without the co-signatures of our children and grandchildren. Now they're paying.

But my own generation is not the only one to blame. Minnesota Senator Dave Durenberger, who is in his 50s, says of his peer group:

> I suspect that my generation will be remembered as the one that invented plastic money: We let the mainspring of American industry run down, so we could have four bedrooms, three baths, and a rec room in the suburbs. And now that we've fallen behind on the payments, we want to borrow the shortfall from our children in order to continue our comforts. The issue of generational equity can't be escaped. It's going to dominate all political debate very soon, I'm sure.

That's not mere political rhetoric. It directly influences all of our lives, particularly the financial lives of not only your current clients and prospective clients, but also their children and your children. As Paul S. Hewitt, former staff assistant to Senator Durenberger in Washington, D.C., notes about young people today, "They must plan their retirement based on the uncertain existence of Social Security, Medicare, and other federal retirement benefits."

Though rare, financial education and planning were important and extremely valuable in the 1960s and 1970s. In the 1980s and 1990s they will be *vital*.

Financial Planning: New and Vital Need

Several years ago, while researching a book on retirement, I found that 60- and 70-year-olds frequently fell into one of two categories.

Members of the first group had conducted their financial lives so that they entered retirement with few or no financial worries. Often, they had deprived themselves of luxuries, trips, second homes, new cars, and other amenities during their income-producing years. Instead, they invested a major portion of their discretionary income into their companys' profit-sharing plans, bought into mutual funds or other securities or even put their money into savings and loan associations while paying off their homes. Gradually, they built up their assets for their golden years.

That frugality during earlier years paid off. These people not only enjoyed a comfortable, even exciting lifestyle filled with travel and recreation, but they also had a financial peace of mind that was obviously playing a part in their good health and enjoyment of retirement.

Those in the other group I observed had done little or no financial planning. In many cases, they had practiced little or no financial self-discipline during their earning years. Too frequently, they were subsisting with little more than their Social Security check. Often, they lived haunted lives from one Social Security check to the next.

What differentiated the latter group from the former was simply financial planning. The first group did it; the second placed the future in the hands of others.

No Longer Ignoring the Figures

"Today, of every 100 people who reach age 65, only two are financially independent; 23 must continue working; and 75 must depend on friends, charity or relatives. Of every 100 Americans reaching age 65 today, a horrifying 98 are flat broke."

We've read and heard those statistics scores of times in dozens of different places. Personally, I don't believe that only two percent of all retired people are financially independent. (Some statistics indicate that four percent may be a more accurate figure.) But my personal belief is less important than what that statement says to those of us who treasure free enterprise. It's a gloomy portrait of the capitalist system we espouse, promote and live under.

Statistics aside, the real motivation for action is the snapshot of life we see when we observe next-door neighbors or others close at hand who are absolutely dependent upon Social Security. They are average people, reliant upon a system that was designed to take care of the poor.

What error placed them in that position? Is the free enterprise system less than what we have proclaimed it to be? Or, have we as people changed? Obviously, somewhere after World War II we misplaced our spirit of independence and drive toward self-sufficiency. Thrift, that virtue of the 1800s, has become far too rare.

Were too many of us seduced by Madison Avenue advertising and the other enticements to spend? When did we lose our resistance to the siren's song of "Buy it now"? When and where did we lose our ability to defer some present pleasures for even greater fulfillment in the future.

Did we falter, financially, because of Social Security and the other aspects of the welfare system? Did the implication that Uncle Sam would take care of us undermine our resolve to plan and prepare for our retirement years?

The answers to these questions, of course, will never be known, though some may hazard guesses. What is clear is that we *must* take action to correct our financial situation. We cannot continue making the mistakes of the past. People, in far greater numbers, must start looking out for their own futures. Delegating the financial future to succeeding generations must cease.

Paul Hewitt, who heads Americans for Generational Equity, wrote the following in a *Washington Post* article, dated February 21, 1984:

> Unlike insurance, Social Security is financed on a pay-as-you-go basis—that is, current benefits are financed by taxes on current workers rather than the contributions of the recipients themselves. Thus, the only guarantee future retirees have of receiving benefits is the willingness of future contributors to support the system.
>
> Such support is bound to atrophy over time. Already polls show that 74 percent of Americans under age 30 do not believe they will ever collect promised benefits—a pessimism supported by the fact that by the time members of the Baby Boom retire, they must either forgo many current benefits or require their children and grandchildren to contribute an unrealistic 25 to 40 percent of their payroll to the system.

The Strongest Argument

Those of us who love the free enterprise system and who also favor helping the needy through our government must do our best to reduce the number of poor. If we don't, our system could collapse.

Can there be any stronger argument for financial education and planning? Can there be any stronger testimonial advocating the need for greater numbers of dedicated financial planners in our future's marketplace?

We need financial planners willing to help the people who need their services most, to help them to avoid becoming a part of that 95 percent that enters retirement destitute. We need financial planners willing to educate and motivate wage earners, at all levels of the income scale.

The need for financial planning and education is great, but so is the opportunity for the financial planners of the future.

AN INTERVIEW WITH
Bob Leary

Bob Leary was an early and continuing advocate of financial planning as a profession. He served as one of the original trustees of the Society for Financial Counselling, Inc. He also helped to structure the International Association of Financial Planners, now known as the International Association for Financial Planning, Inc. In 1982, he was a founding trustee of the National Center for Financial Education. Earlier he worked to assure the establishment of the College for Financial Planning, Inc., the International Council for Financial Planning and *Financial Planning* magazine.

When the IAFP was conceptualized, he was executive vice president of WESTAMERICA Securities, one of the leaders in dual-licensed financial planning, marketing both mutual funds and insurance. He was James Wilson's boss, before Jim was hired as the IAFP's first executive director. Bob also recommended H. L. Jamieson as a source of funding and guidance before we committed the meager assets of our consulting firm to building three nonprofit organizations. The planning firm Bob started in Denver—R. M. Leary & Co., Inc.— is now headed by his daughter, Kate Leary Lee. Here are some observations he shared with me in an interview shortly before his death:

DUNTON: Certainly, you are recognized as a pioneer in the field we now call financial planning. Could you divulge what companies you were associated with when you began in this profession?

LEARY: I entered the business, prior to the passage of the Investment Company Act in 1940, with a company now known as Investors Diversified Services. At that time, we sold Investors Syndicate and its three percent bond, which was a savings plan. That produced most of my income.

DUNTON: Please tell me more about Investors Diversified Services (IDS) and King Merritt, the real pioneers in the field.

LEARY: While I was working with Investors Syndicate, King Merritt was its general sales manager, and I had the good fortune to become personally acquainted with him. When IDS was formed, following passage of the Investment Company Act, King Merritt became vice president of sales. I found him to be the best sales executive and motivator that I have ever worked with. So, in the mid-1950s, instead of opening up my own broker-dealership, I joined King Merritt & Company and sold its mutual funds. By that time, I already had my own life insurance license.

DUNTON: Can you share with me the breadth and scope of King Merritt's company?

LEARY: At that time, King Merritt was operating in 16 countries and generating a tremendous amount of business. That firm gave its managers and representatives great leadership, professional guidance, and incentive. For example, Baron Helbig was nationally recognized for his knowledge of estate tax planning and the first authority I ever ran into who could translate prospects into active clients. We used Baron Helbig on television, as well as for seminar and corporate meetings, with tremendous results. His firm in New York City was the real pioneer when it came to marketing professional advice.

DUNTON: How did King Merritt and H. L. Jamieson get together?

LEARY: During the mid-1950s, King Merritt merged H. L. Jamieson & Company into his own firm and became chairman, while Jamie [Jamieson] became president. Under Jamie's leadership, professional ethics were emphasized and helped to define financial planning in its embryo stage. Later, the firm merged into the Channing Corporation, with Jamie as president.

DUNTON: When we met in 1966, you were with WESTAMERICA. Can you share your experience with WESTAMERICA's operations with me?

LEARY: I became associated with WESTAMERICA Securities, Inc., in 1960, as executive vice president and director of sales. We became one of the largest broker-dealer companies that marketed mutual funds and insurance, utilizing all aspects of estate tax planning procedures and techniques. Through advantageous sales tools and expansion of sales markets, we were able to attract top managers from national firms. In the 1960s, WESTAMERICA had more than 700 representatives in more than 60 divisional offices under the direction of nine regional managers. We also offered our productive management personnel participation in common stock ownership, which expanded their net worth considerably.

DUNTON: In my research, WESTAMERICA's program was the best example of implementing a financial counseling sales approach in the early stages of financial planning. You researched your prospects and their needs, then showed them how to achieve their financial goals. Am I correct about this?

LEARY: Yes, financial and investment inventory data became an integral part of all prospect and account files. From that base, we were able to furnish the proper mutual funds and insurance to complement the client's desires and needs. However, we merely considered it as doing a solid job of full disclosure selling. The term "financial planning" had not entered our vocabulary. You accomplished that with the IAFP, the Society and the College. In fact, we were eager to have someone like Loren Dunton stick his head above the water and get the accreditation necessary for representatives working in this particular area of the investment and insurance business.

DUNTON: Thank you. Now, I've often wondered what type of person you found most successful in selling mutual funds and insurance. Were there any special qualifications?

LEARY: Most of our divisional managers came from the large national mutual fund sales organizations; a few rose from the ranks of member firm offices. The sales personnel, however, came from all walks of life. While a fairly high percentage had previous mutual fund or insurance experience, we didn't use those as criteria for association with WESTAMERICA. We did have an excellent personnel evaluation firm that worked diligently with us in screening applications, however. That may have made the difference, as many of our top producers emerged quickly from successful employment fields outside the securities industry. In addition, many of our managers preferred to hire people new to the field so that they did not have to unlearn any bad habits.

PART TWO

The Way It Was
The Emergence of the Financial Planner

The rise of the financial planner as a professional was not free from resistance to the changes that these new professionals represented. As happens with other changes, people with interests in the status quo tried to deter the developments in the financial field.

Another common problem in adapting to change is failure to appreciate new opportunities. In the 1960s, for instance, some people noted that the railroad industry had lacked the foresight to take over and profit from the fledging airplane industry. They argued that the leaders of the railroad industry could have benefited from considering themselves in the transportation business rather than the railroad business. Similarly, had movie industry executives participated in the growing television industry (defining themselves as part of the entertainment industry), they could have made billions of dollars.

In much the same way, various segments of today's financial services industry had a similar opportunity to expand their role. Many, however, were too insular and too protective of individual financial markets to capitalize on the opportunity that was there. Retrospectively, it seems amazing that none of the three financial giants—banking, insurance, or securities—recognized the potential of positioning its segment to serve the broader financial services industry.

While tradition and regulations offered some stumbling blocks, they weren't insurmountable. With vision and patience, companies could have achieved a considerable payoff. Nevertheless, like the railroad and movie industries, each of the three financial giants was too comfortable in its own niche. I can't help wondering if they would have modified their approach had they peeked into a crystal ball and foreseen the deregulation that would occur in 1980.

To be fair, some segments of the insurance industry did step forward into the larger market that was to become the financial planning industry by buying and starting to market mutual funds. However, a bearish market and some negative mutual fund publicity in the early 1970s soon scared them out.

To understand what is happening and what some think may be contained in the future of the financial planning industry, it's essential to look back at the securities, insurance and banking businesses from which most of today's financial planning professionals have come. Each of these businesses played key parts in setting the course for the financial planner's emergence as a professional.

4 The Stock Broker and The Securities Industry

"It's nothing but legalized gambling at a high level where sophisticated investors sometimes make money; amateurs almost never do, and investment bankers almost always do."

That was the first description of stock brokers and brokerages I encountered as a very young man in Spokane, Washington. Along with that quote goes a story I remember about an investment banker conducting a tour of a yacht harbor on Long Island, N.Y., and noting the yachts belonging to well-known names on Wall Street, all affiliated with investment banks or brokerages. The client confounds the investment banker by asking, "But where are the customers' yachts?"

Possibly there is a grain of truth in the implied and oversimplified criticism of the brokerage community as a legalized Las Vegas casino. If so, there are pounds of truth in saying that stock brokers and brokerage houses play a helpful role in the growth of free enterprise.

Unfortunately, the image of the stock broker was seriously tarnished because of the Great Depression, when a number of people handled the stock market's collapse by leaping from Wall Street windows. During the 1940s, 1950s and 1960s, however, the stock broker's image gradually began gleaming again. In fact, practitioners began to be proud to admit their profession, especially those who worked for the important firms on the New York Stock Exchange.

In the 1970s, however, Wall Street again went through an unstable period. Changing priorities in their profession caused a number of stock brokers to become confused and uncertain once again. The number of stock brokers making a living from four or six hours on the telephone decreased.

The more flexible brokers began selling mutual funds. Indeed, some were elated at being able to help their clients accumulate money in mutuals as opposed to assisting them in speculating on the ups and downs of the stock market.

Early into the 1970s, the leading edge of what was to become a general deregulation trend found a few stock brokers even selling insurance. However, this occupational alternative was overall less successful and less widespread than the marketing of mutual funds.

Early Forays Into Financial Planning

Stock brokers had existing clients. On the surface, it appeared that they should be able to sell those clients a considerable amount of insurance. That didn't occur, however, which led some observers to suggest that stock brokers generally were too set in their ways to change.

Naturally, there were a few exceptions. Some of these gradually began their own form of financial planning for their clients. They set an initial goal for their clients by preparing a comprehensive personal financial plan first. With that agreed upon, they soon were selling their clients insurance, funds, tax shelters, and even stocks and bonds.

Concurrently, having failed to convince insurance industry leaders of the value of financial planning, we approached leaders in the securities industry, hoping they could learn from the history of the movie and railroad industries' past misconceptions. I suggested that they cease considering themselves as the securities industry and start positioning themselves as the logically dominant force in the evolving financial services industry that Donald Pitti, president of Weisenberger Financial Services, Inc., was touting even then (see the interview with Donald Pitti following Chapter 6).

Giving Up on Wall Street

During that period, Wall Street became familiar turf. Other than a pleasant lunch at the New York Stock Exchange, however, little was gained. Perhaps, the location of our fledging Society for Financial Counselling, Inc., in its Littleton, Colorado, headquarters kept brokers from objectively appraising what we were trying to tell and sell them. Back then, most of them had little idea even where Colorado is, let alone our Society. We went elsewhere for support of the IAFP and the College for Financial Planning.

Logically, stock brokers individually and collectively might have been more receptive to the financial planning approach with their clients had mutual funds not performed so poorly during the early 1970s. After all, most brokers who gradually included mutual funds in their sales presentations had—rather than promoting the diversification and safety of dollar-cost averaging—touted short-term performance. They didn't market mutual funds as a safe and prudent method of accumulating long-term capital during the next 10 or 20 years. They sold mutual funds in the same manner as they were accustomed to selling stocks, expecting fast and lucrative profitability in short-term investments.

Instead of recognizing the error inherent in marketing mutual funds in the same way as stocks, stock brokers faulted the mutual funds. Hence, for the next three or four years, the stock exchange community sold relatively few mutual funds.

Meanwhile, many of the funds continued to operate as they were designed to, appealing to the more prudent and patient investor. Some did enter the performance race, trying to compete with the short-term performance of the stock market. Some resorted to questionable evaluations of "letter stock" holdings and similar practices, but most mutual funds avoided this.

Those that did engage in wheeling and dealing operations projected a poor image of the entire mutual fund industry. Some experts say those actions of the few held back the many serious stock brokers, who might otherwise have granted the field of financial planning earlier recognition and support.

Nevertheless, some brokers were creative enough to see beyond the momentary flak produced by overzealous mutual funds. Several New York Stock Exchange firms, mostly regional, were embracing the financial planning approach with their clients. In fact, those pioneers were cognizant that financial planning might be the sole means of survival for most stockbrokers.

One of the primary leaders was the Raymond James organization in Florida. The group began as a fairly typical New York regional firm, but soon blazed new trails by offering its clients financial planning. Today, prominent financial planners and executives in financial planning organizations all over the country credit their early training to the Raymond James organization.

Others also embraced the financial planning concept with vigor and commitment. Still, the average stock broker was at most a reluctant financial planner then and, though to a lesser extent, this is true even today.

A Pioneering Stockbroker

In San Francisco, Mitchell Curtis was typical of concerned and conscientious stock brokers. Another was Churchill C. Peters, founder and chairman of Protected Investors of America, also in San Francisco. One of that firm's more than 40 representatives, Gabe Angell, CFP, was recognized by the San Francisco chapter of the IAFP as Financial Planner of the Year in 1984.

In 1934, when Church Peters founded his company, one of his goals was to help the small investor plan for his or her financial future. His is the earliest instance I can find of a securities broker attempting to apply systematically the insurance industry's concept to the sale of other investments. In fact, his recommendations are remarkably similar to the "thrift saving contract" of California Western States Life Insurance. Churchill Peters also laid the groundwork for marketing many mutual funds, as they became available.

Interestingly, in the *San Francisco Chronicle's* 1984 listing of the 20 largest brokers in that city, Protected Investors, Inc., was the only firm listed as financial planners.

John Watts Proves a Point

Another early conceptualizer was John Watts. In 1981, I realized that E.F. Hutton was marketing billions of dollars of life insurance under the able direction of John Watts. Four years later, he moved to Hartford Life Insurance Company and began building that company's sales as well. He is now a senior vice president of Washington National Corporation in Chicago. In preparing this book, I asked John Watts to share his perspective on that period at E.F. Hutton, and here's how he viewed it:

> What we did [at Hutton] is the only tried and proven method of distributing life insurance efficiently through stockbrokers. *Business Week* succinctly documented the results when the magazine noted that 'only E.F. Hutton to date has demonstrated an ability to sell ordinary life insurance in quantity.' While it wasn't easy, we proved it could be done rapidly and profitably.
>
> When I joined E.F. Hutton, I inherited the remnants of a life specialist system similar to many that are still struggling today—frightfully expensive and totally unsuccessful. The brokers and branch managers were so resentful of what the insurance industry had done to them, that I removed 'CLU' from my business card and stationery.
>
> I did have one ace, which I used to its utmost in gaining broker acceptance. Although I had started in the insurance business, I came to them from an institutional investment counseling firm.
>
> After surveying the industry and seeing the corpses of far wiser failures, I decided not to follow that path. Instead, I turned to the regional vice presidents, branch managers and individual stockbrokers. I conducted extensive interrogations to learn what went wrong, as well as solicited their advice on what they thought would work.
>
> Then I became a registered broker and learned to think, talk, walk and look like a broker. I found them intense, intelligent and fun, so this phase was a pleasure. Simultaneously, I and a small cadre of brokers recruited from Hutton's own ranks began working as a team.
>
> Four years later, 60 percent of Hutton's brokers, themselves (not myself) created one of the world's largest life insurance distribution systems.

While Hartford Life subsequently tempted John Watts away from Hutton, it wasn't before stock brokers proved they could and would sell insurance, thereby contributing to the growth of the financial planning industry.

In 1984, numerous stock brokers saw their jobs cease. Some may have wished they had trained as financial planners, while others already had.

A Historical Note

Jim Anderson of Tillinghast in Atlanta was the U.S. conceptualizer and architect of what we now know as universal life insurance, while Alan Richards of Hutton Life was its early champion and advocate. Paul Green, who heads his own management firm in Green Valley, Arizona, notes that the genesis of "flexible term" insurance—to which a savings element is now added to complete the unbundling of "ordinary" insurance—was the revolutionary Comp-u-term. Continental Assurance, located in Chicago, introduced it under this name in the mid-1960s. It permitted an estimated one million term product variations and, more importantly, was on the forefront of computer-oriented product designs for the financial planning community.

5 The Insurance Agent and The Mutual Fund Rep

Most authorities credit five factors for the tremendous growth the insurance industry experienced during the 19th century and the first half of the 20th century:

1. the general agency system;
2. high first-year sales commissions to agents;
3. continuous recruitment of new agents;
4. outdated mortality tables that didn't reflect the increased life expectancy of the population;
5. competitive interest rates.

Understandably, when drastic changes confronted the insurance industry, the well-entrenched giant companies and the successful general agencies put up considerable resistance.

Solomon Huebner and his successors at The American College in Bryn Mawr, Pennsylvania, had succeeded in bringing stature and respect to the insurance agent, particularly one who could put CLU (Chartered Life Underwriter) after his or her name. However, most trained and experienced life insurance general agents and their leading producers saw little to gain and much to lose in the new approaches that began in the 1950s, accelerated in the 1960s, and engulfed many in the 1970s, primarily those who ignored the winds of change.

Today's objective, multi-product financial planner may find it difficult to believe that his or her own company ever used to threaten dismissal to any life insurance agents attempting to market mutual funds to their clients, for example. But, such was the case in many major firms just a short time ago. Large companies then promoted life insurance as the sole solution to every financial problem. Nor was there much incentive to suggest other financial alternatives to clients, particularly when the profit and commissions were lower.

For 50 years the most successful insurance agents were those who could "back the hearse right up to the door." Then, as the insurance profession matured, it began marketing its product not merely as the answer for emergencies but also a method to finance the children's education and as a tool for preparing for retirement.

Creative insurance policies were not the major reason for the insurance industry's growth. Instead, it was the emergence of selling, including life insurance selling, as a profession. Dynamic, aggressive, hard-charging general agents all over the country were recruiting, training, indoctrinating and inspiring their sales organizations.

Supplementing and often exceeding these sales forces were several large "captive" sales forces. Frequently, they employed thousands of agents, so even those who wrote only a few policies before quitting helped the parent company's premiums swell into millions of dollars.

Credit Is Due

During the 1970s, critics made numerous vocal assaults on the insurance industry. They noted its marble palaces, its resistance to change, its turnover of agents, and its policy regarding certain aspects of whole life–cash value insurance policies, often sold whether or not they were appropriate.

The truth is, however, the insurance industry did give us numerous benefits. Many individuals built considerable nest eggs with their whole life policies. They wouldn't have done so without the forced savings aspect inherent in the design of those policies. Without the threat of forfeiting the money already building in those policies—a penalty feature not present in term insurance—many people might have stopped making the payments.

August Hansch of Los Angeles, a well-respected insurance general agent and pioneer financial planner, observed in *Your Book of Financial Planning:*

> The fixed, level premium of permanent life insurance minimizes this risk, because the deposits to the cash value are built into the plan. In a sense, this means that people with permanent life insurance—if they want their protection to remain in force—are under a semicompulsory obligation to keep their cash values growing steadily at the same time.
>
> Some people insist that they don't need this forced savings feature of permanent life insurance. And, they're probably right if they are disciplined savers, but how many can be self-disciplined over 20 or 30 years?
>
> Putting up with a little forced savings buys a lot of benefits. For one thing, you continually add to a liquid fund that's available for emergencies or opportunities. Even if your other investments are successful, they aren't always liquid. In real estate, for example, many prosperous, high-earning individuals have been grateful for their permanent life insurance cash values when emergencies come up, because it was the only readily available source of funds they had.

Indeed, he is correct.

Changing in the 1980s

Though it took its time in accepting financial planning, the insurance industry by the end of the 1970s was becoming more consumer oriented. By the early 1980s, an increasingly large percentage of innovative interest-sensitive insurance products were available.

In fact, financial planners were eagerly including a number of these new policies in their clients' financial plans. Of these, universal life is possibly the best known. E.F. Hutton, under John Watt's direction, sold $2.2 billion worth of universal life insurance in less than five years; soon Lincoln National outpaced Hutton.

But that was merely the beginning. Variable life insurance and other similar policies were making it possible for insurance agents and financial planners to offer their clients viable options suited to their particular portfolios.

One area where less progress has been made, despite the efforts of Dave Goodwin of Miami, a recognized authority on the subject, is property and casualty insurance. Nevertheless, possibly more financial planners will address this area of their clients' financial plans in subsequent years.

I maintain that next to the computer and possibly the shoe industries, the insurance industry has done more in the last five years to improve the product being offered to the consumer than any other.

The Mutual Fund Rep

During the 1960s, while offering consulting services to mutual fund companies, I began meeting field salespeople who were helping their clients achieve short- and long-range financial goals. These mutual fund sales representatives weren't helping people plan for their death by showing how they could leave an estate. Instead, they were working with their clients to prepare for putting children through college, showing them how to use leverage (often home equity) to accumulate assets more rapidly, and generally assisting their clients with preparing for retirement.

In the 1950s and 1960s, these people didn't call themselves financial planners or even financial counselors, although they were practicing the methodology. In fact, they were tending to two of the most important aspects of today's financial plan: insurance for tragedies and securities to capitalize on the growth potential of American industry.

Many of these mutual fund reps worked for large captive mutual fund organizations, such as Investors Diversified Services in Minneapolis, Waddell & Reed in Kansas City, and Financial Service Corporation of Atlanta.

Smaller firms with a more sophisticated approach, like King Merritt, also entered the market. "Hell, I've been doing financial planning for 20 years. I just didn't call it that," is a claim I have heard at least a dozen times.

An Important Difference

Not everyone who claimed to be doing financial planning, however, actually was. Many who claimed to be offering that service in the 1960s and even the 1970s were actually providing little more than insurance and estate planning.

Many carefully worked out estate plans enabled clients to take good care of surviving family members, but did not put them in an ideal position to enjoy their own retirement. This led to people observing that they often were "insurance poor." A good financial plan, as opposed to an estate plan, recognizes and plans for people retiring sooner and living longer.

AN INTERVIEW WITH H.L. Jamieson

H.L. Jamieson is chairman of the board of Franklin Resources in San Mateo, California. When the concept of financial planning as a profession was first conceived, he cut the first check as a corporate sponsor of the Society for Financial Counseling. He also served as the first chairman of its board of governors, during the structuring of the IAFP and the College for Financial Planning. In this interview, he shares the groundwork laid by a few companies that led to the formation of the financial planning profession.

DUNTON: Could you share with us your beginning years at Investors Syndicate and your approach to marketing?

JAMIESON: I started with Investors Syndicate (now IDS) in 1934 selling savings certificates. During the bank crisis the company had met every obligation and even paid, at maturity, higher than the going rate. There were heavy penalties for early withdrawl, but we used those penalties as a selling feature, by emphasizing forced, disciplined savings.

DUNTON: How did you actually sell this concept to your prospective clients?

JAMIESON: I think I said something like the following: "Mr. Prospect, you have worked for 20 years. During that time, you have earned some $50,000. (Remember, this is 1934 income.) How much have you saved? Is there any reason that you think you will save more in the next 20 years, unless you have a plan that will reward you for saving at its completion but will also penalize you if you stop early?"

Until 1940, we had only one plan to market. After that, Investors Mutual was started and soon became the largest mutual fund in the country. However, we weren't doing financial planning then—only offering our clients a savings program.

DUNTON: But you did come closer to financial planning as we know it today after you left IDS, as I understand it.

JAMIESON: Yes. A group of us founded Jamieson & Company. We soon established a program called "The Balance of Your Life," or "The Power of Positive Planning." While we weren't offering tax shelters, insurance and other of today's tools, we did help our customers plan in the purchase of equity mutual funds.

DUNTON: You also headed sales for King Merritt, correct?

JAMIESON: Yes, and I discovered that many of the salespeople were selling a smattering of financial planning by also offering life insurance. During that time, we hired Baron Helbig, who consulted on financial planning; Bernard Garham who advised on investing techniques; and Tom Fellows, who worked on profit sharing.

When we purchased Federal Life & Casualty, we spent many hours training our personnel on the use of insurance and mutual funds. I suspect that we were the first national company to combine the two products in our planning.

We also had the Key Plan—a single check to purchase mutual funds regularly with insurance protection as well—which was really the first universal life idea.

DUNTON: How did you teach your representatives methods of marketing such a revolutionary concept?

JAMIESON: Basically, we used a simple concept for our representatives. It was to:

1. List your prospect's assets.
2. Establish your client's goal.
3. Sell products that meet those goals.
4. Sell insurance to complete the program, should death or disability occur.

That's what we taught.

DUNTON: I've always admired the work of IDS and King Merritt, particularly their manner of counseling their clients toward a better financial future, during those 30 years from 1935 to 1965.

JAMIESON: Yes, it was a very basic form of financial planning. Later, of course, inflation and high taxes created the need for more sophistication and estate planning. Fortunately, by then the IAFP and the College were operational to train people to meet that need.

DUNTON: Could you share a few predictions about the future, such as where you see financial planning going?

JAMIESON: During the next 50 years, I think that banks will be in financial planning; insurance companies will be in financial planning. I suspect that other types of funds will gain popularity.

In the future, more financial planners will be working with their clients to increase savings and to invest for income and profit rather than merely to avoid taxes, which I think is a negative approach to financial planning. To reflect that changing philosophy, I think IAFP will need to raise its standards.

6 The Banker

Along with others in the financial services industry, banks also resisted change. The average bank opened at 10:00 A.M. and closed at 3:00 P.M., promptly. Those requesting a loan were expected to enter the hallowed banking doors hat in hand and prepared to genuflect before the bank officer.

Missed Opportunities

The reluctance of established banking leaders to incorporate changes is often cited as the reason savings and loan institutions, credit unions, thrift institutions and others grew so rapidly. Even into the 1950s and 1960s, bankers were fostering an unfriendly, austere, and forbidding image that led many people to prefer doing business with other financial organizations. Some also attribute the bankers' emphasis on low-interest passbook savings accounts as primarily responsible for the banking industry's failure to compete with the newcomers.

Bank trust departments provided a classic example of that attitude. They ignored the increasing customer sophistication, just as they ignored the aggressive competition that was changing their marketplace. Instead, they preferred to cling to business-as-usual methodology.

To explain the shift, many bankers used prudent-man rules under which they operated to rationalize why their common stock trust funds were showing such poor performance during the post–World War II period. Meanwhile, conservative mutual funds were showing gains of 5, 10, and 20 percent above inflation rates, though many bank trust fund clients were actually watching their inheritances shrink due to that same inflation.

That inflationary period mocked the bankers' pride in their vaunted responsibility to conserve funds and estates. It simply wasn't enough merely to try to preserve what people had, while inflation eroded its value—particularly when that same culprit, inflation, also offered unprecedented opportunities for growth.

The resistance to change seemed to stem from the bankers' inability to observe objectively the way society was changing and to learn from the rest of the financial services industry's response to those changes. Possibly, even those who could be objective could not envision a manner of responding that would allow them to remain profitable.

Of course, one could argue that what was true in the 1950s and 1960s was surely erroneous by the 1970s and 1980s. A.P. Giannanni, founder of Bank of America, had charted new courses for the banking profession even earlier. Yet, billions of dollars also moved into the money market funds during that period.

Why did bankers let it happen? If they saw the need and the opportunity, why weren't they capitalizing on it? Were government restrictions really the reason for billions of dollars walking away while a number of bankers sat still?

How could they ignore the SRI International (formerly the Stanford Research Institute) study entitled *Financial Planning in the 1980s*? That report's major point was that people desire a financial plan that establishes specific objectives and goals, then develops an overall strategy to reach those goals.

During the mid-1970s, Donald Pitti, then president of Weisenberger Financial Services, Inc., in New York, was an articulate spokesman for those of us who were postulating that banks would be wise to view themselves as financial service centers, with banking merely one of their functions. The historical events of the railroad and movie industries were recurring in the banking profession and the insurance profession. And, like the leaders in the insurance industry, many bank executives were too comfortable as bankers to welcome any other role, even a larger one.

Product Development Opportunities

Fortunately, not everyone was locked into the past. One who wasn't is Anne Lieberman, who left Bank of America to join Larry Krause & Associates, a San Francisco financial planning firm. In her final assignment at Bank of America, in 1981, she headed a new product development group that was working on a financial planning product for the retail side of the bank. She explains the new breed of bankers and the recent trends in banking this way:

> It's important to understand some of the factors that led to banks' interest in financial planning. In the 1970s, Weisenberger and the Stanford Research Institute did a study entitled *Consumer Financial Decisions*. It was an omnibus study of consumer financial behavior.
>
> What bankers discovered from this study was that individuals in the most desirable market segments—the 'upscale' segments—used a large number of financial service providers. Furthermore, the banks tended to have the least profitable part of the upscale customers'

business: the checking account. The question arose naturally, 'What would happen if we captured a larger share of the business of our current customer base?' The answer was straightforward: There was a great deal of money to be made by doing more business with existing customers.

The initial efforts to do this focused on providing price incentives for the use of multiple services, encouraging customers to consolidate financial relations. Financial planning was viewed as the penultimate, if not the ultimate, opportunity to capture the lion's share of a customer's business.

At the same time, deregulation was afoot, putting within the banker's vision, if not grasp, a world with fewer barriers. That future would bring opportunities to serve a broader range of customer needs.

The third thread—persistent high inflation and economic uncertainty—gave the lie to financial strategies that a whole generation had adopted from its parents. Traditional saving and investment vehicles weren't working. A bank savings account guaranteed you'd lose your purchasing power; the Dow Jones declined 55 percent in constant dollars between 1965 and 1978.

In sum, the banks saw that they could harvest existing markets, that financial planning was the tool, and that economic uncertainty had sown the seeds of consumer demand.

Barriers

Anne Lieberman also saw some significant product development barriers that confronted the banking profession. She shared those, as well:

My experience in product development leads me to believe that there are two impediments to the banks' successful entry into the financial planners field—lack of innovative spirit and an inability to adopt a market orientation.

While at Bank of America, I headed a group called 'Concept Development.' In preparation for this assignment, I studied companies (3-M, for example) with reputations for the successful nurturing and development of new product ideas. I learned that bankers get most of their new product ideas from other bankers. This explains why there's been only one new idea in banking in the last 30 years: the bank card. And personally, I consider the application of automatic teller machines as merely using existing technology in business. For many years, banking has been a stable industry protected by regulation. There was no need for a fertile ground to germinate new ideas. Now, while there is a need, there is still no fertile soil.

In addition to the dearth of creativity, there is another barrier to the success of financial planning in banks. Most bankers are unable to step outside the paradigm and think like nonbankers. Financial planners are market-driven, client-oriented, and aggressive business developers. Retail bankers have a different point of view. Their approach is encapsulated in the statement, 'Have efficient operations and good locations, and let the customers come to you.'

There is, however, a trend in banking that goes against the traditional approach. Many banks are struggling to adopt a marketing perspective—a sensitivity to the needs of the marketplace and development of services that fill those needs. This dawning perspective is reflected in banks' interest in hiring marketing people from the packaged goods industry.

I'm not sanguine about banks becoming 'marketeers' in the near term. Banks have been beating the drum about the need for a market orientation for some time. Yet, many bankers still think marketing means advertising; advertising is just one element in the marketing mix of product, price, promotion and distribution.

A Better Educated Public

In 1983, I wondered if banks would be hurt or helped if the public became better educated about the need for financial planning. I also was curious to know whether or not Anne Lieberman thought banks would support our efforts to educate the consumer. Here is her reaction:

> If banks are to profit from customer education, they must adopt a market orientation. If they are still promoting five percent savings, education will hurt. If they are busy assembling a line of products that consumers will value, they can position themselves to profit from consumer education and greater sophistication.
>
> If banks don't educate consumers, someone else will, and perhaps take them away. Banks don't really have a choice. The trend toward greater financial sophistication has been under way for some time. However, they do have an option: They can either meet the needs of their existing customers and their changing market, or they can sit still and let the market pass them by. In business, going the way of the dinosaur is a choice companies make; it is not something thrust upon them.

The Interest Rate Muddle

"One of the reasons people need financial advice is to protect them from banks."

During the 1960s, I heard that remark frequently. Prior to becoming acquainted with some of the pioneers in financial planning, I viewed banks as great repositories of money and trust. It was shocking to hear that others saw banks as experts at obfuscation that were driven by self-interest. Mutual fund and insurance salespeople chortled at my naivete. They gave me countless examples of how banks used "prudent man" rules to defend investment performances well below those of many mutual funds.

When I perused Jane Bryant Quinn's "Staying Ahead" newspaper column in June 1984, those early comments came back to me. She began that column by observing, "Yet another truth-in-savings bill has been introduced in Congress—the latest in a long, and so far futile, effort to deliver honest interest rates to savers."

Confusing language

While Jane Bryant Quinn was not the first to note the confusing language used by banks in presenting their interest rates, she was considered an objective observer. In 1984 in her syndicated newspaper column, she wrote the following:

> As things now stand, it's hard to identify the best and highest interest rate unless you have Ph.D. in math. Take, for example, a five-year Individual Retirement Account advertising a 'simple' interest rate of 15 present. In dollars and cents, that 'simple' account actually pays you less than a five-year account offering 11.5 percent compounded daily. Yet you'd probably choose the 15 percent account, thinking it the better deal.

Even though by the 1980s consumers were aware of and concerned about interest rates, they were still not educated about them. Professionals in the financial services industry knew differently, of course. But unless they were preparing true financial plans for their clients, rather than marketing a particular financial option, they could confuse the customer. It became even more important in the 1980s to have a counselor operating as a professional financial planner.

Certain members of Congress are recognizing that sorting out today's interest-bearing accounts is like solving a maze. They are trying to change this with legislation. For instance, Democratic Representative Richard Lehman of California has introduced a truth-in-savings bill that could clarify much of the confusing information facing the average consumer. In 1984, Congressman Lehman explained his bill this way:

> We would require that when savings institutions advertise interest rates, they must show the simple interest rate, the annual percentage yield, and the frequency of compounding. This will enable customers to compare effective yields and and know where to save for the most interest.

Lehman's bill also requires greater disclosure of advertised rates for credit unions, savings and loan institutions, and others, as well as banks. The disclosure requirements will resemble those for the securities industry.

Deregulation Will Help

More importantly, the deregulation of each segment of the financial services industry is assisting in the continued evolution of the financial planner into a more objective, unbiased professional.

As Harold Gourgues, CFP, of Atlanta noted in a 1985 issue of his monthly newsletter:

> The informed consumer is really the impetus behind the creation of the so-called level playing field, which reflects his or her insistence on understanding who does what, what it costs, and how all that relates to helping to reach personal financial goals. The field has not been leveled merely to help the old order—the traditional industry segments—do more business; it has been leveled to give the consumer more control over his or her financial affairs. Now, all of the participants can compete on an equal basis in attempting to provide a component of the total financial delivery system.

In defense of the banking industry's reluctance to change, however, we should remember that for decades it was controlled by regulation. As the financial services industry began evolving, many bankers were hamstrung by the very regulations that had previously protected them.

What they do during the final years of the 1980s is important. How they handle and respond to the deregulation of the full financial services industry will determine their fate. Much of that deregulation will allow them to be more responsive to their consumer's needs.

If the development of the full financial services industry finds each segment cooperating with the others, the different segments of this new industry can share a much larger pie. The consumer also will benefit from the resources to plan and prepare for a much better financial future.

When that happens, the objectives of the Society for Financial Counselling, Inc., as spelled out in its original Constitution and Membership Application, composed 20 years ago, will deserve to be framed. These objectives are more than an interesting morsel of history, however; they are a foundation that should still serve as a guide for the future.

CODE OF ETHICS

Individual members of the IAFP shall:

1. Promote conceptual financial planning.

2. Understand that conceptual financial planning includes a combination of cash, insurance and equity investments, prudently providing for the realization of financial objectives in the case of life, death, disability and inflation in such a manner as to provide the largest returns consistent with limitations on the ability of the investor to assume risk.

3. Be guided by the highest standards of business ethics, personal integrity, professional conduct, securities laws, and objective counseling.

4. Avoid and discourage sensational, exaggerated and unwarranted statements.

5. Adhere not only to these standards by precept and example, but also encourage, by counsel and advice to others, their adherence to these standards.

AN INTERVIEW WITH
Donald R. Pitti

In 1985, Donald Pitti served as president of the International Association for Financial Planning, Inc. He is currently vice president of John Nuveen & Company, Inc. However, it was his work as president of Weisenberger Financial Services, Inc., in New York that did much to establish financial planning. In fact, Donald Pitti is credited with coining the term *financial services industry* during the 1960s. In 1971 he served as chairman of the board of governors for the Society for Financial Counselling, Inc. In this interview, he addresses the evolution of the financial services industry.

DUNTON: During the 1960s, what caused you to observe that the lines between the banking, securities and mutual fund services would blur to become the financial services industry that we know today?

PITTI: In the late 1960s, the mutual fund industry experienced dramatic growth, both in the number of mutual funds and in assets under management. This period was to become known as the 'go go era,' when a so-called new breed of money managers created and managed mutual funds with an investment objective to maximize capital gains. These aggressive managers achieved spectacular results—often doubling and tripling the assets under their management—as their performance attracted new investors and the Dow Jones Industrial Average soared.

    The growth in mutual fund assets, as well as growing investor interest, attracted other sellers of financial products, most notably the life insurance industry. The life insurance industry was under pressure because its main product, whole life insurance, was being replaced by term insurance. Term insurance was often sold by mutual fund salespeople and by investment brokers under the slogan 'Buy term and invest the difference.' The premise was that an investor could do better in terms of insurance coverage and investment return by purchasing term insurance and a mutual fund that would outperform the savings feature of whole life insurance.

    Simultaneously, life insurance salespeople, faced with a decline in the popularity of whole life and the growing interest of their clients and prospects in aggressive mutual fund investments, were putting pressure on their companies to create mutual funds or allow them to sell the funds of others.

    The insurance industry responded to these pressures by acquiring existing mutual funds organizations, creating mutual funds of their own, or working out arrangements whereby their agents could sell the funds of existing fund organizations. Since Weisenberger was the leading supplier of information on mutual funds, we were asked by many insurance companies to help them enter the mutual fund business.

The securities industry responded to the insurance industry's entrance into mutual funds by marketing the insurance end. Major brokerage firms had their representatives licensed to sell insurance. They either worked with insurance companies to sell their products or created their own insurance companies. Some acquired existing insurance companies.

During this period, the banking industry was not less interested in the growth in mutual funds. However, it was under the restrictions of the Glass-Steagal Act, which prohibited banks from underwriting or distributing mutual funds. So the banking industry had to be content with merely being an observer.

From our vantage point at Weisenberger, it was clear that we were witnessing the beginning of significant change in the way financial products historically had been delivered to consumers in the United States.

DUNTON: What do you mean by change? What was different?

PITTI: Historically, Americans had purchased their financial products through separate, clearly defined industry segments. They bought—or were sold—stocks, bonds and mutual funds from registered securities brokers; life, property and casualty insurance was marketed by insurance salespeople; loans, mortgages and savings accounts were the domain of banks and savings and loan associations. That separateness was traditional and was enforced by the restrictive and protective legislation that had been built around these product suppliers over time.

As a result of these restrictions on competition, the marketing revolution that transformed the rest of American industry after World War II left the financial products business virtually unscathed. In the 1950s and 1960s, consumers began to demand, and get, consumer products that were created to meet their needs, rather than the needs of the seller. The manufacturing creed, 'If we can make it, it is good,' gave way to the marketing creed, 'It is only good if it is what consumers want.' This change in philosophy, combined with the pent up demand of the war years, fueled one of the greatest growth periods in the history of our country.

Through all of this dynamic change, however, financial product suppliers continued to create and distribute financial products in the same way they had historically, virtually ignoring the changing needs and desires of their customers and prospects.

DUNTON: If these single-product suppliers were resisting change so dramatically, why did you predict in the mid-1960s that a new "financial services industry" was evolving?

PITTI: Once the insurance, securities and mutual fund industries began to make and sell each others' products, the tacit, unspoken contract to stay out of each others' businesses was broken. It became obvious that the resulting competition would cut prices and profit margins, forcing single-product suppliers to diversify in order to survive.

That was the simple message we gave our consulting clients at Weisenberger. Although we met resistance from hard-line traditionalists at a number of companies, we had the support of many other executives in those companies that recognized the realities of the changing marketplace. We began to tout a new "financial services industry" that would come about as single-product suppliers merged or diversified to provide customers with more, better, and lower cost financial products and services. From 1969 to 1975, we offered an annual Financial Services Conference, attended by hundreds of financial product company executives who spoke and heard about the evolving industry.

DUNTON: During that time, was the Weisenberger Financial Services Databank conceived?

PITTI: Yes. In 1972, Weisenberger created and sponsored a nationwide study of consumer attitudes toward financial planning services and the companies that supplied them. The survey consisted of a random of 5,000 personal interviews, statistically representing every household in the United States. The study was co-sponsored by 22 major financial service companies, including Metropolitan Life Insurance Company, Chemical Bank and Transamerica. The significance of the study, which was the first of its kind in scope and content, was that it confirmed the views of the most forward-thinking executives.

Consumers did indeed want to be able to buy more or all of their financial products from one source. Of existing organizations, they would most prefer to obtain more services and products from banks. To the surprise of most participants, "a new company set up to meet this need" was the second choice of those interviewed, with insurance companies and brokerage firms finishing near the bottom of the list.

In 1974, the Financial Services Databank was updated. In 1976, it was acquired by SRI International and became the basis for the extensive financial services studies they would conduct later.

DUNTON: How do you see the banking, securities and insurance companies changing in the future?

PITTI: First of all, I think it's important to note that while the three industries are still considered separate, the companies and organizations that make them up are now commonly referred to as financial services. Virtually all of them, particularly the major ones, have broadened their product lines to include products and services that once were the exclusive domain of the others. Even the Fortune 500 now includes a separate listing of the 50 largest financial service companies.

Over the past 15 years, a financial services industry has evolved. What I see in the future is an acceleration of the mergers and acquisitions that have put insurance companies, securities firm and mutual funds under the same corporate umbrella.

Banks, even with the restriction of the Glass-Steagal Act, have entered the securities, mutual fund and insurance businesses in a limited way. And, they will, in my opinion, gain the legislative relief that will allow them to merge freely with, or acquire, other financial services companies. The prototype financial service company of the 1990s will consist of the very largest of the banking, insurance and securities organizations of today.

I believe this will happen because the consumer of financial services, along with the salespeople who sell them and the companies that manufacture them, all want it to happen, albeit for different reasons. Consumers want the convenience and economy of being able to buy more or all of their financial products and services from one source.

While there are studies that show that many consumers do not want one organization to know all of their financial affairs, there isn't any research that shows the consumer wants to return to the days when single-product financial suppliers—free from the pressure of outside competition—"sold" products to the consumer that included the cost of maintaining their expensive selling systems. Consumers are, and will continue, voting with their investment and savings dollars for those financial products that provide lower cost. They also want customized services that prevent them from being squeezed into rigidly structured, single-line products designed to maximize the profits of the manufacturer.

Securities, insurance and mutual fund salespeople, the historic sellers of the majority of consumer financial products, are in the forefront of the changes taking place as this new financial services industry evolves, because of their role as the intermediary between the buyers and the manufacturers of financial products.

Remember, in the 1960s, the insurance, mutual fund and securities salespeople who responded to the needs of their customers by pressuring their companies to begin to offer or at least allow them to offer a wider range of products that were more closely tailored to their customers needs and goals. The companies that recognized and adapted to this need retained their key salespeople; those that didn't have lost and will continue to lose customers to those that have.

Professional financial service people today understand that the best way they can service their customers and, therefore, themselves is to provide them with a variety of investment, insurance and savings alternatives.

They know that the old way of attempting to convince prospects that their single product line is the solution to all insurance, investment and savings needs is not only no longer appropriate, but it also will not work.

Faced with the consumer's desire for more targeted, customized financial services, financial product companies realize that they must respond to the changed marketplace or perish. A number of companies have already recognized this and added new financial services and products to their traditional product lines. Now begun, this trend will continue until consumers have the same kind of options and choices in financial services that they have in other areas of our free economy.

DUNTON: Can you share with us the role you see financial planning playing in the financial services industry scenario you have outlined?

PITTI: As the process that examines and defines a consumer's current and future financial needs and provides a written plan to meet them, financial planning is at the very heart of these changes. It is both the agent of these changes and the result of them.

Still at issue is the major question: How will companies that manufacture financial products fit into the financial planning movement? Many still view financial planning as merely a new way to distribute financial products and services. They are making more products available to their salespeople and training them to deliver those products within a financial planning context, thereby amortizing the cost of product development and distribution over a wider product base.

Other companies, realizing that they may no longer be able to afford to support both a manufacturing and a distribution capability, have decided to be either manufacturers or distributors of financial products.

The result of the changes is a massive realignment in the distribution of financial services, unprecedented in the financial history of our country. At the core of this battle for distribution and a larger share of the consumer's financial services dollar is the fact that companies can no longer afford to control the people who sell or provide financial products to consumers.

The golden opportunity for financial planners, whether they are operating on a fee-only or a fee-plus-commission basis, is to use this independence truly to become the consumer's advocate for all of his or her financial affairs.

PART THREE

The Influences of Change
Others Begin Noticing the Change

Not until the 1970s did the financial planning profession and the financial planner begin to get national recognition and attention. Certainly, the Society for Financial Counselling, Inc. and its two divisions—the International Association of Financial Planners and the College for Financial Planning—contributed to early notice by other professionals within the financial services community. In addition, *The Financial Planner* magazine, now known as *Financial Planning,* kept new subscribers and those already in the profession informed. However, these groups were not the only ones fanning the winds of change.

While it's difficult to locate early references to financial planning as such, a number of individuals, companies and books were discussing and addressing the need for objective and detailed analysis of the typical consumer's personal finances. Some even were practicing financial planning, but not calling it by that title.

In tandem with their work was the gradual evolution of the securities, insurance and banking industries into what we now refer to as the financial services industry. The Society for Financial Counselling also was going through a maturation process. Established groups, such as the National Association of Securities Dealers and the Securities and Exchange Commission, began at least noticing the fledgling group headquartered in Littleton, Colorado. In the early years, the NASD and SEC didn't necessarily embrace the young upstart with open arms. Still, they did begin to recognize that just maybe something new was beginning there.

7 Financial Writers and Talkers

By 1985, the term *financial planning* was widely used all over the country. More importantly, planning for one's financial future had become almost a must in our society. Although the evolution of financial planning organizations certainly deserves considerable credit for this, there were also a number of individuals in the financial community who helped pave the way.

One of them, Dr. Israel Unterman, now a tenured professor at San Diego State University, offered a number of groups leadership in thinking of personal finances more directly. His book, *Creative Money Management for the Executive,* published by Doubleday & Company, startled many executives in 1962, particularly when they compared what they were doing with what Dr. Unterman was suggesting to protect their assets. That book did something else as well: It focused the spotlight on the possibility of a new career for financial counselors, who could advise executives about their finances.

Lorraine Blair

Another book that influenced a broader segment of people, including many who were active in the financial field during the 1960s and 1970s, was *Your Financial Guide for Living,* written by Lorraine L. Blair and published by Prentice-Hall in 1963. While it failed to gain the recognition of Napoleon Hill's *Think and Grow Rich,* a long-time best-seller, it did uniquely present a great deal of information that could help early financial planners structure the information they needed to assist others in managing their money. As such, Blair's book exerted a powerful influence on a number of mutual fund and insurance salespeople all over the country.

The sample forms Blair included in her book were the forerunners to the thousands of forms in use by financial planners today. Here are some of their original titles:

- Personal and Family Data
- Personal and Family Records

- Your Personal Financial Statement
- Itemized Estimated Expenditures
- Estimate of Present Income, Expenditures, and Savings
- Estimated Expenses and Savings Until Retirement
- Your Goals and Desires for Now and for the Future
- Actual Record of Expenses

Blair also included in that book a plan for recording savings, insurance policies and personal property.

Having counseled people about their financial affairs for almost 30 years, Blair spoke and wrote with great insight and authority. That she was recognized as an expert in both mutual funds and insurance added to her influence.

Older readers may be familiar with such classics as Orison Swett Marden's booklet titled *The Law of Financial Independence* and George Classen's *The Richest Man in Babylon*. Both of these authors, like Napoleon Hill and W. Clement Stone of Chicago, played a major part in motivating people to accumulate wealth and teaching them how to do it. However, Lorraine Blair's book came closest to providing a model along with the real tools needed for the financial planners of the 1960s. Hers was a guide for those in the 1970s who were writing books, training sales organizations, preparing manuals, or setting up procedures for financial planning firms.

Jerrold Glass and Hy Yurman

Jerrold Glass and Hy Yurman were leaders in the Mutual Fund Council of Million Dollar Producers and were helpful pioneers in expanding the new organizations, as well as in creating the financial planning profession. Their writing projects—*A Financial Planner's Guide,* published by Society Publishers in 1972 and *Conceptual Financial Planning,* published for the College for Financial Planning three years later—not only were milestones, but also gave direction to the evolution of the financial planning profession.

The Investment Dealers Digest

One of the early and great contributors to financial planning as a profession was Eliot Sharp, publisher of *The Investment Dealers Digest,* an influential magazine published in the heart of Wall Street. Along with producing the Digest, Eliot also had a good eye for people. For example, he hired Lucille Tomlinson, who wrote a booklet series on mutual funds, which was titled *Frannie Goes to College* and was extremely influential in the 1960s. Eliot also chose Ben Cascio, who ran the Mutual Fund Dealers Conference, which the Digest offered for years. Assisted by Pat Tisch and others, Cascio made that conference so successful that by 1971 almost 5,000 people attended its San Francisco meeting.

Although Eliot and his son Tim, who served for a time as one of the trustees of the Society for Financial Counselling, were helpful, neither was willing to embrace the financial planning concept. As a result, *The Investment Dealers Digest* considered the activities of the financial planning pioneers as competitive. Still, by its contributions to the mutual fund industry, *The Investment Dealers Digest* was a true source of help to the fledgling financial planning profession.

Advice Through the Media

"How can they possibly give all the advice they do, sometimes even being specific to individuals, when they know little or nothing about the person they are advising?"

Many financial planners are voicing that question about the writers of financial columns, radio and television commentators, and talk show hosts who have proliferated in the 1980s. They're concerned, of course, because they believe so strongly in learning a great deal about a client or prospect *before* giving any financial advice, much less preparing a financial plan.

In defense of the writers and broadcasters, a number of them are extremely knowledgeable and effective communicators. When they qualify their advice, or keep it general, they provide a real service to the consumer.

In fact, some media financial authorities are fully qualified to offer financial planning services, which distinguishes them noticeably from others, less qualified, in their profession.

Some Popular Examples

An outstanding example is Venita Van Caspel of Texas, who appears on many talk shows. In 1982, she started her own television show, "Money Makers," which has been aired on public broadcasting stations for four years. She is also the author of the *Money Dynamics* book series, published by Reston/Prentice-Hall. The reason Van Caspel is so knowledgeable about the topic is that she has been doing financial planning for more than 20 years. An outspoken critic of cash value life insurance, she has done more to polarize the proponents and the opponents of cash value/whole life insurance than probably anyone else.

Another notable writer, less well liked by the financial planning profession but probably better known to consumers, is Sylvia Porter, who has been writing about money, very readably, for almost 50 years. For years, in the early days of her career, she wrote under S.F. Porter, to disguise the fact that a woman was giving out financial advice at the *New York Post*. Undoubtedly, the advice in her widely syndicated column, her lectures, her magazine articles, and her best-selling books has been of great help to many thousands of people. In fact, she deserves credit for popularizing money as a topic worth reading about.

Some observers, however, including this one, have found it hard to forgive her for the role she played in causing Social Security to be viewed as a retirement plan. Indeed, she still questions, even publicly, those of us who are worried about the future of Social Security.

There are many others, of course, who have contributed to the consumers' growing interest in financial planning and managing their money wisely, but space precludes covering them all here.

Shortcomings of Talk Show Advice

Many cities, including smaller ones, also have excellent money-oriented talk shows. These programs serve to stimulate people's interest in matters financial and also frequently have financial planners as guests.

However, not all financial planners who are guests on these shows are as careful in their responses as they should be. Some give advice with little information, pointing up the difference between the way a trained, conscientious financial planner answers questions and gives advice and the way an inexperienced one might. Financial planning professionals give answers, advise and counsel only after a long series, sometimes hours, of searching questions and fact finding.

Occasionally, we still hear a caller add a final bit of information that causes the quest expert or the host to observe, "Oh, you didn't tell me that. If that's the case, then you shouldn't tie up your money at all. Neither one of the options you outlined to us are right for you." However, more and more each year, media authorities are being careful to point out the need for integrated financial decisions and urging people to visit a qualified financial planner.

Helpful Answers

In the newspaper area, William Doyle, a longtime syndicated columnist, is a superb financial journalist. For years, he's proved himself a knowledgeable source for specific answers to questions. Here's an example from one of his 1983 columns, illustrating how he approaches his craft:

> Question: In 1982, when my wife and I were both 67, we sold our home of 10 years for $98,000, at a profit of $50,000. A few days later, we bought a new home for $105,000. This house now is worth about $130,000.
>
> I did not realize we had the option of postponing the tax on the profit from the sale. On our 1982 income tax return, we took the once-in-a-lifetime exclusion and did not pay tax on the $50,000 profit.
>
> Can I write to the IRS and ask them to let me use the exclusion later? In view of the above figures, would this be the wise thing to do?

Answer: You can file a 1982 1040X amended return and a new From 2119—the form used to either postpone or exclude tax on the profit from the sale of the principal residence and which you used to take the exclusion on your 1982 return.

It will be to your advantage to do just that. By amending your 1982 return, you can postpone, rather than exclude, the $50,000 profit from the sale of your first house. You'll also adjust the cost basis of your present home downward by $50,000.

That will make the basis of your present home $55,000—the $105,000 you paid for it, minus the $50,000 adjustment.

If you sell your present home for $130,000 after having lived in it for at least three of the five years before the sale, you'll then be able to take the once-in-a-lifetime exclusion and not pay tax on the $75,000 profit.

Question: How much time does a person have to file a Form 1040X amended federal income tax return?

Answer: In almost all situations, you must file an amended return within three years of the date on which you filed the return you want to amend or within two years from the time you paid your tax, whichever is later.

The major exception is with worthless securities. In that unhappy situation, you can file an amended return and take a capital loss equal to the price you paid or whatever other basis you have—back for seven years.

That exception recognizes the fact that it often is difficult to determine exactly when a worthless security lost all its value.

Answers like these provide a useful service and make a valuable newspaper feature.

The New Writing Standards

Undoubtedly, the best writing being done today on the financial planning industry can be found in *Financial Planning* magazine. Chapter 19 is entirely devoted to the magazine and the important role it has played in establishing financial planning as a profession and the financial planner as a professional. The success of that magazine has permitted editor Jack Lange to attract some of the best financial writers, who now contribute to *Financial Planning*.

Two consumer financial magazines are also running excellent, well-researched articles on financial planning subject. *Money* magazine, owned by Time, Inc., was a little slow in recognizing the emergence of the financial planner as a leading player on the field, but the magazine has made up for that slow start in its coverage since 1983.

The *Sylvia F. Porter Financial Magazine,* under editor Patricia Estess, didn't begin publishing until 1983 but lost no time establishing itself with both consumers and professionals. Just a few of the articles on financial planning that were published during its first year are:

- New, Low-Cost Financial Plans
- SFPFM's Guide to Financial Plans
- Checking Out Financial Supermarkets
- Financial Planning: A Lifetime Affair

In addition, managing editor Arthur Rogoff ranked the quality of financial counseling obtained from qualified advisors. He listed accountants, bankers, insurance agents, stock brokers and lawyers. Ahead of all of them, he put financial planners.

8 The Society and Its Divisions

"It was an organization and a concept whose time had come," said Richard T. White, editor of *The Financial Planner* from 1977 to 1980. He was speaking of the Society for Financial Counselling, Inc., founded in 1969.

Originally, the Society had the word *ethics* in its title. Later the word was dropped, however, and the subject was covered in the Society's Code of Ethics. When it was founded, the Society had three stated goals:

1. Increasing the percentage of people able to retire in a sound financial position (without depending on government subsidy) by improving, broadening, and professionalizing the financial counseling available to the public;
2. Increasing the number of people all over the world whose future can be brighter because of the intelligent, forward-thinking financial planning they are encouraged to do; and
3. Increasing the professionalism of and recognition earned by those engaged in areas of ethical financial planning and counseling.

The Early Years of the Society

After researching other professions, we determined that the foundation that worked best was a combination of a professional association with an educational institution. Clearly, if helping people plan their financial futures was to become a profession, then these important cornerstones had to be laid. So, from its beginning, the Society was organized with two divisions: the International Association of Financial Counsellors (the professional association) and the College for Financial Counsellors (the educational arm).

Unfortunately, the financial centers of the East, including the National Association of Securities Dealers and the Securities and Exchange Commission, had difficulty visualizing, much less supporting, any such organizations, particularly headquartered in Littleton, Colorado. Rumblings about our group began, and our first concession to them was to agree not to use the term *counselor* for our group. It took help from Ferd Nauheim, a financial consultant and author in Washington, D.C., but the term *financial planner* was eventually approved.

I vividly recall meeting with Irving Pollack, who later became a commissioner of the SEC, during the formative years of our Society. In a Washington interview in 1972, he posed some key questions about our new society. His first question was, "How many Certified Financial Planners have you created, Mr. Dunton?" I told him we hadn't created any.

"Well, didn't the NASD just conduct your examinations for you?" he asked. I admitted the NASD had indeed conducted them and that we were very grateful.

"Then, don't you have any CFPs? Didn't anyone pass?" Mr. Pollack challenged. I explained that about half had passed the test, but that it was merely the first examination. To become a CFP, one needed to take five courses and pass five examinations, which would take about two years.

We discussed in depth the courses and examinations, designed by Jim Johnston, Lew Kerns and others. Mr. Pollack also queried me about our plans for the future of the College for Financial Planning and the IAFP. When he learned how the Society later planned to educate the public as well, he offered suggestions as to where we might seek funding to create our new profession. I returned to Denver thinking the Society's financial problems might be soon solved; that my little company, my sister, and my family might even get back the money advanced to set up the College and the almost 30 IAFP chapters across the country.

Forrest Wallace Cato's Contributions

Forrest Wallace (Wally) Cato became editor of *Financial Planning* magazine in 1979, when Vernon Gwynne was IAFP executive director and publisher. Wally was interested in the history of our organizations and of the new financial planning profession. An article he wrote for the *Financial Securities Digest,* titled "An Interview with Loren Dunton: The Man Who Created a Profession Without Ever Practicing It," appeared in the magazine's October-November 1983 issue. Here are some of the questions he asked after I told him about my interview at the SEC:

> CATO: *Did any government agencies solve your financial problems?*
>
> DUNTON: No, because at the next board of governors meeting, they vetoed the idea of us going to any government agency. As I recall, about the time my wife and I cosigned for another $5,000 loan so we could pay some IAFP bills and part of Jim Johnston's back salary. Jim was doing a tremendous job in structuring the college and the CFP courses, even though he usually had to wait to be paid for the conservative $1,000 a month he agreed to work for.

CATO: *Speaking of salary, what was yours at the time?*

DUNTON: $1,000 a month, when there was enough to pay me, that is.

CATO: *You wore a lot of hats: which one did that pay?*

DUNTON: That $1,000 was it. At one time I was executive director of the IAFP, first president of the college, president and executive director of the society, as well as editor and publisher of *The Financial Planner* magazine. Oh yes, I was also selling all the ads and have to work at being amused remembering that my replacement got himself a contract for $45,000 a year for just two of those jobs.

CATO: *What really made it possible to wear all those hats?*

DUNTON: A helpful and understanding wife, of course, but what really made the most difference was Jim Johnston doing almost all of the work involved in setting up the college and CFP courses. His secret was getting Lew Kerns and all those other good people to help him.

CATO: *Yes, but what about the IAFP? Who were the guiding lights in the beginning?*

DUNTON: First the people who came on the society board, of course, like H.L. Jamieson, Donald Pitti and Julius Cahn, and then the IAFP chairmen like Walter Fisher, John Keeble and Hy Yurman. Richard W.A. Davis and June Davis picked me up in their airplane, and we flew all over Florida setting up four chapters from the preliminary organization work he did. They were in the first 15.

CATO: *It's all tied together of course, but let's get back to the financial planning profession. When did you really feel that the Financial Planner would be recognized as a professional?*

DUNTON: Well, first finding that many people around the country wanted us to help them set up IAFP chapters inspired a lot of confidence. But the great job that Jim Johnston, Lew Kearns, Ferd Nauheim and those early trustees of the College were doing creating the CFP courses made a tremendous difference also.

CATO: *Where were the first chapters you set up? And how many of them made it?*

DUNTON: A couple of years ago it was said that over half of the almost 30 chapters we set up are still very active. Others that died have since been reborn until there are now over 100. The first 10 were listed in The Financial Planner Newsletter, which became *The Financial Planner* magazine:

1. Knoxville Association of Financial Planners,
   Kemp Fain, Jr., President.
2. San Diego Association of Financial Planners,
   Allyn B. Ostroski, President.
3. Los Angeles County Association of Financial Planners,
   Stuart Raffel, President.
4. Santa Clara County Association of Financial Planners,
   Gilbert J. Gray, President.
5. Seattle-Tacoma Association of Financial Planners,
   Dickinson W. Sparks, President.
6. Portland Association of Financial Planners,
   Dr. Shannon P. Pratt, President.
7. Orange County Association of Financial Planners,
   Ted Koziatek, President.
8. San Francisco Association of Financial Planners,
   Clarence "Al" Swearingen, President.
9. Chicago Association of Financial Planners,
   Patrick J. McEvoy, President.
10. Baltimore Association of Financial Planners,
    Dennis D. Wielech, CLU, President.

CATO: *Which came first, the financial planning profession or the financial planners?*

DUNTON: We used to think of it more as a chorus. They had to move ahead together. As more and more IAFP chapters were formed, more and more individuals began calling themselves financial planners. Most of them were licensed to sell both securities and insurance, and this increased their objectivity and their image of objectivity which played a large part. As the Institute for Certified Financial Planners has grown, it has done the most to enhance the professionalism and establish the function as a profession.

CATO: *Something had to come even before that, didn't it?*

DUNTON: Initially, as with all new professions, and old ones, come to think of it, the *need* is what comes first. And I'm sure that I wasn't the first to recognize the almost universal need for more helpful and objective financial counseling. A few enlightened insurance men and a large number of mutual fund pioneers were actually doing it for their clients. Dr. Israel Unterman even wrote a book way back then that was very helpful.

CATO: *I understand the insurance, banking and security groups turned a deaf ear to you but that some mutual funds were helpful. Is that right?*

The Society and Its Divisions

DUNTON: Yes, and especially the Mutual Fund Council of Million Dollar Producers. Its members helped form Chapters and spoke without charge at the first IAFC and IAFP sales seminars.

CATO: *You started that, I understand.*

DUNTON: No, I didn't, but because of the book I had written on selling mutual funds they called me in to help. Later I served as their executive director. That was in '67 and '68...before the IAFP.

CATO: *After you got your organizations started, weren't there a lot of people calling themselves financial planners who were just using the image to sell more insurance?*

DUNTON: Yes, there were, and we resented it of course. Jim and I reminded ourselves, however, that they would experience a certain amount of living up to the image they created that would be a plus for the public. And, I think it has worked out that way.

CATO: *As a writer, I'm of course interested in the role* The Financial Planner *magazine played.*

DUNTON: Well, it started out as a four-page quarterly newsletter. Same name of course. By the third issue (January '71) it was eight pages, and in January '72 it became a 48-page magazine.

In that first issue we ran the William A. Doyle newspaper column of March 12, 1968 which had influenced me so greatly. Here's a quote from that column:

> We need financial advice badly and do not know where to turn. Our insurance man wants us to get more insurance. The bankers advise us to put more money into savings accounts. Mutual fund salesmen urge us to invest in funds.
>
> We have five children and very little extra money, but we do want to use it to our best advantage. We need a disinterested person who will study our situation and advise us on what is best to us. Is there such an animal as a financial adviser?

CATO: *There weren't any, were there?*

DUNTON: Yes, of course there were. But only rich people could afford them. What we had as our vision was a general practitioner who would make a good living working with people of average means. Dennis Weilech, a CLU and early chapter president, wrote one of the first newsletter articles and titled it 'On the Threshold of a Dream.'

CATO: *Apparently there was a lot of idealism present in those days?*

DUNTON: Yes, lots of it. It is powerful fuel for the job that had to be done then, and I'm glad to see that there is still a lot of idealism for the big job that remains to be done. My favorite perhaps was Kemp Fain's article in 1971 titled; 'What Financial Planning Has Done for My Clients and for Me.' Here are his first three paragraphs:

"Kemp, why don't you write about the very things you've mentioned?"

He had gotten me talking enthusiastically about how sold I was on doing *real* financial planning for my clients rather than just trying to sell them mutual funds or insurance. This was Loren Dunton's way of getting an article written for his IAFP newsletter, *The Financial Planner*.

As a charter member of the IAFP (International Association of Financial Planners) and president of the first local chapter, it was a logical request. Having given talks on the same subject, it didn't seem too difficult an assignment.

CATO: *What about publicity? When did you first start getting any?*

DUNTON: One of the first [articles] was by Dave Goodwin. He wrote about our organization in the November 26, 1970, insurance column he wrote for newspapers. We reproduced the entire column in our January newsletter. Other articles gradually appeared, forerunners of the publicity the financial planning movement is now getting.

CATO: *What else was in the first two or three issues?*

DUNTON: In that first one I answered the question, 'Why the IAFC?' this way:

We are often asked what got us started on the IAFC. Reading Mr. Doyle's column two years ago made me realize the one way to bring about more objective financial counseling to more people would be through such an organization. We suggested it to other larger organizations but finally after visiting with leaders in the industry, we decided to tackle it ourselves. Much time, effort and money has been expended, but we're confident it can be a good thing for the public, the salesmen, and the industry itself.

CATO: *Did you have any letters or columnists?*

DUNTON: Stuart Raffel wrote the first letter in the first issue, and when the newsletter grew to become a magazine, Dave Goodwin, Jerrold Glass and Hy Yurman, all of Florida, were our first columnists. Don Pitti wrote a very prophetic lead article, 'You and the Financial Services Industry of the Future.' Ferd Nauheim, Hamilton Gregg, Walter Fischer and William Kendall wrote articles, and Mack McDonald of Texas was interviewed on how to run seminars.

CATO: *What was your editorial about?"*

DUNTON: On why companies should join the society and thereby support the IAFP and the college. I also wrote an article titled, like my speeches, 'Let's Quit Fighting the Wrong Wars,' in which I deplored the 95 percent figure [retirees dependent upon Social Security] and encouraged the various segments of the financial services industry to join together to compete more successfully with the forces in our society trying to get people to *spend* their money. Here's a direct quote:

> ...if those who are concerned, and especially those who are marketing long-range investments, don't work together to create a better climate for *INVESTING* for the future as opposed to all-out *SPENDING* for today, not only will the securities and mutual fund industries be badly hurt, but even the insurance industry.
>
> This could result in an even smaller percentage of people able to retire in comfort, and increasingly justified criticism of our free enterprise system.

CATO: *That certainly gave a clue that someday you would be doing just what you're doing now with the National Center for Financial Education.*

DUNTON: Yes, you're right.

CATO: *Before we get on to that, however, I'm curious as to how the IAFP obtained ownership of* The Financial Planner *magazine when you and the publishing company you set up founded and financed it.*

DUNTON: The minority stockholders who owned about 20%, with the exception of Jay Smith, agreed to sell half and donate half their stock to the IAFP. This worked out to fifty cents a share. Jay was really angry that his other board members were allowing their new Executive Director to get all the stock so the IAFP could sell the magazine.

CATO: *The IAFP did sell the magazine for a while, I understand, but what happened to Ratterman?*

DUNTON: He ended up as editor for the new owners with a forty-five thousand a year contract. But that didn't last long. The IAFP got the magazine back and the following year hired Rich White as Editor.

CATO: *Does Jay still have his stock?*

DUNTON: Yes, he kept his stock but at that time agreed to hold off on the legal action he was considering.

CATO: *Who owned the majority of the stock?*

DUNTON: Loren Dunton Associates, Inc. [LDA], my wife and I.

CATO: *What happened to your stock?*

DUNTON: We donated outright our sixty-two thousand shares to the IAFP.

CATO: *So that's how they got the magazine.*

DUNTON: George Ratterman who was running the IAFP insisted of course that when the IAFP could afford it they would be anxious to reciprocate our generosity.

CATO: *What about the other money you had invested?*

DUNTON: He also agreed to pay LDA a thousand dollars a month until it had recovered the thirty-four thousand dollars we had put up to get the IAFP and the college going.

CATO: *You said you never received anything for the sixty-two thousand dollars worth of publishers stock you donated to the IAFP, but did you or LDA ever get the thirty-four thousand in cash it owed you?*

DUNTON: Partly. Fred Harris, who had taken over from Ratterman as executive director said the IAFP was too poor to pay thirty-four but would we settle for twelve? It was a good cause and, in a way, our own child, so we did.

CATO: *Well, your generous donation and that of the other stockholders has certainly paid off. The magazine is still playing a big role in the growth of the IAFP and the financial planning profession.*
But McGraw-Hill had published your book on salesmanship, and you had consulting clients on both coasts, London, Zurich and Frankfurt. How come you gave this up to do something like trying to create a new profession? It was bound to cost you a lot of money.

DUNTON: In the first place I had achieved my last big financial goal in taking my family on a year's trip around the world, so making a lot of money wasn't very important. Besides, it was a unique challenge and it appealed to me. Also, since neither my grandfather, my father, nor I had ever done any financial planning, the need was obvious. Besides, since I had never sold any kind of financial products we figured I would meet less objection than someone coming from either the securities or insurance industries. Less, that is, than someone who sold one or the other.

CATO: One saying you used while building the IAFP is that 'one of the measurements of success is the amount of time you can afford to spend helping others in your profession.' Do you have any other pet sayings?

DUNTON: Yes. One of them is to the effect that most creative things are done by people who aren't too busy making money.

AN INTERVIEW WITH
John Keeble

John Keeble is president and chief executive officer of Financial Service Corporation, International, of Atlanta (FSC). He and his firm were involved in the beginnings of the financial planning movement. He also was one of the early supporters of the IAFP and was an early chairman of its governing committee. A lawyer, John Keeble also had experience in life insurance, investments, estate planning and tax work, before entering into financial planning. In this interview, he shares how he and his firm began doing financial planning and how he views the financial planning profession today.

DUNTON: When did you and your firm enter into the financial planning profession?

KEEBLE: I entered the mutual fund business 25 years ago on the theory that 90 percent of people would do better with mutual funds than they would by fooling around with their own stocks. And, I found out I was wrong: it's more like 99 percent!

DUNTON: Yes, but selling mutual funds doesn't constitute financial planning any more than selling insurance does. You did more than market mutual funds, didn't you?

KEEBLE: Our experience started back in the 1950s. I remember writing what was the first financial planning case I ever saw in early 1963. I adapted it from a mutual benefits life analagraph, which is a programming method of selling. Toward the end of the 1960s, we were doing 150 financial planning cases every month. We were also recruiting the best people out of companies like Waddell & Reed, IDS, Mutual Benefit Life, Massachusetts Mutual, and so on. We had 300 full-time reps, and we were averaging half a case a month per rep.

DUNTON: How would you define financial planning?

KEEBLE: Financial planning is a profession. It is also something people do in order to reach short- and long- range financial goals.

DUNTON: How many people really need financial planning or a financial planner, in your opinion?

KEEBLE: Everyone who wants to accumulate money or assets or who wants to protect the money or assets that they have or who wants to make those assets grow needs financial planning. The average person needs someone who will sit down and give him or her a complete financial physical, make a knowledgeable diagnosis, and write out a prescription for financial well-being.

DUNTON: In your firm, you address three things that can happen to an average person that spotlight the need for financial planning. Can you share those with us?

KEEBLE: First, you can die young. Life insurance is the most urgent need, because if you die young there is no other way to raise the capital to provide an estate. If you buy it [insurance] as part of an overall financial plan, you can buy a lot of coverage at a very low cost.

Second, you can become disabled. Being disabled for three to six months is probably not a real hardship. But what if you can never work again? Your life insurance doesn't pay, because you are not dead. You can't accumulate capital to become financially independent, because you can't work. The answer is you need disability insurance, an extremely important part of financial planning.

Third, you can live a long, healthy life. If you don't die early, you need "money at work" to replace "person at work" for your retirement years. You need to accumulate capital.

The most important objective of financial planning is to accumulate enough capital so you can become financially independent.

DUNTON: How do your financial planners convince the average person to put aside $4,000 a year for his or her retirement?

KEEBLE: In FSC, they point out that given reasonable control of inflation, a reasonable amount of growth in income, and a continued amount of discipline, a $40,000-a-year person could end up with an estate of $500,000 in 20 years. With a 12 percent yield, that would give the person $60,000 a year on which to retire.

DUNTON: What do you think will represent the biggest change in the future of the financial planning profession

KEEBLE: Automation—that has already changed things; it hasn't changed them yet as much as it's going to change them. Automation allows more people to perform the financial planning function without getting bogged down. It also makes it easier, or at least possible, to track products and to see the results of an account at once and to compare those results to six months or a year ago. Automation is coming on stronger and stronger, and it's one of the major directions of our firm.

DUNTON: Could you share some of your personal observations on financial planning, particularly fee-only financial planning?

KEEBLE: I'll give you a personal experience. I have a Keogh plan. I used to get a lot of my income in commissions, so I put some of that money in a Keogh account with my bank. I also had some of my company stock in that account. When I sold that stock, the bank had a choice of giving me a passbook savings account or a money market account for six months. Can you guess which one they put my money in?

Yes, they put it for six months in a passbook savings account. I wanted to take that money and roll it over into my IRA and start applying it in something more interesting.

One of my friends, Richard Stoker, is a wholesaler. I told him of the story and my desire to put my money in something else. We talked about it for several weeks. He came in one day with an application for some mutual funds. I noted that they were load funds, whereupon he said, "Well, OK, then call your no-load rep and have him or her come over here and help you." Then, I noted the "ABC Fund" had performed better in the last five years. He said, "Well, call somebody from the ABC Fund." I ended up signing for the funds he recommended.

DUNTON: How do you feel about the giant companies that are now entering financial planning?

KEEBLE: American Express bought Shearson; Shearson bought Robinson-Humphrey—we're familiar with that story here. Sears bought Coldwell Banker and Dean Witter; Prudential bought Bache.

The big insurance companies also are entering the market by buying broker-dealers and getting into the investment business; banks are getting into it too.

We're not afraid of the big insurance companies, the banks, or Sears, because we think we have the advantage. We understand the business; the guts of that understanding, in my opinion, is the professional salespeople. Nothing happens unless somebody sells something, and banks, historically, have not been able to sell very successfully. While life insurance companies have proved they can sell, the big companies are so rich that they may not be motivated enough to really learn and adopt true financial planning. Sears has also not proved that it will ever commit to the concept of financial planning; the brokerage houses are more interested in transactions than financial planning. So, I think a certain segment of the financial services industry, which we represent, will be where financial planning really is.

PART FOUR

Financial Counseling Today
Change and Need Yield Growth

We have already noted that the development of a middle class, the effects of the Baby Boom generation, the rise in the number of college students, the increasing number of retirement years, higher income taxes, more discretionary income, mutual funds, tax shelters, and more were part of the post–World War II changes. It became obvious in the 1960s and 1970s that we needed to do more intelligent planning for our personal financial future.

That need brought about the function of financial planning. Mutual fund sales representatives and insurance agents began taking an active interest in counseling their clients. Gradually, others noted that the counseling posture was more effective in selling than were their previous practices. This, too, speeded up the growth of the profession.

As more people in their 50s and 60s found themselves in higher tax brackets, they became more willing to seek and pay for financial advice, resulting in an increasing number of fee-only financial planners.

What also evolved, however, is a type of financial counseling—sometimes even called "financial planning"—that is rendered by people in other professions, sometimes merely as an added service, sometimes only to sell one financial product or another.

Part Four covers the different types of financial counseling, as opposed to true financial planning. Because the term *financial planning* has become so popular, it is being used by insurance agents, stockbrokers, bankers, accountants and lawyers.

9 Financial Planning as an Add-On

Lawyers are doing it; accountants are doing it. Doing what? Financial planning, that's what. Now some of them are saying that they've been doing financial planning all along. If you ask them to show you a five-year-old financial plan, however, they start hedging.

Nevertheless, more and more lawyers and accountants actually are learning financial planning techniques, according to Dr. Bill Anthes, president of the College for Financial Planning, by enrolling in the college and studying for their CFP designation. In fact, a number of them have already graduated.

Attorney John Freeman Blake, formerly of the Bank of America, now works with the Tax Management Institute in Washington, D.C. He reminded me recently that 50 years ago a lawyer often advised the head of a family about financial matters. With the growing sophistication of many Americans, however, lawyers gradually lost ground in this important area. "Moreover," he maintained, "if the legal profession is smart, it will use [Americans'] growing interest in financial planning to recapture some of that earlier relationship."

Shortly thereafter, I began a little research of my own to assess the likelihood of things coming out the way he implied they might. Would lawyers become a dominant force in the financial planning movement?

I observed that more of them are attending financial planning seminars, and a number of legal programs and meetings contain sessions and speeches that prominently address financial planning subjects and techniques. I also noted that a number of lawyers are subscribing to and reading financial planning literature.

However, in practice, I also observed that many lawyers and accountants were offering financial planning to their clients as an add-on service. After all, they reasoned, they knew about taxes, wills and estate planning; have an insurance rep they can turn to; and know a stock broker "if you want some investments." Still, if you asked them about tax shelters, investments, risk management, retirement planning, or particularly how to integrate the overall plan to the maximum advantage of the client, they frequently floundered.

Still a One-Sided Ball Game

The sophisticated financial planner frequently calls in other professionals or works with those the client already has retained to develop and execute a real financial plan. For the business executive with a family, a profit-sharing plan, a deferred income arrangement, a few ignored investments, and college expenses looming, the team approach is almost essential and the one most financial planners prefer.

However, accountants and lawyers rarely call in a financial planner if their client needs to pay more attention to his or her finances. They generally prefer the add-on approach, seeing to all of it themselves. This reluctance to expose their clients to others, opting instead to investigate financial matters themselves, has led many of them to enroll in the College for Financial Planning.

In the future, instead of adding on financial planning services for their clients, will accountants and lawyers follow the lead of so many insurance brokers and actually change to financial planning as their primary profession? Apparently, they are interested in doing just that, at least in progressive regions of the country, like San Francisco, California.

Jim Hermann, CPA, is chairman of the California CPA Society's Financial Planning Task Force. He is also a CFP and chairman of the National Center for Financial Education National Accounting Committee. Here's what he recently had to say about the topic:

> It's high time that accountants realize that 'financial planning' is here to stay as a recognized and accepted client service.
>
> A study, commissioned by the California CPA Society and performed by the Management Advisory Center, would indicate that the consumer wants financial services but feels that the current CPA lacks the broad educational skills to adequately perform these services.
>
> If the accountant wants to plug into this viable market of financial planning, he or she will need to become more acquainted with the skills necessary to do this. In my estimation, it will take the accountant's commitment to become more specialized in this field, if he or she is going to adequately be able to service his or her clients in this area. Otherwise, [the accountant's] clients may soon become the clients of another financial planner.

Herb Perluss, another San Francisco accountant, has an interesting observation about the future of the accountant in the financial planning profession. He thinks that the average accountant has far more time now, thanks to automation and computerization. "Financial planning should be an excellent place to put that time," he says.

An East Coast CPA Speaks Out

In Cherry Hill, New Jersey, Harry Scheyer, CPA, decided several years ago to expand his practice to include financial planning. He soon qualified for his CFP designation and became active in the profession. Here's why he thinks that CPAs should become CFPs:

> The emerging personal financial planning movement is in great need of high-quality, dedicated professionals to provide objective, comprehensive financial planning services to the public. The CPA professional, properly trained in the body of knowledge, methodology and concepts of the personal financial planning process, is in an excellent position to meet that demand.
>
> One of the best ways a CPA can attain this knowledge is to successfully complete the CFP professional education program given by the College for Financial Planning. The required study and exams, like the CPA program, will help the professional attain the necessary skills and confidence in the field.
>
> The CPA profession has earned the highly regarded and accepted role as the public's independent business and tax adviser. Today, this independent and objective image is greatly needed and sought after by prudent individuals, in regard to personal financial planning services.
>
> The CPA profession is becoming more aware of the supply and current demand for independent, comprehensive personal financial counseling. CPAs are starting to organize their practices to develop financial planning services. Therefore, the CPA/CFP professional will be ideally suited for and sought after by those firms requiring their expertise. In addition, the CPA can better serve his or her existing clientele by being more well-rounded and by knowing the financial planning process.
>
> A CPA does not have to have a CFP to provide financial counseling for his or her client. But, an important professional standard is that a CPA should only accept those engagements for which he or she has adequate expertise and can successfully perform. The CFP program is an excellent way to help develop the expertise needed for those professionals wanting to provide personal financial planning services.
>
> It should be important to note that the CFP educational program has been recognized by some states as meeting some of the continuing education requirements for CPAs. Finally, at a recent marketing seminar, attendees were informed that one of the best referral sources for new business was the CPA!

One accountant who is apparently doing financial planning is advertising in his local newspaper. "Whose Financial Planning?" is the ad's headline. The ad maintains, "We sell no investments, so our advice is unbiased. We consider your resources and goals, then suggest a program that is right for you—not one that produces the largest commissions for us." Then, in bold print, it gives the name of the CPA, his address, and his phone number.

For some reason, that phrase "suggest a program" caught my eye. It didn't say "prepare a plan," so I wonder if this accountant is like others who talk about financial planning and suggest a program without realizing how much less effective and helpful that is than preparing and helping the client implement a financial plan, which is what the good financial planner does.

Bankers with Their Toes in the Water

What about bankers? Can and should they add financial planning, in some form, to their present banking functions? Robert Metzger's bank consulting firm in Tustin, California, is one of those trying to help banks capitalize on their growing opportunities in broader-based financial counseling for their clients, again as an add-on to their other services.

He and his partner, Susan Rau, as well as other firms like theirs, are trying to help banks expand their services. However, banks will probably not play a dominant role in offering financial planning to their clients until they become more effective at basic financial counseling. Here's how Robert Metzger sees it:

> Retail customers, in general, and the upscale customer, in particular, have become much better educated and more sophisticated in their product knowledge. In fact, some customers know more about their options and opportunities than the average customer service personnel hired to counsel them.
>
> In spite of the dollars committed to these projects in both marketing promotion and personnel training, there has yet to be a real success story in the financial counseling area. Not a day goes by in the industry without some announcement of the newest Sears Financial Center opening; the latest training efforts at E.F. Hutton, Dean Witter, and Shearson; the attempts by Empire Savings in upstate New York to emulate Sears; Scudder and Fidelity opening mutual fund storefront operations; or ITT Insurance training bank and savings and loan managers as licensed insurance agents.
>
> But none of these efforts at financial counseling has been clearly successful. Why? The primary reason is that none of these institutions has been very clear as to exactly what financial planning is or should be. The Sears and Empire Savings centers are a concentration of different sales booths in one central location, with each attempting to sell its own narrow product line. The Registered Representative training program at the brokerage houses have been an effort to

develop more reasons and ways to sell a prospect on a brokerage account. None of this is true financial counseling.

From Robert Metzger's perspective, banks have a long way to go before they become one of the dominant forces in the financial planning movement.

A Banker's View

"Are Banks the Financial Planners of Tomorrow?" was the title of an article that appeared in the February, 1983, issue of *Financial Planning* magazine by John Tapley, senior vice president of the Flagship Bank of Tampa, Florida. I thought it would be interesting to get his answer to that question now, more than two years later. "Things are moving very slowly in that direction," he said, "but I still feel that if banks come out with the right program, they can become a real force in financial planning."

Perhaps the American Banking Association (ABA) will speed things up. In a press release issued in 1984, ABA observed the following:

> More than 360 bankers have applied for and been awarded the ABA Trust Division's Certified Financial Services Counselor (CFSC) designation—an indication of their advanced training and experience in financial counseling.
>
> The specific title of the designation, formerly known as Certified Financial Counselor (CFC), was recently changed to eliminate possible confusion with another organization which uses a 'CFC' title.
>
> ABA's Certified Financial Services Counselor designation is conferred upon those who complete with distinction the current expanded curriculum of the ABA National Graduate Trust School (NGTS), or who graduated from NGTS, or the Stonier School of Banking's former three-year trust major program, and have three years of trust banking experience since graduation.
>
> 'The CFSC designation is awarded for high-level academic achievement,' said Van R. Gathany, chairman of ABA's Trust Division. 'The emphasis for the award is on professional responsibility—encompassing effective functioning within the bank trust department, maintaining a current level of knowledge and expertise throughout the financial counseling career, and seeking outside assistance as necessary.' Gathany is senior vice president, Northern Trust Co., Chicago.
>
> The CFSC designation acknowledges that the NGTS graduate has met stringent requirements in a variety of courses including, but not limited to, investments, asset management, new business, business and personal tax planning, estate planning, employee benefits, fiduciary law, trust operations, and administration. High scores on examinations in each year of the two-year graduate session are

required, as well as superior performance in a comprehensive work program. The extension program may include, over a two-year period, completion of 18 problems or a combination of problems with a major thesis or research paper on a topic of current interest to the industry.

Recipients of the CFSC designation will also be issued a seal, similar to that used by a notary public, which may be affixed to relevant documents prepared in their capacity as Certified Financial Services Counselors. 'Along with the name change, this seal will help distinguish CFSCs from the numerous other "financial counselors," Gathany noted.

Interestingly, the term *financial planner* is never used by ABA in its release.

I also wonder how successful this add-on approach will be for bankers, accountants and lawyers, particularly over a long period of time. Will it become even more important than their present function? Will they be able to get new clients for whom to do financial planning? Are they real threats to the present financial planning firms? Chapter 26 will look into some of those questions.

The Money Manager

While it's just one of many developements in financial counseling today, the "money manager" could represent another career possibility in financial counseling and one that could lead to a financial planning career.

The money manager concept was created and pioneered by the 24 banks of the First Wyoming Bank Corporation. It began with deregulation in 1983 and was First Wyoming's response to the growing competition among financial institutions.

"The money manager represents a new customer-oriented concept and was established as a highly visible service," according to John Olafson, First Wyoming's vice president for marketing. "Our money managers assess the customer's needs personally with the aim of building customer trust, cross-selling products, and collecting demographic data. At the same time, they are working to increase core deposits and attempting to sell free-income services for the bank."

The approach took the bank two years to develop. But it appears to be paying off, as money managers increased core deposits by more than half of the entire 12-month projected total in just two months, according to Olafson. In the same period, more than 50 percent of the customers handled by the money managers were sold at least one additional service or product.

In explaining the money managers' success, Olafson says:

> Operating as a financial counselor, with knowledge of the entire range of bank services and products, along with a strong sales

background, this person could effectively build customer confidence and cross-sell the banking services and products.

The customer service objective is to provide proper service for all customers, regardless of the account balance. The feeling was that all customers were willing to pay for good customer service—not just those we commonly identify as the high-net worth customer. We remember well the type of customers who have afforded us low-interest savings balances in the past.

The program's success rests in the fact that the banking institution is visibly willing to meet customer needs and to give people the kind of service they feel they deserve. The customers who tell one of our money managers that their bank neglected to give them beneficial information on available interest—or whatever—are customers who move accounts. The bank that can successfully develop the image of a trusted advocate is the bank developing an image essential to profitability in this highly competitive marketplace.

Can actual financial planning by banks, even in small towns, be far behind?

Well, smart financial planners are already spotting and capitalizing on the possibilities. One of them is Marilyn Capelli, CFP, who set up a financial plans center for the Naperville (Illinois) National Bank on a shared-fee basis. By 1985, she had left that one bank to provide the service for several banks. As she explained it:

> The smaller banks are finding that it is often too expensive to set up their own financial planning centers. Besides, they occasionally lose bank deposits to different investments.
>
> It can be done, however, by using a CFP without hiring a CFP. A joint venture might be the answer.

It seemed to me that she was offering further proof of how positive the future is for the trained financial planner, provided he or she is flexible enough to take advantage of the opportunities opening up.

10 The Sales Approach

Chapter 9 covered some of the professions that are adding financial planning to the services they offer their clients. The accounting and legal professions, however, are not yet offering financial services to build their clientele. Instead, they are offering these services to maintain their current clients.

This chapter addresses a different group—the insurance agents and stock brokers who offer financial planning solely to sell insurance or securities. These people differ greatly from the true financial planner, whose initial goal is to prepare a financial plan for the client. He or she might well suggest the purchase of both securities and insurance, if the plan requires that kind of implementation. However, the financial planner is willing to prepare a financial plan with or without a fee and regardless of earning a sales commission. In that capacity, some insurance agents and stock brokers are financial planners.

However, the majority of the ones addressed in this chapter are the insurance agents or stock brokers who have no intention of preparing any financial plan, have not trained themselves to do so, are not dually licensed, and wouldn't recognize a comprehensive financial plan from a business plan. These people are merely taking advantage of the growing interest in financial planning and using the term as a buzzword and come-on. To back up their advertising, some even will offer a computerized, boiler plate financial plan, which the salespeople can get for you from the home office, if you insist.

As part of my research, I've responded to a few telephone prospecting pitches and almost felt guilty embarrassing the friendly deceiver, which some of them truly are. Of course, some are more honest—and their number is increasing—and will be upfront with you. Some are even working toward becoming legitimate financial planners and are enrolled in a CFP program.

A Reason for Antagonism

Almost 15 years ago, when I was traveling around the country setting up the first IAFP chapters and Jim Johnston was staying in Denver to organize the first CFP courses and exams, we realized that as financial planning became more widely recognized, there would be salespeople who would use the term as a posture to sell more insurance or securities.

We knew it would happen. But, we figured that even if people used the term *financial planner* without the education or commitment to the real thing, at least it would get consumers thinking about planning for their financial futures. We also thought that it might force salespeople to do a little better job for their clients, rather than just push the hot stock of the week or pretend that more insurance was the answer to almost any future financial problem.

We didn't realize how soon use of the term would start, but we were prepared for that eventually. What we weren't prepared for was the 1981-82 Prudential-Bache advertising campaign. This highly visible company was claiming to offer "total financial planning" to millions of people, when it didn't have enough qualified financial planners to do financial plans for hundreds. When Prudential-Bache began running its 1982 full-page and two-page ads offering "total financial planning," not one in 10—probably closer to one in 100—of its 4,000 account executives in its 200-plus offices around the country were qualified to discuss intelligently the more sophisticated financial planning techniques regularly practiced by any experienced financial planner. In fact, one of Prudential-Bache's senior executives defined a financial planner as merely someone having "a fair degree of training and one who practices financial planning on a regular basis." Prudential-Bache was far from the only company bannering ads with the claim for "total financial planning," but it was such a large and prestigious firm that was misusing the term that we felt the need to take corrective steps. So, in 1984, the National Center for Financial Education issued a consumer-alert press release calling attention to the dangers that unwary consumers (and our members) might do well to avoid. That press release is reproduced on the next page.

an ncfe
News Release

"CONSUMER ALERT #2" FOR IMMEDIATE RELEASE

A consumer alert has been issued by the San Francisco based National Center for Financial Education, a non-profit consumer organization. It is targeted at recent full-page ads and TV commercials promising total financial planning.

"Some of the very large companies, seeing the growing interest in financial planning and finally entering the field themselves are making offers they might be in no position to fulfill," according to Loren Dunton, NCFE president. He went on to say:

"Some of the giants, with thousands of insurance agents and/or stockbrokers, actually have only a handful of trained financial planners and yet they are inviting millions of Americans to come to them for financial planning."

According to P. Kemp Fain, president of the Institute of Certified Financial Planners and John Cahill, Board Chairman of the International Association for Financial Planning, only a small percentage of those purporting to be really are financial planners. Even fewer have passed the examinations to become Certified Financial Planners.

Fain points out: "Financial Planners usually enroll in the College for Financial Planning and take six courses. They must pass all proctored examinations and it normally takes about two years to become certified."

According to Dunton and the NCFE, total financial planning should be done by a trained (usually certified) Financial Planner, or Chartered Financial Consultant, or an accountant or lawyer trained in financial planning techniques. Dunton fears that many

MORE

─────── NCFE ───────
National Center for Financial Education, Inc.

The non-profit corporation for public education, dedicated to helping consumers do a better job of spending, saving, investing, insuring and planning for their financial future.

2107 Van Ness Avenue, Suite 308, San Francisco, California 94109 (415) 474-8496

"CONSUMER ALERT #2"
Page two

people seeing the ads by large companies offering total financial planning are being attracted to stockbrokers and/or insurance agents whose primary motive may be to sell securities or insurance, not to help people decide on short- and long-range financial plans.

The NCFE literature strongly endorses financial planning but only by those educationally qualified to do so. It also suggests using "financial planners" who have subscribed to and follow a professional Code of Ethics such as required by the ICFP, the industry's professional association, or the IAFP, the industry's trade association.

"We stress to our members and other consumers" Dunton says, "not to be overly influenced by big corporate names since they usually end up dealing with an individual anyway."

"It is often logical to go to an insurance agent or stockbroker to buy insurance or securities. What isn't wise is to go to either one assuming you automatically receive informed and objective financial planning advice. It is important to find out whether the individual is qualified to give that type of assistance." The NCFE educational programs for consumers covers the five areas of spending, saving, investing, insuring and planning. Its members are encouraged to ask questions and explore six subjects with anyone who offers to help them with their financial planning:

1. What experience has the individual had in the financial services industry?
2. What educational qualifications?
3. What professional certifications?
4. Membership in what professional organizations with a Code of Ethics?
5. Who have you done financial planning for?
6. How are you paid?

"It is perfectly okay for your financial planner to earn a commission on financial products you might buy from him or

MORE

"CONSUMER ALERT #2"
Page three

her" says Dunton. "What isn't of course wise is to expect objective advise about securities or other froms of investments and savings from someone wanting to sell only insurance. Or vice versa."

Dunton points out that "you improve your chances of getting objective advice from a financial planner who is duly licensed and can sell both securities and insurance."

"Even worse than putting off educating oneself about financial matters" he stresses "is to pay good money for a carefully prepared financial plan and then never get around to implementing it."

$ $ $ $ $

FOR MORE INFORMATION:

Loren Dunton, President
National Center for Financial Education
2107 Van Ness Avenue, Suite 308
San Francisco, CA 94109
(415) 474-8946 or 474-0232

As a result of our press release magazines and newspapers called our office and asked us to name specific companies. With just a little research, they were able to note what had concerned us for some time. For example, financial writer Cliff Pletschett has a thrice-weekly column that appears in the *Oakland Tribune*. His column of September 6, 1984, addressed the growing problem, as follows:

> Loren Dunton, regarded as the 'father of financial planning,' is up in arms.
>
> He dislikes the current ad campaigns of some nationwide financial services firms—including large brokerage houses—which claim to offer customers 'total financial planning.'
>
> Dunton, founder and president of the nonprofit National Center for Financial Education in San Francisco, says the big houses don't have enough trained financial planners to fulfill the offer.
>
> In a widely circulated 'consumer alert,' Dunton says, 'Some of the giant [firms] actually have only a handful of trained financial planners, and yet they are inviting millions of Americans to come to them for financial planning.'
>
> He fears many people are 'being solicited by stock brokers and/or insurance companies whose primary motive may be to sell securities or insurance, not to help people decide on short- and long-range financial plans.'
>
> Dunton, a founder of both Atlanta-based International Association for Financial Planning and the College for Financial Planning in Denver, doesn't name any firms. He says he wanted to, but his board of directors rejected the idea.
>
> Prudential-Bache Securities, Inc., however, could be one of his targets, since 'total financial planning' is a slogan now appearing in Prudential-Bache's national television and print media advertising campaign.
>
> Charles Wilmot, a Prudential-Bache senior vice president in New York, is not worried. He says his company has enough trained financial planners among its 4,800 account executives in its 300 office across the country.
>
> The controversy, it seems, is really over the definition of a financial planner.
>
> Dunton asserts, 'Financial planning should be done by a trained (usually certified) financial planner, chartered financial consultant (the insurance industry equivalent), or an accountant or lawyer trained in financial planning techniques.'
>
> The certified financial planner (CFP) designation is earned by passing a stiff exam administered by the College for Financial Planning. The college offers a two-year course leading to the exam,

but other colleges—notably Golden Gate University in San Francisco—also offer CFP courses.

Wilmot of Prudential-Bache defines a financial planner as having a 'fair degree of training and one who practices financial planning on a regular basis.'

He said his company has its own training program, encourages account executives to take college courses and hires people who have been 'doing financial planning for a number of years.'

I think the definitions on both sides are too fuzzy. Uniformity is needed. To settle matters, a true financial planner should hold the designation of certified financial planner or chartered financial consultant.

In addition, the planner should be put through an additional testing program to make sure he or she is properly serving clients. The International Association for Financial Planning has started such a program with its referral service called 'The Registry.'

I asked Wilmot how many certified financial planners Prudential-Bache has on its staff. He said he didn't know.

Although this is perturbing, the company deserves credit for at least trying. Too many other firms are content to simply sell commission-paying securities and not worry about their customers' broader financial planning needs.

The Insurance Industry

Deserving of Credit

As Cliff Pletschett noted, Prudential-Bache does deserve some credit for trying to fulfill the promises of "total financial planning" that it has been making for more than two years. In 1984 the company began to hire experienced financial planners and is now encouraging its executives and salespeople to take financial planning courses.

In fact, the entire insurance industry deserves praise for greatly improving the products it offers the consumer. Some of the old companies, of course, are not changing, perhaps assuming that an improved product even without different marketing methods will be enough to withstand the winds of change. However, the majority are changing.

Another Giant with Another Approach

In 1984 the Sears Financial Services network began using actor Hal Holbrook to reassure customers that Sears was able to take care of all their financial needs. Sears had Coldwell Banker for real estate, Dean Witter for securities, and Allstate for insurance. The bigger question was, who does Sears have to prepare the individual's financial plan? As one critic noted recently, "They have made it possible, actually very easy, for the average bewildered consumer...to listen to three different salespeople, all under the same roof." Fair criticism or not, that observation makes it clear that consumers need objective, unbiased financial planning more than ever before.

An Encouraging Start That Fizzled

Early in the 1970s, even before our financial planning organizations were garnering much attention in insurance circles, particularly among the giants, mutual funds were attracting the attention of bottom-line people in insurance. No doubt some of this attention was due to the efforts of earlier mutual fund groups such as IDS in Minneapolis, Waddell & Reed in Kansas City, and Hamilton Funds and Financial Industrial Funds in Denver, who were well on their way to success by the mid-1960s.

During the 1970s, a number of even the largest insurance companies entered the mutual fund business. Some bought companies, others bought separate funds, and still others started their own mutual funds.

It wasn't that they were thinking of offering their clients financial planning, however, that spurred them into mutual funds. A number of them were influenced by how the stock exchange firms were selling mutual funds, which was by performance.

Unfortunately, they chose the wrong time to enter into mutual fund marketing. The early 1970s saw two years of a bearish market, low mutual fund performance, adverse publicity for mutuals in general, and a disappointing performance for their agents in specific. Even the insurance companies that moved in earlier and that had powerful sales forces found it difficult to motivate their agents to accept a portion of an eight-percent sales charge when they could realize a much higher commission by selling a whole life policy.

Few of those insurance people were doing financial planning. They weren't selling mutual funds for long either. Today, the scenario has changed, so that nearly all of the giant insurance companies are getting into financial planning in one form or another.

In April 1984, *Financial Planning* editor Jack Lange featured a number of large insurance companies in a series of articles, highlighting what they were doing in their second go-around at selling equities and their first attempt at offering financial counseling or financial planning to their customers. The articles featured George Trotta of Metropolitan, Henry Kates of Mutual Benefit, James Zilinsky of New England Mutual, Robert Dalton of Connecticut Mutual, Ted Bohner of John Hancock, and Jim Mayfield of Travelers.

These people represented a new breed of insurance company executives with an obvious interest in providing what the consumer wanted...and needed. Not only were they leading the way in selling *new* products, but they were also charting new ways of *improving* the product they were offering the insurance consumer.

The full series is well worth reading, but let me quote a few paragraphs from an article by Henry Kates:

> Insurance companies which have sworn off securities would do well to study the kind of response Mutual Benefit's broker-dealer subsidiary received in its first three years of operation. Of a total of 1,600 Mutual Benefit sales agents, 1,400 have either made the week-long pilgrimage to Providence or signed up for classes. The sales figures are just as interesting. In 1981, the company's gross revenues climbed from zero to $20 million, passed $100 million the following year and reached $169 million in 1983. Put another way, that represents a 67.3 percent increase. The comparable figures for life and group insurance last year were 5.1 percent and 13 percent respectively.
>
> The growing broker-dealer operation in Providence is an unusual—possibly unique—version of a story unfolding in every corner of today's insurance industry. While the larger companies, like Prudential, purchase their brokerage distribution system outright, others are establishing their own broker-dealer operations or purchasing companies which began as general agencies and subsequently became clearing houses for the new diversity of financial products. Still others, like The Travelers, are making expensive overtures directly to financial planners, offering computerization and other incentives in return for what many insurance executives regard as the most sophisticated product pipeline in the marketplace. And some—still in the minority—are training an upscale cadre of financial planners to serve an increasingly sophisticated customer base.
>
> Although a number of analysts have talked about the corporate advantages of diversification, the movement into securities has primarily been driven from the grass roots. Like their counterparts 12 to 15 years ago, life agents in the 1980–82 period encountered a new customer resistance to the pure sales role they have adopted, coupled with a demand to see more products. 'The life insurance policy was a beautiful product back in the fifties, sixties and seventies,' says one agent-turned-planner. 'It was very easy to understand and maintain, and you could get in without a great deal of up-front cash. With the advent of money market funds, unit trusts, bank CDs and public partnership offerings, you could say that niche has become a lot more crowded.'
>
> The net effect has been to create a marketplace more amenable to the investment advisor than to the sales agent. Agents were quick to

respond. At this writing, some 5,250 CLU-holders have added the educational supplement of a ChFC degree from The American College in Bryn Mawr, Pennsylvania, with another class due to graduate shortly. Others lobbied their professional associations for a new professional description. The American Society of Chartered Life Underwriters, which has in excess of 30,000 members, recently completed a 20-month study of the issue, hiring a number of consultants and university research centers, polling members who reportedly expressed a widespread desire to change the society's name. A new Committee on the Society's Name eventually recommended changing to the 'American Society of Insurance and Financial Consultants'—a recommendation unanimously defeated by the board of directors.

In Need of Better PR

Another problem is that although the insurance industry has done so much in the last five years to improve its consumer products, it has done little to communicate those improvements to the public. New chief executives and association heads are showing a gratifying concern for the consumer, especially as compared to their predecessors of 20 years ago. But they're doing that communicating among themselves.

These leaders must show their concern for the consumer to the public through the insurance organizations or through another organization such as NCFE. Instead of fretting about the future plight of the insurance industry in the consumer media, they need to express more concern about the future of the individual, possibly by talking more about the need for us all to plan actively for our financial futures.

Should selling insurance lead to true financial planning? Ed Morrow, of Confidential Planning Services in Ohio, and Ben Baldwin, of Equitable Life in Chicago, are two successful insurance agents turned financial planners. They are far from the only ones who have gone from selling insurance to doing true and professional financial planning for their clients.

Academicians are also teaching insurance salespeople how to become financial planners. One of them is Dale S. Johnson, who has been with both the College for Financial Planning in Denver and The American College in Bryn Mawr, Pennsylvania. To help his clients decide whether they should be planners, Johnson asks them to address the following:

- What kind of business am I really in?
- What sort of business do I want to be in?
- What resources—personal, financial and client-based—do I have for making my business what I would like it to be?
- Which marketing, economic and company-related conditions are favorable for change? Which are not favorable?

- What realistic possibilities and alternative are open to me?
- How willing am I to make changes?

Johnson also points out some differences and some challenges to the insurance professional considering a change. Here's the way he advises his clients:

> If the name of the new financial services game is money management, then to remain competitive, sales professionals in insurance must at least acquire the knowledge and experience to effect the transition to sophisticated marketers of a broad array of both insurance and investment products. Products placed in this way can more effectively meet the needs of consumers in a manner consistent with their expectations for participating fully in the money management game. The same holds true for registered securities representatives and other sales professionals in financial services. This change, in response to current market conditions, would be a career transition.
>
> This transition and evolution means that insurance agents—like all financial services professionals and specialists—must position themselves to service the generalized life-planning and related financial needs of their clients, as determined either by a more sophisticated consultative marketing effort, or by the full implementation of the financial planning process in their practice. This process begins with sophisticated marketing research—the thorough gathering of the facts, feelings, attitudes, values, needs and financial objectives of clients. It proceeds to a determination of their total financial resources. The process, through counseling, helps clients become willing to allocate their resources to a strategic planning and decision-making process—one that integrates their risk management, investment and tax-planning initiatives in a financial plan custom-tailored to their particular lifestyles.
>
> The essential and radical difference between pure marketing approaches to providing financial products and services and the financial planning approach is that the former are product-driven, while the latter is process-driven. In this distinction lies a very large—and very threatening—challenge to insurance professionals who confront the necessities of transition and evolution in the contemporary marketplace. It is, in fact, a challenge to the very basis of their professional success.

AN INTERVIEW WITH Edward W. Chin and Oliver M. Stafford

AIS Financial Services, Inc., is a firm in Oakland, California, that graduated from an insurance operation into a full-fledged financial planning firm. Edward W. Chin is the company's founder and president, and Oliver M. Stafford is the executive vice president. They shared with me some of their activities that have contributed to the incredible growth of their client base in this interview:

DUNTON: You talk a great deal about "financial independence." What exactly is your definition of financial independence?

CHIN/STAFFORD: We refer to it as Independence Day—that date in the future, which the clients have picked, when they can enjoy the same standard of living they enjoyed during their highest income—producing years without having to work, if they don't want to, and without being dependent on someone else or charity.

DUNTON: You use computer graphics as part of your written financial plan. Do you find clients relate well to this technique?

CHIN/STAFFORD: Definitely! Many people do not relate to a lot of numbers, so we give them a visual representation of where they stand. It puts everything in perspective. This is particularly true for financial statements, such as balance sheets and income statements. They are very revealing, particularly when they are presented visually. They let people see how much they are paying in taxes, how much discretionary income is available, how liquid their assets are, and what retirement benefits are available, just to name a few. In addition, they let a client know exactly how compatible his or her investments are to his or her goals and objectives.

DUNTON: Could you explain that further?

CHIN/STAFFORD: One of the many things a balance sheet reveals is the kind of investments a person has and what percentage these invested assets are of total assets. Financial statements are very revealing and are an important part of the total client profile. For example, if a 40-year-old client tells us that he wants to retire at 55, but all of his investments are in CDs and money funds, his investments are not compatible with his investment objective. Interest-bearing fixed-income investments are not going to build an equity base of sufficient capital to permit early financial independence. At this point, he needs growth. Based on his objectives, we might recommend repositioning some of those dollars into growth-oriented investments that also afford a degree of tax shelter, such as real estate, professionally managed growth stock funds, etc.

DUNTON: Do you always insist on doing a complete financial profile for a client?

CHIN/STAFFORD: In the majority of cases, yes. A profile lets you examine the details of where a person stands financially today. It involves the development of basic financial statements and an evaluation of the strengths and weaknesses of all the major areas of a person's economic makeup, including risk management, investments, tax and retirement planning, estate planning, and business planning. It also sets forth the qualitative side of a person's goals, dreams and hopes for the future—what's important to that person in life.

Without this base to work from, without knowing where you stand right now, it is very difficult to set goals and chart a course. Recommendations made in a vacuum, without knowledge as to how they interface within the total picture, cannot have the same accuracy or validity as those made in the context of a total plan design.

As an example that we do practice what we preach, last December a woman was referred to us whose only concern was the investing of $200,000. She wanted current tax shelter and was not interested in anything else. Under those circumstances, we refused to take her. Three weeks later, she called back to say that everyone she had gone to had something to sell her, except us. She had thought it over and had realized that our comprehensive financial planning approach made sense and she would like to come back and do things the "right way." Today, she is a very happy client of AIS.

DUNTON: You are doing considerable work in the employee benefits area. Do you work only with key executives and high–net worth clients?

CHIN/STAFFORD: While we do work with a large number of key businesspersons, we also have many clients who are of very modest means, many of whom are just getting started. That is the best time to start a basic plan in motion. Everyone has some income to protect from taxes and/or inflation. We would never turn away a client with a low net worth. After all, they probably will be worth a lot more someday, and we do not want them saying, 'If only I had started a fi-

DUNTON: I understand that several large stockbrokerage firms in the area send clients to you. Why would they do that?

CHIN/STAFFORD: Many people do not take their investing seriously. When seen in the context of a complete financial plan, investments, people realize, are crucial to their economic well-being. After completing the financial plan and making generic recommendations, we send the client back to the account executive, who then implements our recommendations. From the broker's point of view, clients generally invest more than they would have before the financial plan. Furthermore, we provide them credibility, which is sometimes difficult for a commission salesperson to achieve.

DUNTON: How large is your company?

CHIN/STAFFORD: AIS has more than 40 full-time professionals on staff. They work closely with a network of professionals serving more than 350 planners and brokers in the greater [San Francisco] Bay Area than use one or more aspects of our professional services.

DUNTON: At AIS, you have three levels of planners. Can you explain each of them?

CHIN/STAFFORD: The Senior Staff Planner must be a Certified Financial Planner (CFP), licensed in securities, real estate and insurance. Such people assist in teaching and must have at least five years in the business.

A Staff Planner should also be a CFP and licensed in at least two areas, with a minimum of two years' experience.

An Associate Staff Planner is not a CFP, but must have taken a minimum of CFP I or a paraplanning course with a minimum of two years of supervision under a Senior Staff Planner.

Once planning has begun, an associate staff planner gathers data and begins research, under the supervision of a senior staff planner. When a plan is near completion, it is reviewed by at least three people—a combination of senior staff planners and/or executive staff. If anyone on our staff knows the client or is associated with the client in any way, that person cannot work on the client's plan without the client's consent, in order to maintain full confidentiality.

DUNTON: What would you say is the key to your tremendous growth?

CHIN/STAFFORD: We are totally committed to the marketing and delivery system of a fee-based comprehensive financial plan, and the placing of the client's interest first. Our overriding objective, which we practice faithfully, is to recognize that the client basically needs someone to help him or her figure out where the client stands today financially, where he or she wants to be at certain points in the future, and what the best ways to get there are. By helping people help themselves, we establish a close and *ongoing* relationship through periodic reviews and updates.

PART FIVE

The Step Beyond
Financial Planning Gets Clout

George Orwell made *Nineteen Eighty-Four* a household word, and 1984 made financial planning a household word.

A front-page article in the October 6, 1983, issue of *USA Today* by Richard Eisenberg (now with *Money* magazine) was titled "Fiscal Needs Give Birth to New Profession." The article noted that financial planning was still struggling with its image and the need for regulation, but it also noted that financial planning had arrived with clout.

Both terms—"financial planning" and "financial planner"—began appearing in regional as well as such prestigious national newspapers as the *New York Times* and *The Wall Street Journal.* Magazines of every type also began running articles on financial planning even more often than on investing, insuring or saving.

Financial planners started appearing on radio and television talk shows constantly, not just occasionally, as was the case in 1982 and 1983. In 1985, the trend accelerated; even publications that had avoided the term started using it.

Not all of the publicity was favorable, of course. As with any new, or old profession, financial planning took its share of media knocks. Some writers found it easier to focus on the negative; some editors attracted attention the same way. For the most part, however, the media coverage in 1984 and 1985 culminated by finally establishing financial planning as a profession necessary for the times.

The next three chapters will cover the three modes of operation most prevalent for financial planners in the last half of the 1980s.

11 Financial Planning: Upper and Lower Case

For some time now, three types of financial planning have been offered to the consumer. First, there is the fee-only, sophisticated financial planning being offered to executives, professionals, business owners, entertainers, sports figures, scientists, and other high-income or wealthy people. Often done by business managers, CPAs, tax lawyers, and knowledgeable and sophisticated CFPs, this type of financial planning will be covered in detail in Chapter 13.

Another type of financial planning is the straight-commission, product-oriented work being done by some trained and conscientious insurance agents—often with a Chartered Financial Counselor (ChFC) designation—or stock broker willing to take a financial planning approach. A significant number of experienced financial planners, frequently CFPs, also use this approach to earning a living and helping people have a better financial future. We'll discuss this form, "financial planning: lower case," in Chapter 12.

This chapter addresses the third form of financial planning, which is most frequently used for the large and growing middle-income group—"financial planning: upper and lower case." The financial planner working in this mode usually charges a smaller fee, with the intention (assuming the client agrees) of supplementing that fee with the commissions the client will pay on some of the financial products purchased in order to implement the plan.

Fees, Commissions and Plan Implementation

Financial planners still disagree about how best to fulfill their responsibility to their clients. Here is an excerpt from a letter I received from David Hokanson, CFP, MSFS, ChFC, of Kansas City:

> First of all, I will make the assumption that our shop is not unusual. We do full, total, comprehensive financial planning and market our services strictly to the upscale market. Based solely on the comprehensive nature of our planning and the significant amount of

time that needs to be spent on each plan, we feel this is the appropriate market for our type of service.

Thus, [my partner] Jim Stevens and I have come to the realization that developing the best of plans is only half of the financial planning process. The most successful and busy individuals need someone to take over the responsibility of helping with the implementation of the plan, once it has been put together.

I think it is important to understand that we have come to the realization that not only do they need help, but in many cases they need someone actually 'selling' the concepts to them. While our clients may believe those concepts, they need to be motivated to take action as soon as possible in order to reach their objectives in a timely and successful manner. With this thought in mind, we put together a summary after the written recommendations, known as a 'checklist,' that we run down during the interview. This checklist has three columns following the summary recommendation. The first column says that the client accepts the recommendation, the second column asks for whose responsibility it is to carry out the recommendation, and the final column requests the time frame for completion of the recommendation.

The other significant point is that when we are making a recommendation we think is important, and yet we feel the client will have some misgivings, we place that item in two or three places following an obviously acceptable recommendation. Therefore, psychologically, the client is in a rhythm and feeling comfortable with the recommendations before he reaches the one that we think will require the most help from us in terms of implementation.

An example of a recommendation checklist Stevens has used is included here. It seemed to me a good answer to the questions people often ask as to what financial planners do that other financial counselors don't do.

RECOMMENDATION CHECKLIST

	Accept	Reject	Implement
1. Reposition retirement plan funds into real estate limited partnership and common stock mutual funds.	_____	_____	_____
2. Establish tax-exempt money market fund.			
3. Consider the use of a Clifford Trust to accumulate educational funds for the grandchildren.	_____	_____	_____

4. Use Crown loans as a method for making gifts to the children.
5. Purchase a personal umbrella liability policy in the amount of $2 million.
6. Implement a cash flow management system to systematically reduce the profit sharing plan.
7. Change beneficiaries on Don's retirement plans to "Johnson Country National Bank under Trust Agreement dated January 25, 1986."
8. File amended tax returns for 1984 and 1985 to claim a refund for the overpayment of taxes in regard to the Broadway Plaza Medical Building.
9. Consider an investment in a real estate limited partnership program with a life of five to ten years.
10. Change the debts and taxes clause in your wills.
11. Change the beneficiaries on the New England Life split-dollar policy to Don's living trust.
12. Transfer up to one-half of Don's life insurance to Myrle's ownership and change beneficiaries to Myrle (primary) and Trust (secondary).

David Hokanson and James Stevens, Jr., CLU, ChFC are using a method that is becoming more common among financial planners. They make a full disclosure to the client, explaining that the personalized financial plan will be prepared by their firm for a fee. They also explain, however, that they have a separate company that can implement the plan—or portions of it—should the client wish. When they began in the 1970s, almost 90 percent of their income was from commissions. In 1985, it will be about fifty-fifty.

Financial planners taking fees and commissions have different ways of broaching the topic with their clients. A number of them use variations of this opener, which I like best:

> Obviously, there are going to be commissions paid on certain types of securities, insurance, and even savings vehicles. We find that our clients would rather have these commissions come to us, especially when it reduces the fees they pay for the preparation of their financial plan.

Others use different methods to address this question. I don't know how financial planning pioneer Lee Pennington, CFP, actually tells his clients, but here's what he told me:

> We do not agree with those who, by statement or by implication, think that those who implement are less objective than those who don't. What does that have to do with integrity? Those who make such statements imply to me that they personally could not be objective if they also implemented. We believe that we should be concerned about the quality of the plan—and the integrity of the implementor—rather than whether it's a fee-only or a fee and commission-only account. No one is objective, if he or she really believes anything; surely, such a totally objective person would be very dull.

When the topic of being objective or avoiding possible conflicts of interest comes up, I'm always reminded of the story of a judge down in Ozark bootleg country, who told the defendant that since he was in possession of equipment to produce alcohol, even though he wasn't caught using it, the judge was going to find him guilty. "Well," the defendant quipped, "then you'd better find me guilty of rape, too." It's an old illustration but a good reminder. The potential is always there, of course, and should be guarded against, but that in itself is no crime and doesn't of itself demand that financial planners defend their capabilities.

Financial Planning and Management Consulting

Many financial planners find themselves acquiring a high degree of expertise by working with one particular group of clients or specializing in one client category. One of them is Karl E. Byrd of Jackson, Mississippi. His university training was in business management and, despite his youth, he soon became a consultant to medical and dental practitioners in Mississippi. Here's how he describes the two parts of his unusual practice:

> In our management consulting practice, we will get involved in such things as design and implementation of medical records systems,

design and implementation of accounting systems, clinic staffing, office automation, practice valuations for buy-in and buy-out purposes, contractual negotiations for representing physicians entering into private practice, fringe benefits planning, accounts receivable management, etc. In short, we help our professional clients manage the business aspects of their practice, regardless of what that might entail.

Curious, I asked Byrd to explain how he became so involved in his clients' business.

> I recognized that while physicians are highly trained in clinical medicine, they have had very little education and experience in running the business applications of their practice. I tell each and every client that I work with that there are two sides to a medical practice: the clinical and the business. As such, the success of the practice often hinges on how well the practice is managed as a business.

It sounded so natural that one couldn't help wondering why it also seemed unique.

> In addition to the management consulting work that we do with the health care profession, we are very much involved in coordinating the personal financial objectives of our clients with their practices. We explain that financial planning is an ongoing process. As such, we help our clients define realistic financial objectives, consider alternative methods for meeting those particular objectives, and then select the best alternative to help the client reach his particular financial goal.

Naturally, I wondered whether or not Byrd's relations with his clients could possibly stop short of implementation.

> When the client desires our help, we also have the capability of implementing the financial planning recommendations as far as products are concerned. After the initial plan is formalized, we update, on an annual basis, our client's financial plan to take into consideration changes that occur in the tax laws, and the client's personal situation, thus enforcing the premise that financial planning is an ongoing process. If the plan calls for legal accounting work, [clients] are referred to qualified CPA's and attorneys that we work very closely with, that are specialists in the specific areas of our client's financial needs.

When asked to be more specific for the benefit or readers of this book, Byrd answered:

> In the financial planning process, we do a lot of work in the area of cash flow management, or budget planning; risk management; investment management; and income and estate tax planning. We feel that it is imperative to help the client obtain control of his monthly cash flow before any meaningful progress can be made through the financial planning process.

This combination of consulting, planning, and implementation may indicate that another group, the business consultants, are entering into financial planning.

Making a Transition

J. Pierre Maurer, executive vice president of Metropolitan Life, estimates that 10 percent of his company's sales force has the potential to make the transition from life insurance to financial planning. His company, along with others, now pays for its agents to take the ChFC course from the American College. He also notes that the best life insurance agents develop long-term relationships with their clients, which really makes them ideal financial planners.

Fifteen years ago, insurance exectutives—except for a few like Gus Hansch of Los Angeles—didn't want to talk about financial planning. We couldn't find any of the big insurance companies' executives to say what Pierre Maurer says now, even 10 years ago. Today, a new breed of big insurance company executives are rising into positions of authority in their companies.

Insurance companies are not the only ones entering into fee-plus-commission financial planning programs. In a variety of banks around the country, arrangements are being made whereby the fees and commissions might bring in enough for the bank and the planner to capitalize on the interest in financial planning, as well as avoid losing so many depositors.

Director of Financial Planning

Seeing "Director of Financial Planning" on Jane Mary McEnroe's business card is not surprising, until you notice that it also reads "First National Bank—Cincinnati." Some astute observers of the financial services industry believe what the bank and McEnroe are doing portends the future. Here are some excerpts from a talk she gave in Middleton, Ohio, in November, 1984:

> Personal financial planning offered by banks is definitely becoming one of the most talked-about marketing opportunities in our industry. Many bankers see it as an essential service to help ensure continued growth...to attract new customers...and to maintain our existing customer base.

The reason is fundamental. In today's complex financial environment, planning ranks right up there at the top of the list of unserved consumer needs.

Ours is a joint venture between the First National Bank of Cincinnati and Financial Planning Consultants, Inc., to offer financial planning services in Ohio's Hamilton County market.

Studies conducted this year as part of Payment System, Inc.'s affluent-market research program showed banks to be a *preferred* source for various financial planning services.

Banks also offer a *strong base* of existing relationships, existing lending relationships, and an established distribution system. This large personal and corporate base is a customer segment that is already favorably inclined toward working with a bank. Consumers who are already comfortable with a particular bank also are more inclined to feel positive about new services offered by that bank. Plus, the larger channels of distribution of most banks conveniently allow financial services to be offered to the total customer base.

Together...banks and financial planning firms can offer the best of financial services. The combined resources and experiences of both organizations can only result in more professional, detailed financial planning services. The planning company will broaden its customer-base and benefit from the established name of a bank. The bank in turn has a good opportunity to retain current customers and build new ones to increase profits...and to move toward the idea of offering a total service package.

Does this new practice indicate a way of the future? Is it a solution to the problem banks have as to what to do about financial planning? Time will tell.

12 Financial Planning: Lower Case

The preceding chapter looked at fee-plus-commission financial planners, who make up the largest group of professional financial planners today. However, they are not the largest group that *calls* its work "financial planning." Some authorities estimate that this group numbers almost 200,000.

Its largest segment includes thousands of established insurance agents, often with large companies, who are using a financial planning posture to market only insurance. Most of these people are not dually licensed, not knowledgeable about what constitutes financial planning, and not dedicated to helping people achieve financial goals by better financial planning. Instead, they are interested in selling insurance.

Nevertheless, there is a large group of people who do deserve to be called financial planners, even though they are straight-commission salespeople who elect not to collect fees for the financial planning they do. Their position is that preparing a financial plan is what they do to deserve the commissions they will make by helping the client implement the plan with the appropriate financial products. Many of these people are dedicated, professional, and adhere to the strict codes of ethics of the financial planning organizations to which they belong.

Like many of the financial planning pioneers, they work strictly on commission. In fact, many of them were in that pioneer group of leaders who sponsored the financial planning movement and its organizations. Among their ranks are some of the most professional and experienced financial planners today. As a group, they probably help more people to accumulate wealth and have a better retirement than the other two groups of financial planners put together. I've chosen to call this group the "lower case" because lower-case letters are used more than any other kind.

Financial planners, lower case, often attach less importance to the *plan itself* and more importance to their *implementation* of the plan. They don't wish to design fee-only financial plans that sit on dressers or in desk drawers because the client isn't motivated by the financial planner to take action.

Some stay with a straight-commission operation because they don't know how to begin charging a fee for a service they've been supplying their clients at no charge. Others are working toward charging a fee as one method of making up for the increase in the amount of no-load or low-commission products they recommend.

Looking Back Helps

During the 1960s, as a sales and marketing consultant with clients in New York, San Francisco, Los Angeles, Denver and Chicago, as well as London, Frankfurt and Zurich, our small consulting firm started specializing in helping insurance and mutual fund companies. That specialization brought me in contact with pioneers of dually licensed selling, the real forerunners of the largest segment of financial planners today.

Many of the mutual fund sales representatives with whom we worked had acquired dual licenses, so they could sell both insurance and mutual funds. We were able to teach them a counseling sales approach that helped their clients achieve financial goals. It was not only more client oriented, but it also was more lucrative than the prevalent "pushing one product" posture of many insurance agents, mutual fund representatives, or stock brokers.

Unlike the mutual fund companies, the large insurance companies were primarily one-product marketers. Insurance agents who realized and said that one product was not the answer to all their clients' financial needs were often disparaged or fired.

In the 1960s and 1970s, a rivalry developed between established insurance agents and the newer, more progressive financial planners. In fact, the replacement of cash value life insurance with the greater coverage and lesser expense of term insurance was a hot and much debated issue. Even state commissioners across the country joined the furor with regulations to make replacement more difficult.

One critic of cash value life insurance was Jay Smith, CLU, of Sausalito, California. He set up a firm called Life Insurance RX, which was designed with the aid of computers to help the agent or financial planner comply with the onerous regulations necessary to replace an insurance policy without getting into trouble with the insurance commissioners. In the last decade, Life Insurance RX has grown tremendously and now provides computerized assistance to several very large life insurance companies.

The A.L. Williams Approach

In 1984, both the *Saturday Evening Post* and *Financial Planning* magazine ran in-depth articles on A.L. (Art) Williams of Atlanta and his multi-level term insurance sales organization, A.L. Williams Corporation, of almost 70,000 part-time agents.

Here are a few paragraphs from Bob Johnson's article, which appeared in the December, 1984 issue of *Financial Planning* and was subtitled, "Art

Williams and his 70,000 recruits have targeted financial planning for their next marketing invasion":

> In 1971, Williams decided to move his family to Atlanta to sell insurance full-time. This led to his first of many encounters with the established insurance order. Not satisfied with the company's support for his 'buy term and invest the difference' campaign, Williams left the Waddell and Reed agency to launch his own company in 1977, taking his top seven managers with him.
>
> The new company's mission was to take the 'buy term...' argument to its logical conclusion: convince as many Americans as possible to replace cash value life insurance with a term policy issued by Massachusetts Indemnity and Life Insurance Company (MILICO). In 1981, the firm was restructured as A.L. Williams Corp., with two subsidiaries, the insurance company and First American National Securities—a discount brokerage firm. The following year, a $27 million stock sale was offered, characteristically, to ALW agents, recruits, and associated personnel to capitalize the new companies. They responded by oversubscribing sale by $8 million."

Representatives of the A.L. Williams organization occasionally introduce themselves as insurance agents, but more often as financial counselors or financial planners, although what they are doing is not true financial planning. One of the recurring themes in the Williams organization is, as one of their agents confided to me in 1983, "educating the public; not just selling them a cheaper insurance."

Williams has many critics, of course, particularly among the more professional financial planners. They criticize the multi-level sales organization, the part-time sales people he uses, and the high cost of the products he gives to his people to sell.

One reason so many people respond to A.L. Williams representatives is that most of the financial planners who could have helped them earlier were too busy selling to clients with higher incomes and/or more money, or were offering them tax shelters, as those, too, were highly lucrative for financial planners. Everyone seems to agree that the high commissions for tax shelters could soon be mostly rosy memories. If so, many financial planners will have to look to other financial choices for their clients.

Obviously, there won't be enough wealthy and high-income people to go around. So, some of those professional financial planners may have to spend their time and talents helping people *become* wealthy.

Actually, that's where a number of financial planners began, back when they realized how satisfying it was to help the average consumer do a little financial planning. And, maybe someday, if the A.L. Williams agents really graduate to true financial planning, they'll experience the same greater satisfaction financial planners enjoy.

Financial Planning Is Not Just Selling

Financial planners are often successful because they *don't* put selling first. That fact distinguishes the financial planner from the successful stock broker or insurance agent.

Even professional and experienced planners who have elected to continue operating solely on commissions have learned there is no more effective preselling they can do than to concentrate all their initial efforts on finding out everything they can about their prospects so that they may prepare the most logical and helpful plan possible. As several financial planners have put it to me: "We know that the best way to sell a lot of insurance and a number of investments, especially in the long run, is to put together a financial plan that is obviously ideal for that particular couple or family." Since few families have enough savings, investments or insurance, the financial planner who takes the time to get their spending under control and prepares a road map to a better financial future provides a noticeable contrast to the broker or agent who won't take that time.

Will Consumers Pay Fees?

Naturally some customers will pay fees and are already doing so. More interesting, however, is whether many people will agree to pay a fee that is kept low by the ability of the financial planner to make a commission.

One astute observer of that aspect of financial planning is R. Lamar Brantley, director of retail funds acquisition for the U.S. League of Savings Institutions, in Chicago. He recently drew some interesting conclusions, based on elaborate surveys by the Financial Institutions Marketing Association. The surveys showed that many people were "very" or "extremely" interested in financial planning. But while a great number of them will pay for it, many don't want to pay very much—$50 or less.

Based on those surveys, Brantley wrote the following in his report to the U.S. League of Savings Institutions in 1984:

> Financial planning means different things to different people. As a result, the tendency is to discuss the concept as being just another financial service fad that will soon disappear.
>
> Perhaps that fate ultimately awaits financial planning, but I am impressed with an undercurrent that runs through this concept. Our economy and the financial service offerings that drive it have never been more complex. The public seems to be saying in several ways that it needs help.
>
> The problems with tapping this market are two-fold. Can anyone—but particularly a savings institution—develop a process that can consistently provide sound advice on personal financial matters?

And, can it be done in a way that maintains the trust of the public?

The savings institutions that successfully solve these problems will raise the concept of financial services to a higher and potentially rewarding plane.

So far, we have yet to see any large-scale effort by the savings and loans to capitalize on the public's interest in financial planning.

13 Financial Planning: Upper Case

It is hard to find an analogy, in other professions, to the types of financial planners, broken down by remuneration, that are now evolving in the financial services industry. They cannot be divided by specialty, as in the medical profession. While it can be argued that the fee-only planner prepares a plan that is usually more complicated, even that is not always the case.

It is interesting to note that while both the straight-commission and fee-plus-commission groups are found in small, medium, and giant organizations, fee-only planners usually practice in small, highly professional offices, or are affiliated with major corporations, such as some of the Big Eight accounting firms and some of the major stock brokers or insurance companies.

To provide insight into both types of fee-only financial planning, this chapter looks first at Leonetti & Associates of Arlington Heights, Illinois, then at the Bank of America's Executive Financial Planning Department, which was headed by Tim Kochis. (The Bank of America has since closed this department, but its structure and scope are well worth looking at for an understanding of the fee-only planner in a large corporation.)

A Simple, Effective Approach

Michael Leonetti, CFP, calls his firm "financial consultants" on his letterhead, and, in his company literature, frequently describes his financial planning and investment management services this way:

> Leonetti & Associates provides financial planning and/or investment management services attuned to the objectives and desires of its clients. Therefore, the company is registered with the Securities and Exchange Commission as an investment adviser. This Description of Financial Planning and Investment Management Services ('Brochure') is provided in accordance with Rule 204-3 ('Brochure Rule') under the Investment Advisor's Act of 1940, and should be reviewed prior to entering into a financial planning and/or investment management agreement with Leonetti & Associates.

To give you a picture of this particular seven-member, fee-only financial planning firm, the following pages show Leonetti's cover sheet and several of the pages from his prospectus.

---

125 S. WILKE RD.
SUITE 204
ARLINGTON HEIGHTS, IL 60005

LEONETTI & ASSOCIATES

FINANCIAL CONSULTANTS

(312) 577-4450

WHAT WE OFFER

Leonetti & Associates is a fee-based planning firm offering comprehensive financial planning and investment management services. Our plans cover the areas of insurance and estate planning, investment analysis, retirement planning, education funding, employee benefits review, tax planning, and wills and trusts.

Once it is determined what type of planning is needed, data is collected, objectives are set, and the plan is created. Since financial planning is a continuing process, periodic reviews are made to assure our clients are kept on track to met their goals.

We assist our clients in implementation of their plans, because a plan without action, no matter how well designed, is worthless. We differ from most planning firms in that we use non-commission products to help our clients achieve their objectives.

In addition, we provide investment management services on a fee-only basis. Our clients receive frequent statements showing their investment positions and how they're doing. They also receive our bi-monthly market and financial planning newletters to keep them informed on what is happening in the investment markets and the latest financial planning tools and techniques.

CREDENTIALS

— Certified Financial Planner
— Registered Investment Advisor
— Member, Registry of Financial Planning Practitioners
— Vice President and Director, National Association of Personal Financial Advisors (NAPFA)
— Member, Institute of Certified Financial Planners
— Director, International Association for Financial Planning (IAFP), Greater O'Hare Chapter
— Member, American Association of Financial Professionals
— Past Member, Estate and Financial Planning Council, American National Bank
— Teacher, Financial Planning, Harper College

- Featured in Chicago Sun-Times, Sylvia Porter's Personal Finance, and on nationally syndicated television
- Listed on Who's Who in Financial Planning
- Vice President, Chicago Society of Certified Financial Planners
- Member, Financial Professional Advisory Panel

INTRODUCTION

Leonetti & Associates believe that most individuals, partnerships and corporations need assistance in managing their financial affairs in a knowledgeable, effective manner. This is evidenced most often by the lack of coordination of the various aspects of financial planning. Most successful individuals have accountants, attorneys, stock brokers, life insurance consultants and/or other advisers whose efforts, though well founded, may not necessarily coordinate into a sound financial plan.

Our company accepts the responsibility of becoming a working partner with its client and his/her other advisers, undertaking a thorough review of the client's financial affairs, and creating a written financial plan. Furthermore, Leonetti & Associates will assist you in the implementation of recommendations made in your financial plan. Once implemented, our company provides a thorough and constant tracking of your financial situation.

We also believe that most individuals have a need for professional guidance in managing their investments. This is because:

1) Today's securities market is intensely competitive and dominated by professionals;
2) Investment decisions should be based on skillful, in-depth research and analysis, which the average investor seldom has time to undertake; and
3) Full-time supervision of investments is vital for consistent success.

We endeavor to provide this service to our investment management clients.

SERVICES

....Comprehensive Personal Financial Planning
....Complete organization of personal/family finances
....Personal cash management—budget analysis
....Income tax analysis and planning
....Savings, annuity and investment analysis

.... Complete insurance analysis
.... Estate planning analysis
.... Retirement planning analysis
.... Recommendations regarding insurance, investments and taxes
.... Professional investment management

INVESTMENT MANAGEMENT

Constant analysis and management of investments is essential to a successful financial plan. For this reason, Leonetti & Associates provide ongoing investment management services for its clients.
These services include:

— monitoring of investment portfolio
— making adjustments in portfolio as necessary
— researching new investment alternatives
— managing investments with respect to client's objectives and tax situation
— timely reporting to client of his/her investment position
— bi-monthly of "Market Review" letter to keep the client informed of what is happening in the market place.

FINANCIAL PLANNING

The financial planning process normally includes the following steps:

1) The Financial Planning Agreement is prepared and executed.

2) A detailed gathering of data is accomplished and an analysis is made of the client's present position in light of his/her circumstances and objectives.

3) A written financial plan is prepared, including a profile of the client, a statement of estimated net worth, an analysis of cash flow and tax position, a description of current investments and insurance programs, a first-second death analysis program, a statement of estimated estate tax computations, a summary of estate liquidity needs, etc.

4) Recommendations for meeting short and long term living goals, projected cash flow analyses, estate planning goals, etc. will be furnished.

5) After discussion of the written financial plan, a program for implementation of recommendations is outlined. On going consultation is provided to the client in this regard.

INVESTMENT STRATEGIES

In conjunction with its investment management services, Leonetti & Associates analyzes the current investments of its clients and makes recommendations regarding retention, disposition, and/or repositioning of investments. The company is registered as an Investment Adviser with the Securities and Exchange Commission; however, the company shall not take possession of any assets of its clients.

The general guidelines to which Leonetti and Associates adheres in recommending investment strategies include:

1) DIVERSIFICATION. Diversification in a variety of investment vehicles is beneficial to balance risk while maintaining the possibility of gain.

2) UNDERSTANDING RISK. Investment decisions should take into consideration the risk of loss of capital (i.e., "market risk") and risk of loss of purchasing power (i.e., "inflation risk") as well as other risks.

3) BALANCE OF ASSETS. Proper investment planning requires a balanced approach, with due consideration to short and long term liquidity needs, blending of lower and higher risk approaches, combining income and growth concepts, etc.

4) PROFESSIONAL MANAGEMENT. The unsophisticated investor should rely upon qualified experts to oversee investment decisions.

5) DISCIPLINE. Investment planning requires a disciplined approach. The investor should commit to an investment approach for a reasonable period of time to allow it to work, since short term emotional decisions often defeat a well designed investment program.

6) INCOME TAX CONSIDERATIONS. Income tax considerations should not supplant economic benefits as the primary determinant of investment decisions.

OUTSIDE CONSULTANTS

Leonetti & Associates, in addition to its own qualified staff, maintains a consulting relationship with outside specialists. The company recognizes that quality financial planning services require a high degree of specialization in various areas. Such specialists include, among others: investment advisory firms, financial planners, fringe benefit consultants, income and estate tax experts, insurance specialists, attorneys, and accountants. The company is also aware of the necessity of coordinating its work with the client's other financial advisers.

It is expressly understood and agreed between the parties hereto that the company is not qualified to prepare any accounting or legal documents for the implementation of the client's financial plan. The client agrees that his personal accountant and/or attorney, shall be solely responsible for all the following:

1) Legal Advice
2) Legal Opinions
3) Legal Documents
4) Tax Returns
5) Accounting
6) Due Diligence

MANAGEMENT

The education and background of the President of Leonetti and Associates is outlined below:

Michael E. Leonetti, CFP

Michael E. Leonetti, CFP, is President of Leonetti & Associates. He received his Bachelor of Arts Degree from St. Mary's College with a major in Finance and a minor in Economics. In addition, he received a Certified Financial Planner designation from the Denver-based College for Financial Planning after completing the required courses and successfully passing the qualifying examinations. Mr. Leonetti is also an NASD Registered Representative, a licensed Insurance Broker, and registered with the Securities and Exchange Commission as an Investment Adviser.

Mr. Leonetti is currently a member of the International Association for Financial Planning, The Institute of Certified Financial Planners, the American Association of Individual Investors, The National Association of Personal Financial Advisers, the Registry of Financial Planning Practitioners, and the American Association of Financial Professionals. He has also taught financial planning courses at Roosevelt University and Harper College, and has appeared in various national publications such as the <u>Chicago Sun-Times</u> and <u>Sylvia Porter's Personal Money Management</u>.

FEES

Financial Planning Service

The company charges a fee for the creation of a personal financial plan for its individual clients. The fee is payable in four installments: 25 percent of the charge in advance of services rendered (collected when data form is returned), with the balance payable in three quarterly installments upon receipt of bill after presentation of your financial plan.

Leonetti & Associates provides consultation regarding initial implementation at no further charge to client. The company's fee structure is set out in Exhibit A.

Financial planning is an ongoing process. Changes occur in tax laws, the economic environment, investments, and in the personal circumstances of the client. Therefore, Leonetti & Associates establishes a long term consulting relationship with its clients. However, in most cases the work involved in annual review and service is less intensive than the initial services described above. Therefore, the company normally charges a reduced fee, as illustrated in Exhibit B, to provide subsequent annual reviews.

Investment Management Service

For many of its clients Leonetti & Associates provide constant and ongoing investment management services. Fees for these services are outlined in exhibit C.

FEE SCHEDULE

Financial Planning—Exhibit A

First year financial planning fees are calculated by applying the percentages below to the dollar amount listed. These dollar amounts are the sum of personal gross income and active assets. Active assets are only investment assets and do not include home, personal property, or business value. They do include company retirement plan balances, trust account balances, etc. Identification of what is included will be shown in each individual case.

Income + Assets	%
First $200,000	1%
Next $300,000	.5%
In excess of $500,000	.25%

Reviews—Exhibit B

Fees normally run from 50 percent to 100 percent of first year's planning fee as calculated in Exhibit A.

Asset and Investment Management—Exhibit C

Portfolio Setup: Estimated charge based on complexity with average charge being $100–$200.

Portfolio Value	% of Portfolio Value
First $500,000	1%
Next $500,000	3/4 of 1%
In excess of $1,000,000	1/2 of 1%

Portfolio values* are computed each quarter and multiplied by appropriate percentage listed above. This amount is then multiplied by 1/4 to determine that quarter's charge.

Miscellaneous—Exhibit D

There is a charge of $50.00 per hour for miscellaneous work done such as re-registration of investments, separate research work requested by client, etc. Client will be notified prior to work being done if such work incurs these charges.

*Values of vehicles such as stocks, bonds, mutual funds, annuities, etc. are based on the closing value on the last business day of the month in which the quarter starts. Limited Partnerships and other non-static investments will be valued at cost basis until liquidated.

A Much More Elaborate Approach

As you might expect, the descriptive literature of the Bank of America's Executive Financial Counseling Department was considerably more elaborate. On the inside cover of a Bank of America brochure was the following:

> The need for truly professional financial planning has never been greater...As President of Bank of America, I'm proud of Executive Financial Counseling for the leadership role it has taken within the financial planning industry. As a client, my personal experience with this group's professionalism and technical competence has yielded significant benefit to my family and me.—Samuel H. Armacost, President and C.E.O., Bank of America NT&SA.

It's an impressive endorsement, isn't it?

Why Did It Close?

As 1985 was drawing to a close the *San Francisco Chronicle* devoted a large part of its daily business section to the Bank of America.

The bank not only sold its own building to raise cash; it also sold some large subsidiaries, namely FINANCE AMERICA. Despite opposition from some highly-placed executives, Bank of America also closed down its Executive Financial Counseling Department. Some observers took it as proof that fee-only planning was not consistently profitable. They compared it to the short-lived experience of Merrill-Lynch in the fee-only planning business.

According to Tim Kochis, "The bank has not abandoned the use of financial planning as a tool in its general retail efforts. What it has done is discontinue providing financial counseling as a distinct professional fee-based service."

Time will tell whether that was a wise decision.

Obviously Deloitte, Haskins & Sells, one of the most respected of the top eight accounting firms, saw a profit in fee-only planning. Tim Kochis and five of his top planners have now joined that firm both in New York and San Francisco, and, with no objections from the bank, they have taken their clients and practice with them. For the most part, according to Tim, they will be establishing a very similar operation to supplement that already in effect at Deloitte, Haskins & Sells. Tim Kochis himself will be taking on similar responsibilities to those he had at the bank. My guess is that with the help of this nationally respected financial planning executive, Deloitte, Haskins & Sells will soon be a real leader in the fee-only segment of this exciting new profession.

AN INTERVIEW WITH
Edwin P. Morrow

Edwin P. Morrow is chairman of the board of Confidential Planning Services, Inc., and president of Financial Planning Consultants of Middletown, Ohio. During our interview, I asked him to elaborate on the reasons he entered financial planning and why he thought the financial planning profession might need help. Here are excerpts from that interview:

DUNTON: When did you first realize that the independent financial planners might need help if they were to survive?

MORROW: In 1970, I started my own fee-based financial planning firm, Financial Planning Consultants, Inc. For the next six years, we struggled to develop materials that were suitable for supporting a financial planning practice. Then, in 1976, I organized a meeting of six other financial planners to see what we could accomplish if we worked together and shared common knowledge, successes, problems, and things to avoid.

As a result of that meeting and others, in which we realized a need in the industry for a definitive support program, we started Confidential Planning Services, as a nonprofit trade association. In 1985, CPS converted to a franchising operation; however, each firm retains its independence and identity.

DUNTON: Were your initial members all connected with a particular produce vendor?

MORROW: The original CPS members brought different strengths to the organization. They came from different backgrounds and had different degrees of experience in financial planning.

All initial participants agreed, unanimously, at the beginning to develop CPS as a non-product oriented organization. It was a deliberate effort to be attractive to a variety of professionals who could become affiliates, regardless of their own product orientation.

DUNTON: How did the original affiliates differ from the ones you are signing up now?

MORROW: Today's CPS affiliates are like and unlike the early affiliates. We still see some people making a transition from one profession to financial planning, where continued education is needed so that they can eventually provide comprehensive financial planning services. On the other hand, many of our new affiliates are CPAs, attorneys, stock brokers, and bankers who already have a high degree of sophistication in financial planning.

DUNTON: How do you test the services that you are now offering your affiliates?

MORROW: Financial Planning Consultants, Inc., my financial planning firm that specializes in the corporate executive market, is located in the same facilities as CPS. It was and is the guinea pig for all tests and trial runs for our services and programs. FPC is an active financial planning firm that must stay ahead of the pack in services and marketing in order to allow CPS affiliates in the network to benefit from proven and tested programs.

DUNTON: Are your services on an optional basis? Or do prospective affiliates have to take the whole package?

MORROW: CPS offers a wide variety of services that come as a package called "affiliation." This package allows access to the CPS system, professionals and knowledge, including the CPS operations manual system, comprehensive training programs, public relations, advertising and marketing programs, office supplies, printed materials, brochures, and optional hardware, as well as ProPlan software, developed by Financial Planning Consultants, Inc.

Our training program is quite intensive, with four different schools focusing on distinct areas of financial planning practice management. In our classroom, the planners refer to many of the more than 35 operations and more than 100 slides used to promote their practice.

In addition, CPS will send field consultants to affiliate offices to advise on office management, practice image, marketing, and client development. These specialized services may involve additional expense.

DUNTON: When did you change to a corporation and why?

MORROW: In 1982, to respond to the increased requests for support from affiliates, the association became a for-profit corporation, to facilitate the capitalization that would allow for expansion. Association dues are not enough to keep up with the growth potential and the increased services being requested by our affiliates.

DUNTON: What type of financial planner do you look for as an affiliate?

MORROW: Our affiliates run the gamut, from new firms in the first steps of transition, through growth firms that are fully aware of what needs to be done and are growing, to the mature firm that has been supplying financial planning services for some years and continues to benefit from our network and information distribution to keep up with the industry's trends and changes.

DUNTON: What type do you avoid?

MORROW: We do not encourage affiliation by persons or firms who intend to remain totally commission oriented. The CPS process presumes a desire for fee-based service and development of a long-term trust relationship with the client that indicates more labor-intensive effort on the part of the firm and loyalty from the client.

DUNTON: You have an internship program in CPS. Would you elaborate?

MORROW: CPS has developed an internship program that is very successful for us and our affiliates. Currently, we provide lodging, as well as education. The interns come to us as college seniors, recent graduates, and graduate students from departments of finance, computer science, marketing, and public relations. Many come from such universities as Purdue in Indiana and Wright State in Ohio, which have curricula in financial planning. The internship familiarizes students with our ProPlan software and the internal workings of an active financial planning firm.

The internships are flexible enough to allow the students to emphasize their interests, as we recognize that young people will enter the industry as counselors, planners or marketers, and each specialty in our industry requires different gifts and abilities. In addition, it gives them a sense of our network and contacts throughout the country.

So far, every intern to complete our 12-week program has found instant employment with a CPS affiliate, or we have hired them ourselves. The internship program continues to grow as it adjusts to provide tailored training programs for employees of our affiliated firms.

DUNTON: Of all the services you provide the new financial planning firm, what is it that most increases their chances of success in this profession?

MORROW: Success in the financial planning profession relies on a wide variety of efforts that must be made by the firm and its principals. CPS's most important service is to break down into chewable pieces the process of beginning and maintaining a financial planning practice: It is a variety of well-thought out processes that all come together to support a well-functioning, successful firm. Success in financial planning is the same as success in any other business or field. It depends on the effort put forth by the individuals involved. We provide the tools that make the effort given by the financial planner come back to him or her through a profitable practice.

PART SIX

Important Scenes in the Picture
Financial Planning Becomes More Than a Household Word

In 1984, financial planning became a household word; in 1985, the light on the financial planning picture illuminated new scenes. These new scenes concerned three powerful forces: giant companies and professional groups, the computer, and the academic community.

By 1985, all three were dominating much of the media and occupying a large part of the thoughts of those in or planning to enter into the financial planning profession. Each of these segments was now playing a key role in the evolution of the financial services industry.

Even companies that had disparaged the concept of financial planning in the 1970s were deeply committed to the concept by the mid-1980s. As a result, the new breed of executives calling the shots were far more often on target. In addition, many colleges and universities were now willing to incorporate financial planning into their curricula.

In 1985, the computer also came into its own as a financial planning tool. While there were some who promoted it as a substitute for the work of the financial planner, more and more the computer became a tool that allowed financial planners to make projections they formerly would only dream of doing for their clients.

Large companies and professional groups, academia, and computers were not the only important new scenes in the financial planning picture. However, they were some of the more interesting.

14 The Giants: A New Force

In his interview on page 41, Donald Pitti made some interesting predictions about the financial services industry and how it was evolving. Obviously, deregulation is playing and will continue to play an important part with regard to the banking, securities and insurance segments. What may be more interesting is the influx of giant companies into the field. Large companies providing and/or setting up financial planning services or departments are coming not only from banking, securities and insurance, but also from accounting.

Until 1984, large companies' efforts to provide financial planning services were often tentative and half-hearted. They did recognize several years ago that financial planning was evolving and increasing in popularity as a prerequisite for top executives. By 1982 and 1983, financial planning as a perk had worked its way down to middle management. The use of financial planning as a perk is often credited for the interest shown by the large companies in getting into financial planning in the mid-1980s.

Also influential in the last five years has been the impressive scope of and attendance at the IAFP's annual conventions. At the Dallas convention in 1978, followed by the Chicago, San Francisco, Boston, New Orleans, Las Vegas and Anaheim conventions, there was a trend toward a greater number of representatives from the largest firms in the country. By the time of the Atlanta convention in 1984, it was already obvious that many of those same large companies had embarked on one planning approach or another.

Merrill Lynch's Experience

Testing the Waters

Merrill Lynch's first attempt at financial planning—the $5,000 per plan operation—opened and closed during the early 1980s. The company's second overture was aimed at a much broader market and was called Financial Pathfinder Service, headed by experienced financial planner Jay Rabinowitz.

Today, Financial Pathfinder Service is a growing department that provides, for $250, a computerized plan for Merrill Lynch clients and prospective clients. The plans are prepared by Merrill Lynch account executives in their various offices.

The term "financial planner" is apparently reserved for Jay Rabinowitz's department and has not spread to the field offices, or even the corporate offices, if my recent experience with the switchboard operator is any example. I was assured that Merrill Lynch did not have a financial counseling or financial planning department, though the company did have a sales department, a real estate department, an accounting department, a legal department, a public relations department, etc. But no financial counseling or planning department.

Nevertheless, Jay Rabinowitz believes that the financial planner, not the account executive, will prevail at Merrill Lynch as time passes. In a recent discussion, he elaborated on the subject:

> As evidence of this trend, the number of account executives who have enrolled in financial planning courses is growing dramatically. In fact, our Donald T. Regan School of Continuing Education offers a course of study in financial planning that leads to a Certified Financial Manager (CFM) designation.
>
> In terms of a specific offering, Merrill Lynch is proud to provide the Financial Pathfinder Service to our clients. As you know, Merrill Lynch has been involved in financial planning since 1976. The Pathfinder report is the culmination of what we have learned over the years.

Because of Merrill Lynch's wide and deep market penetration, as well as its leadership role in the industry, I encouraged Rabinowitz to discuss the topic further with me. He said:

> A surprising number of affluent individuals have no financial plan or strategy at all. Financial planning is very much like motherhood and apple pie. Everyone agrees it is important, but most have gone no further than that.
>
> Therefore, it became important to provide a service that overcame some of the obstacles. Our service mails the questionnaire to the client and provides a staff of financial planners via a toll-free number. The client completes the booklet at his convenience and in the privacy of his home. Thus, it is relatively easy, and the time commitment is minimized.
>
> The second factor that is important is cost. Again, in spite of knowing they should have a plan, many hesitate as a result of the fees. By having a quality service at a relatively modest cost [$250], we hope to avoid high price as an obstacle. Mind you, many clients will

subsequently have a second, more expensive plan done after receiving their Pathfinder. Having the Pathfinder started the process and got the client on the track. Of course, for a very large number of clients, the Pathfinder will be more than sufficient.

One of Rabinowitz's more interesting comments had to do with financial education, which, of course, is what the NCFE is all about. I asked him about it.

> A third element in our approach to financial planning is education. It is important that a plan indicate how and why conclusions are reached and recommendations made. It is our philosophy that we want the client actively involved in the decision-making process, and that can only be done if we act to educate our client.

I also asked him about implementation and potential conflict of interest, and here's his response:

> A financial plan is of no value without implementation. I believe that our greatest successes have been with the clients who had a Merrill Lynch broker available to review the choices and put their plans into action. Those clients who claim to be able to do it on their own usually fail to do so. At the risk of sounding self-serving, I do not believe that planners (and the writers about financial planning) are doing their clients a favor by providing advice only. Once the client leaves the planner's office, I am afraid the probability of implementation drops dramatically. I suggest that the best favor we can do our clients is assist in putting their plans into action.
>
> I say this being fully aware of the problem of one-product salespeople or commission-hungry "financial planners." Merrill Lynch's goal in taking a financial planning approach is that it will inevitably lead to a longer and deeper relationship with the client. Certainly, selling that client an inappropriate product or service contradicts our entire philosophy and strategy of relationship building. Running a profitable business and serving client needs are by no means mutually exclusive.

Not All Rose Petals

While Merrill Lynch was making inroads, it also was giving professional financial planners some migraines. In 1985, I wrote the following open letter to the Merrill Lynch executives, voicing my concerns:

> Three times I have heard your brokers claim to be financial planners. When questioned more closely, they took the position that "it's the same thing."

If I've had it happen to me three times, imagine how many times the public at large is being misled.

As you know, or should know, brokers are not the same as financial planners. They do not have the same training and certainly do not have the same obligations to prepare and operate within a financial plan.

As one who played a key role in establishing the financial planner as a new professional and is now, through the NCFE, trying to bring greater education and sophistication to the average consumer, this false claim by your brokers offends me. One even said "yes" (at first) when I asked if he was a CFP. I'm sure it bothers financial planners all over the country, especially those who have worked hard at qualifying themselves to prepare financial plans for their clients.

It would be appreciated if you would pass the word to your offices that the use of the term "financial planner" by those not qualified to prepare financial plans could be interpreted as misleading the public. Until we can get regulations promulgated to stop it, it should be stopped voluntarily.

The Accountants' Role

While companies like Merrill Lynch are making inroads into financial planning, astute observers such as Lew Wallensky, CFP, of Los Angeles are going on record as saying that accountants will dominate the financial planning profession in the future.

The Big Eight Accounting Firms

W. Thomas Porter is a partner and chairman of Touche Ross's Personal Financial Management (PFM) program, as well as a leader in the Big Eight firms' entrance into financial planning.

In fact, Tom Porter composed Touche Ross's impressive *Guide to Personal Financial Management* manual. Essentially, it is a do-it-yourself guide, replete with elaborate forms to fill out. Although the "financial planner" is only a three-ring binder holding all the necessary forms, Porter added wisely, "Once you have your 'financial planner' prepared, you can use financial advisers in a much more cost effective way and better evaluate their advice."

Touche Ross is still experimenting with ways to make its PFM program most effective for its clients and its own bottom line; coordinators have been appointed in each of its offices to work with the program. The company also conducts many seminars and, in cooperation with Prentice-Hall, which publishes the *Personal Financial Management Guide,* has issued the Lumen software program.

Arthur Young Gets into the Act

Arthur Young & Company also has a financial planning division that offers elaborate fee-only planning for executives. One of that accounting firm's top people recently noted that financial planning is not only lucrative in and of itself, it also helps solidify relationships with clients.

The Struggle Ahead

With the move into financial planning services, accounting firms are losing some of the financial planners they train. Some go to work directly for the clients, while others, with more entrepreneurial spirit, set up their own financial planning offices.

Most of the Big Eight accounting firms are committed to the financial planning field, in one way or another. As a result of their interest, the financial planning field has garnered greater respectability, both as a process and as a profession. Undoubtedly, the entrance of the Big Eight, albeit a tentative one, is speeding up recognition of the financial planner as a true professional.

What has yet to be established is the ability of these CPAs now doing financial planning to compete successfully with the experienced financial planner, operating his or her own financial planning boutique. Nevertheless, from amid the giants will come some of the future financial planners.

Two Interesting Observations

"How quickly do you think the big accounting firms will expand their operations to include financial planning as an additional service they offer their clients?"

That question is asked of all of us who speak or write about the financial planning profession. Here's the response of William Mayberry, a financial planner in New York of whom I recently asked that question:

> I set up a meeting with the head of the Personal Financial Department of Arthur Young & Company in New York City. I intended to develop a potential source for referral business and to learn more about what was going on with the Big Eight firms, regarding their efforts to bring financial counseling to their clients.
>
> The person I met was perhaps 35 years old, had a background in personal taxation, and looked thoroughly confused about his role. He explained that the New York office was waiting for official word from headquarters as to what extent Arthur Young would be involved with personal financial planning, if at all. While he sat and waited, two plans piled up on his desk, awaiting completion. He confided to me that he was literally 'reading the next chapters' in the manual he had been provided so that he might complete the two plans.

> I pressed on, asking what his recommendations might consist of, once the plan was completed. 'We will shy away from specific investment recommendations,' he replied. 'We would rather the client develop his or her own sources in the investment area.' In addition, they plan to house several 'experts' in the local offices, rather than utilize outside expertise.

I'm not sure that experience is typical, any more than I'm positive the next observation is objective, although it comes from one of the most respected and forward-thinking financial planners in the country. Ben Baldwin, who is profiled later in this book, began three years ago composing a computer-based comprehensive financial planning system with one of the Big Eight accounting firms in mind. Baldwin contends that the large accounting firms will play an increasingly important role in financial planning. In a recent discussion, he observed:

> Right now, they are doing it for perhaps the top two percent of the executives of their client firms. It won't be long, however, until many of those client firms will want financial planning done for the top 30 percent. Not a single Big Eight firm is equipped to handle an assignment like that. To be able to take on such an assignment, they will need a system like mine.

What About the Supermarkets?

One financial supermarket executive, who asked not to be named, thinks financial supermarkets will continue to thrive, "if only because they'll make comparison shopping available." When pressed, he cited IRAs as an example. "People could go from the bank in a multiservice center to the insurance office to the stock broker, all without getting back in their car."

I didn't argue with him, but realized from my years of involvement with financial planners and their customers that most people are delighted when they discover that this type of comparison shopping can be done for them by their financial planner. "The average person doesn't even know the right questions to ask about today's complicated financial choices," points out experienced stock broker–turned–financial-planner Pat Bonnet, CFP, of Sherman Oaks, California.

Banks and S&Ls: Collective Giants

If 1985's headlines and scare stories reporting on bank failures and multi-million dollar mistakes are indicative of a trend, banks will have to look for something to recapture their solid and dependable image. Financial planning might well be the answer, as whether Bank of America thinks so or not. (See Chapter 13, pages 104–115, for more details). Undoubtedly, some banks will follow its lead, but I suspect more will form joint ventures with small financial planning firms.

Some observers predict that even before the banks enter financial planning, the savings and loan associations will. Lynette King, executive vice president of Security Savings, headquartered in Scottsdale, Arizona, has extensively researched this new profession. In our conversation, she made the following observations:

> Yes, I believe that S&Ls are even better positioned than banks to offer financial planning. S&Ls have, historically, been service-oriented vehicles, while most banks have become very transaction-oriented with their automatic teller machines and their commitment to electronic banking.

I asked King to explain how she thought S&Ls would get involved. Using her successful S&L group of 23 offices as an example, she replied:

> We are more interested in helping educate people than in doing financial planning for them. There are a great many people who need to be educated in the very basics; we feel we can do that as part of our personal service for our customers. S&Ls are in a unique position to provide the financial education people need *before* they do financial planning. We don't have tellers, we have customer service representatives.

That's at least a step in the direction of financial planning.

The Insurance Giants: Once Over Lightly

Prudential-Bache was not the first to entertain the concept of financial planning as a method of selling more insurance and securities. It was, however, the first to start running full-page and double-page ads promising "Total Financial Planning." It may have accelerated the entrance by other insurance giants into the field of financial planning, although they used different tactics.

In 1983, for example, the Travelers Corporation announced that in 1984 it was forming a new subsidiary, First Financial Planner Services (FFPS), which would be "providing independent financial planners with the financial tools and products needed to serve their customers." One competitor describes the new service as "a franchise operation, charging fees of $25,000 per year and requiring them to become security broker dealers."

As early as 1981, possibly sooner, many authorities in the insurance industry were predicting the end of the typical general agency system as a profitable insurance marketing approach. Some credited this directly to the emergence of the financial planner, while others saw it as a force in the marketing of insurance, pointing to the number of well-established general agents who had converted their operations to do financial planning and were selling equity products, as was Robert Pogue of Sacramento, California, who is profiled at the end of this book.

By 1983, most of the large insurance companies were doing something about financial planning. They might have tried sooner, except for their abortive experiments in the early 1970s. Contrary to what some companies professed, however, they had not actually tried financial planning. Instead, they were trying to market mutual funds, based on the success of mutual fund companies' marketing of insurance, by dually-licensed salespeople.

As the giant insurance companies knew they were stronger in the sales department, they may have thought it would be an easy matter to sell mutual funds as well. But their timing couldn't have been worse, unfortunately. In the early 1970s many fund groups received poor publicity and had poor performance. Many insurance companies therefore took their losses and forgot the fund business, with the exception of companies that bought large funds rather than forming their own.

For the reader who wishes to pursue this particular subject in depth, *Financial Planning* magazine's April 1984 issue covers Metropolitan, Mutual Benefit, John Hancock, Connecticut Mutual, CIGNA, New England Life and others. Among the new insurance executive leaders mentioned are J. Pierre Maurer, Henry Kates, Tom Dooley, Larry English, Dennis Mullane, George Trotta, Ted Bohner, Tom McAboy, Jim Mayfield. They, along with others, are already making an impact on the financial planning industry.

CIGNA Individual Financial Services Company

One of the Leaders

Many large and medium-sized companies are watching CIGNA Financial Services Company of Hartford, Connecticut, one of the obvious leaders in converting a sizeable portion of its sales forces and activities to a financial planning approach. Leading the way with CIGNA's field forces was Edward Berube of Houston and Nelson Jones of Denver.

For a quick update, I recently contacted Chic Finn, vice president for financial planning sales and marketing for CIGNA:

> We began a study in 1981 on how to market the services and products of CIGNA's Individual Financial Division (IFD) during the coming decade. We knew that life insurance premiums were down, that term insurance sales were increasing, and that our costs of doing business were going up.
>
> As a result of that study, on April 15, 1982, the company announced a new business strategy for IFD. The linchpin of that strategy was financial planning for a fee. And, it caused us to restructure the organization. We now do business as CIGNA

Individual Financial Services Company, which includes not only Connecticut General Life Insurance Company, but also CIGNA Securities, Inc., a broker-dealer and registered investment adviser, as well as CIGNA Associates, Inc., which we believe to be the largest general agency in the United States.

On August 1, 1982, we kicked off financial planning for a fee in five locations across the United States.

Tom Dooley, Finn's boss at CIGNA, had already explained the new strategy as follows in a company brochure:

> In 1982, when the Individual Financial Division unveiled its new business strategy with an overall objective of diversifying its revenues, we announced our intention to create and develop financial planning services. There was little question then, and there has been no question since, that this was a bold undertaking for the division and certainly not one devoid of risk. Financial planning for a fee had been tried before by some very large, impressive companies, not the least of which was Merrill Lynch. From their perspective, these programs were not successful.
>
> For us, there were some questions about the marketing of the service. Was there really a market for it? Would the client pay a fee up front for this diagnostic and prescriptive planning? Could we train our people within a reasonable time frame and at a reasonable cost? Would the client feel it was too complex?
>
> From the outset, we recognized that the list of open issues, while not endless, was long. But we felt the service was a natural for us. First, we were in the right market. For many years Connecticut General's individual life business has been in the affluent small business market. Second, we believed we had the best trained and the most sophisticated producers [agents] in the industry. And, we felt that the planning service was a natural extension of what we've been doing for decades.
>
> We also recognized that success with financial planning would have multiple payoffs. It could become a major contributor to revenues and earnings, and it would be an outstanding recruiting tool.

Growth Achieved

Two years after CIGNA's financial services company had entered into financial planning, Larry English, the company's president, commented on the growth his segment had achieved:

> We're pleased with our results today. We began in 1982 with six offices in financial planning. By the end of 1983, we had 16, and we are projecting that by the end of 1984, 24 of our major marketing

offices will be in the financial planning business. That represents a 50 percent increase. We have a total of 34 marketing offices out there, and by 1985 we expect to have them all in the financial planning business.

Keeping in mind that we began the year with only 16 offices in financial planning and recognizing that the heaviest selling season in our business is in the latter half of the year (especially in the fourth quarter), our average sales per month rose rapidly to an average of 50 cases per month level. We had a significant uptick in the spring, thanks to a very large—what I would refer to as a cluster—sale in one of our new offices that got us almost up to 100 cases in the month of April.

We expect to continue to rise through the second half of the year and expect that we will average 75 to 100 new financial planning customers per month by the end of the year.

In 1983 we billed and collected a total of $715,000 in fees for financial planning. Our projection for 1984 is $2.75 million. That's 380 percent growth over last year. I can't promise you we're going to sustain that kind of growth on a year-to-year basis, but we are very comfortable we're going to make that number and we're going to have substantial growth in 1985 and 1986.

Later, in an interview with *Financial Planning* that appeared in its April, 1984 issue, Larry English made this key observation:

> We used to have the problem with our agents, where we'd spend a great deal of time and money training them about the process of planning and giving value-added services, English says, and then there would always be the day where they come into the office and say, "Oh, I'm just a salesman." We don't get that with our planners anymore, and our employee turnover has started to turn around.

Some Held Back Progress

While some were leading and continue to lead in the financial planning arena, others drag their feet. Some still refuse to grant financial planning the status it has earned in today's marketplace.

For example, even after 10 years, Nelson Broms, a key executive with Equitable Life, had not changed his stance. I was still hearing the same disparaging remarks in 1982, in San Francisco, as I had heard in 1972, in New York. I was shocked by that, but not surprised to hear that the Equitable would not urge support of NCFE efforts to educate the consumer.

It *was* surprising, however, more than a year later to meet Ben Baldwin, then chairman of the Greater O'Hare [Chicago-area] IAFP chapter as well as an Equitable agent, and to discover that he was obviously one of the most knowledgeable of financial planners in the country. Ben and I were both surprised with Equitable's position, but he was having no success in getting his company to move into a financial planning posture. That, too, changed by 1985, when Equitable began offering what the other insurance giants had been providing for about two years. Now, like MONY, Massachusetts Mutual, New York Life, and Northwestern Mutual, Equitable is playing catch-up to the more progressive life insurance companies. When I learned of Equitable's move, I requested and received its financial planning material and discovered much of Ben Baldwin's thinking but, not surprisingly, no mention of Ben Baldwin.

15 The Computer and Its Roles

To give inside expertise to this chapter, I asked Paul Morey to be "guest author." Morey is currently a financial planner with Financial Network Investment Corporation's Concord, California, office. In the early 1980s, he was an independent consultant in the application of microcomputer technology, after eight years with Rapidata and four years with G.E. Information Services. In addition to his experience with computers, Morey has a bachelor's degree in marketing and a master's in finance from San Jose State University in California.

Not only is this chapter an overview of the impact of computers, it is also almost a small course for the financial planner or any reader who may be contemplating entering this profession. While it is only one man's look at the subject, it does shed considerable light on the topic of computers and their role in financial planning offices. And now here's what Paul has to say about computers.

The Computer Generation Arrives

Since so much of what a financial planner does is analytical, it seems natural that the computer should become a vital tool. More than 15 years ago, Computone introduced a "briefcase terminal" for insurance agents to use in preparing projections of future policy benefits. From this pioneering effort, the use of computer-generated analysis and illustration has grown substantially, though it is still far from reaching its potential.

In 1970, access to computer power was limited. The spreading availability of the remote timesharing terminal, however, was changing the way that financial analysts arrived at investment decisions. Financial planners then worked for corporations and seldom were involved with personal financial planning, yet the first experiments were being conducted in applying computer analysis to personal decision making.

The leading supplier of remote computer power was General Electric Corporation, which founded the timesharing industry in the mid-1960s. In 1971, G.E. began marketing FAL, the Financial Analysis Language, which is a powerful tool for preparing financial reports, spreadsheet projections, corporate models, and investment analysis. FAL helped G.E. expand the use of interactive computer power into the business community, becoming its leading product for the 1970s and being copied by other firms, just as VisiCalc has been in the 1980s.

In 1972, the trust department of the Wells Fargo Bank, in San Francisco, began developing a personal financial planning model, using FAL. The trust department succeeded in producing a highly accurate model that projected taxation, cash flow, and wealth buildup for many years into the future. This initial effort resulted in a service that was marketed to Wells Fargo's major corporate clients as a fringe benefit for senior executives. However, the model cost thousands of dollars to develop and hundreds of dollars in processing charges to complete an analysis for a single individual. In turn, corporations paid thousands of dollars per executive for completion of a financial plan, limiting the use of computers for personal financial planning to those who could afford to spend large sums of money.

New Horizons for Financial Planners

These limitations did not change much during the 1970s, until the potential of the microcomputer exploded upon the scene. The growth and affordability of the microcomputer already is revolutionizing the financial planning industry. Within a few years, planners simply will not be able to remain competitive without using a microcomputer.

In 1985, the use of the computer in financial planning was spreading rapidly, but well-established firms were still only experimenting with its capabilities. However, the costs for purchasing microcomputers are so low today that virtually every financial planner can afford to begin implementing computer applications.

Traditionally, financial planners have prospered by serving the needs of the already wealthy. For them, the planner could afford to spend many hours, perhaps days, preparing a tax analysis and plan for clients who could afford to spend thousands of dollars for that service.

Serving the Middle Class

Our future challenge, as financial planners, is to provide professional quality services to the middle class—those who need to learn how to acquire wealth. While the marketplace for such services is much broader, the cost of providing the service must be reduced. The computer answers that need by offering greater efficiency.

Consumer Financial Institute (CFI) in Newton, Massachusetts, has used the computer to pioneer what is sometimes called the "store-bought" plan. The plan is standardized and created with information from client-prepared questionnaires. In addition, the plan is delivered by mail, without any interpretation or guidance from a financial counselor. CFI has sold more than 100,000 such plans, charging the consumer $175 for the service. Similar mass production planning services are being offered by most of the major brokerage houses, at prices ranging from $40 to $250.

Nevertheless, turning over the middle class to such impersonal marketing giants, just because they offer a product the average consumer can afford, seems almost unethical. If a client is to look forward to financial security and possible future affluence, he or she still needs training and personal guidance.

The Role of the Commissioned Planner

Planners who earn commissions from the products they recommend are in a position to offer inexpensive, personal services to their clients, providing the planners have the right tools. Generally, the sales commissions are sufficient to offset the costs of a modest financial planning and counseling effort. Many commissioned people enter the field from sales careers in insurance, real estate, mutual funds or securities. While their professionalism is sometimes challenged, their service is greatly needed and may be all that many people can afford. These salespeople/planners, however, do require adequate training in personal finance and counseling. To offer true planning services to the middle class, they need even more. They must be able to offer inexpensive, computer-generated plans that will allow them to compete with the store-bought services.

It Can Be and Is Being Done

To support these planners, software must be professionally developed and specifically targeted to those with assets falling in the range of $30,000 to $250,000. In our office, we met this challenge with a custom-designed system.

Our software is immediately usable, with little training; the total time required to input the data and print out a complete plan is usually less than one hour. We made the data collection forms self-guiding, so that clients can enter most of their financial data themselves, provided they are careful and willing to take the time.

We don't think the plan should be a sterile financial document, nor so long as to discourage clients from reading it. In addition, the software plan I designed has individual pages with explanations as well as numbers, and it is relatively easy for the nonprofessional to read.

Planners Using the Computer

How do financial planners use the computer to reduce the costs of providing service to their clients?

Let me explain how I do it. I begin by preparing rough, handwritten recommendations for insertion into the plan, which is then prepared by a secretary or other nonplanner. The client completes a detailed questionnaire, which we jointly review, and I complete sections that the client may not understand. These data, along with the handwritten text, are entered into the computer and used to create the plan.

After all data are inputted, the computer formats them into reports via a planning program, while a word processing program formats the text portion. Computer-generated plans, prepared in this fashion, can cost the planner less than $20 for the secretary's time, making the cost of preparing the final written plan almost incidental.

In addition, using the computer frees the financial planner to help the client understand the wealth-building process, explore needs and priorities, and help in the establishment of goals. Following development of the plan, the financial planner should also guide the client through its implementation. Charges can be limited to the time spent with the client, plus one or two hours for formulating the recommendations.

Forget Fears of HAL

Many people fear computers and the threat of new technology, possibly goaded on by Arthur C. Clarke's story, *2001: A Space Odyssey,* in which a computer named "HAL" is not very user-friendly. Others have had dreadful experiences with computers, either with poorly designed software or equipment that was ill-suited to their needs. However, when software is well designed, almost anyone can use the computer.

In our case, the program simply displays a menu, a list of options for what data to enter, corresponding to sections on the detailed questionnaire. The operator fills in the blanks on the screen by typing in data in precisely the same order as on the questionnaire. So, entering a client's assets, for instance, takes the typist about 30 seconds, as does the entry of liabilities. Naturally, descriptions of investments take longer. The whole data entry process often can be completed in 15 minutes.

Following data entry, the computer screen shows a menu of reports, from which one or more may be selected for printing. After the selections are made, the printer often begins typing the report in no more than five seconds, freeing the operator to work on other business, away from the computer, while the report is automatically printing out.

This software is truly user-friendly. There are no lengthy, predefined data entry sequences. Only the information important to the client need be entered; the menu allows it to be entered in any order. Likewise, the menus permit the operator to select only the reports needed, skipping those that don't apply. All reports are prepared from a common source of data, so a modification of any value will automatically be reflected throughout the report. If the system sounds expensive, take heart. These programs will run on an inexpensive personal computer.

Is the microcomputer destined to become an essential part of the financial planner's business? You'd better believe it is. Those who put off the introduction of computers into their business are simply going to be left behind.

Tools, Templates and Black Boxes

The July 1984 issue of *Financial Planning* contained an article that accurately addressed the three levels of computer software being used today. Let's look at each: tools, templates and black boxes.

Tools

Tools do not perform any specific task, but they do allow the novice to develop computerized solutions to unique needs. If you cannot find an existing program that does what you need it to do, it may be possible to create one, using a tool. To date, the best-selling software programs have been tools for spreadsheet analysis and database management, as they both have such broad applications.

However, customizing solutions takes hours and hours of time. You may spend hours tinkering with the computer, only to discover that what you have created has only marginal usefulness. One such episode can easily cost you $2,000 or more, as measured by the value of your time. Remember, the time required to develop quality computer programs is not usually measured in hours, or even weeks, but most often in months.

Templates

The term *templates* is often used to describe software applications built with tools. A set of instructions is written, directing the tool to read, store, manipulate and print the data that you want to have analyzed.

Generally, the software developer has spent the months required to complete this solution and will share the results with you for a price. The benefits of templates to buyers are that the cost is usually modest and you have the ability to modify, enhance, or further customize the templates to match your own needs.

Unfortunately, there are also some major drawbacks. First, you must purchase the underlying tools, as well as the template. Then, to use the template application, you must learn something about how to operate the tool, even if you don't plan to modify the application. Also, template applications seldom perform smoothly, requiring much user intervention and some degree of skill; errors are easy to make. Template applications often require extensive training, skilled personnel, and hours of operation until the personnel are proficient at using the software.

Black Boxes

A compiled computer program is sometimes referred to as a "black box." The information goes in one end, and analysis and reports mysteriously pop out the other end.

The user doesn't need to know anything about what happens inside the black box, but some people wonder if they can trust the results if they don't know how those results were achieved. Another drawback is inflexibility; such programs cannot be modified to suit the user's individual needs. They are also usually more expensive to purchase.

The advantages of such programs can be substantial, however. Professionally designed application programs can be a dream to use. Unskilled personnel can learn relatively quickly how to input the data and prepare the reports. The computer may even catch some kinds of errors as they are made and give the operator another chance to input the correct information.

The time required to complete a job is often reduced to one third or less of the time needed to perform the same job with a tool or a template. The virtues are elegant design, ease of use, and efficient processing in a user-friendly environment.

Certainly, all these virtues are not assured by the mere purchase of a black box program rather than a template. These are the potentials, however, when the software is developed by skilled professionals. Unfortunately, there are a number of poor-quality software packages offered, and much of the good software is still quite expensive.

Getting Started

If only it were easy to computerize your office. It isn't. As you computerize, you're bound to make mistakes, and some of them may be costly. You probably don't know anything about computers, for one thing, and most people who know computers don't know anything about your business.

Consider this scenario (it's one that many first-time computer buyers are afraid of): You finally gather enough courage to enter a computer store. The salesperson asks what you want, and you explain that you need a computer to use in your financial planning business. After asking a few more questions, the salesperson determines that you need a business-quality computer and printer, plus word processing software, a spreadsheet program, a database manager to keep your records, and "something financial," which the salesperson may interpret as, perhaps, Andrew Tobias's program, "Managing Your Money."

You buy the total package for about $5,000 and take it proudly to the office. In addition to the equipment, you have a stack of manuals about two feet high. Where do you start? Well, what about this manual? Oops, it's written in Greek; you realize it would take months and an interpreter even to begin to comprehend it. You put the book down and make a mental note to have your college-bound child take a look at what you just bought. The next day, you tell your secretary to learn "word processing." But, six months later, guess where that computer is? Chances are, still in the boxes, not even unwrapped, or unwrapped and dusted by the cleaning people but not even plugged in.

Getting to Know Your Computer

How do you get off on the right foot with your new computer? Let me offer a few simple Don'ts and Do's that will solve many of your potential problems.

What *not* to do:

- Buy a computer before determining what you will use it for and what software you need.
- Try to implement several applications all at once.
- Buy more software than you need for your first application.
- Buy any software that you don't completely understand before you get it.
- Buy anything that the store is not prepared to teach you to use.
- Buy an Apple or any other CP/M (eight-bit) computer. (They are too slow for most applications.)
- Buy any database or spreadsheet software without first knowing exactly what you will use it for.
- Start with a modem and a subscription to a database service. This should be the *last* use that you try to implement.

What you *should* do:

- Plan to set aside at least two full weeks to prepare for purchasing the computer and implementing your first application.
- Decide in advance which personnel will be using the computer and involve them in the selection process.
- Buy from a computer store that caters to businesses and will help by

preparing a needs analysis, offering training, and providing after-sale support.

- Keep visiting different stores until you find people who can talk your language. They should have some understanding of your business environment and should be truly helpful in defining your needs. Make them demonstrate any software they recommend and show you exactly how it can be applied to your business needs.
- Before buying, create a plan that states exactly what you want to do with your computer. Prioritize the applications and work with only one computer until it is working correctly.
- Attend a class and learn the fundamentals of operating your computer—before buying it.

Working with computer stores will help you avoid many initial problems. However, it probably will do little more than get you started, usually with word processing, because computer stores do not carry the application programs used by financial planners.

Where to Learn About Software

You can learn about financial planning software by reading advertisements in financial journals, attending demonstrations at IAFP conferences, or asking other financial planners what they use. If you can order a demonstration version of a software package, do so. No matter how attractive the vendor makes the software sound, you will not know whether or not it suits your needs until you test it.

Also, decide what your market is. Don't buy elaborate taxation analysis, estate planning, and portfolio tracking programs if your typical clients are not millionaires. Don't purchase spreadsheet programs, database managers, or template applications unless you have hours of time to spend learning them. In short, know the environment in which you could achieve success with your computer and be sure that what you buy is consistent with that environment.

Can You Avoid Mistakes?

Even with these precautions, be prepared to make mistakes. You may end up with a printer that is too slow or an expensive hard disk system when floppy disks might have worked just fine. No doubt, you'll purchase software that looks good but doesn't perform as you expected. Take heart. When you overcome your mistakes and get a system that works for you, it will pay for itself in a few months. If you avoid the major mistakes by following the previous suggestions and forgo purchasing any $5,000 software packages until you are sure you really need them, the cost of computerizing can be moderate.

If you're watching your dollars, I recommend starting with an IBM-compatible computer with dual floppy disk drives.

As for printers, I prefer a letter-quality dot matrix or the Hewlett Packard ink jet printer over many letter-quality impact printers, which can be too slow. However, that is changing. Do avoid the very cheap dot matrix printers; their print quality is too poor for professional use.

Costs vary and are dropping all the time, but this is what your initial investment could look like today:

Microcomputer	$2,000
Printer and cables	550
10 Extra diskettes	40
Paper	30
Word processing software	350
Comprehensive planning program	1,500
Total first cost	$4,470

There are, of course, many other items you can purchase, and probably will, once you have experienced success. However, you are better off to start modestly with only one or two applications and to build up from there.

16 The Academic World

The American College, originally called the American College of Life Underwriters, is an impressive academic institution, located in the lush suburban area of Bryn Mawr, Pennsylvania. Started by Solomon S. Huebner in 1927 and supported by tuition as well as grants from the major insurance companies, the school has earned an enviable reputation among professional institutions of advanced learning. In the 1970s, it began its master's program in financial sciences.

Through its nontraditional, "open university" approach to education, the college provides its students—many of whom are already established in business—with the opportunity to study at centers in all 50 states, the District of Columbia, and 25 foreign countries. Students may pursue their course work through participation in organized classes in their local communities, informal study groups, or independent study.

The American College is best known for its Chartered Life Underwriter (CLU) professional designation program. Through its Graduate School of Financial Sciences, the college also offers an advanced program leading to the master's degree.

During the 1980s, the American College created a more comprehensive and objective program aimed at accrediting its graduates as Chartered Financial Consultants (ChFCs). By 1985, there were more than 10,000 ChFCs, many of whom already were CLUs.

The program is designed to provide the ChFC with a comprehensive understanding of the financial services environment, which is much broader than life insurance. It qualifies its graduates to do financial planning. According to Gordon Rose, vice president for society and industry relations:

> The curriculum includes client counseling, economics, income taxation, insurance, investments, financial analysis, tax shelters, real estate, gift and estate planning, and planning for business owners and professionals.
>
> Special emphasis is placed on comprehensive fact finding, counseling techniques, the development of effective working

relationships with other financial services professionals, and issues of professionalism and ethics. The program culminates in a comprehensive financial planning case course that provides a practical means of integrating previously covered tools, techniques and products into the financial planning process.

In addition to completing the rigorous educational requirements, candidates for the Chartered Financial Consultant certification must meet strict experience and ethical requirements. They must also pledge to keep their knowledge relevant through lifelong continuing education.

With more than 10,000 ChFCs forming the advance guard and qualified to do more than sell insurance, the message is plain. The insurance industry has taken an important turn; financial planning is one way of the future, and it may be one of the most successful.

The move confirms the growing feeling that the consumer has graduated from his or her traditional willingness to buy financial products, even insurance, from one-dimensional product purveyors. However, don't count out the general agents. Many of them are smart, experienced, highly capable, and dedicated to helping their clients. Some are affiliating themselves with networks such as Edwin Morrow's Confidential Planning Services (described on pages 113—115) and expanding their operations to encompass financial planning. Others, helped by the American College, are preparing to deal with at least more aspects of the risk management side of financial planning.

The Colleges and Universities

Many academic institutions now offer financial planning courses. In addition, a number offer specialized degrees in various aspects of financial planning.

At last count, there were 82 colleges and universities authorized to use the College of Financial Planning CFP course material.

The new arrangement is that other colleges who devise their own financial planning curriculum can have their courses reviewed by the International Board of Standards and Practices for Certified Financial Planners (IBCFP). If these courses meet the standards established, the students taking them will be approved to sit for the CFP examinations without first taking the courses from the College of Financial Planning.

Professionals in the financial services industry who have academic and professional degrees, e.g., a J.D., a C.L.U./Ch.F.C. or a C.P.A. degree, may sit for the examinations and thereby earn the CFP designation, assuming they meet the other requirements.

Another avenue for academic preparation in financial planning can be taken with the standard management/finance (or similarly oriented) MBA program. Traditionally, the MBA program is broadly structured to provide knowledge in finance, management, economics, marketing and business policy. Therefore, most good MBA programs, when combined with special training in taxation, personal insurance, and investment strategies, along with appropriate business experience, are good backgrounds for entering the personal financial planning field.

Golden Gate's Expansion

Indicative of the way the academic community has embraced the study of financial planning is Golden Gate University in San Francisco, Sacramento, Los Altos, Walnut Creek, Los Angeles, and Orange County. Its comprehensive program is headed by Dr. Robert F. Bohn, who founded the pioneering program at Brigham Young University about 10 years ago. In a brochure describing the university's programs, Dr. Bohn offers his views on the rise of the profession:

> 'Put not your trust in money, but put your money in trust,' Oliver Wendell Holmes said, a century and a half ago; the rich, for the most part, have taken that advice and become richer. The rest of the population has made do by rather haphazardly putting its money in banks, savings and loan companies, and perhaps stocks or a little real estate, as its means allowed.
>
> However, in the 1970s, the escalating inflation rate not only exceeded the interest earned on most savings accounts, but it also pushed many incomes into a higher tax bracket. Middle-income Americans, as well as the affluent, began to realize that a more astute approach to planning for their financial future was necessary. They started taking their money out of established financial institutions and not putting it back.
>
> But, where should they put it instead? There were money market funds, annuities, real estate, IRAs, securities, hard assets, and a myriad of other options, which were confusing. The confusion and need for advice gave rise to a whole new profession—that of the financial planner.
>
> Many specialized professionals in the 1970s were frustrated. They were trying to help the individual, but were doing so in a fragmented way. There was the life insurance agent, the property/casualty agent, the stock broker, the mutual fund salesperson, the accountant for tax advice, the attorney for estate planning documents, the real estate broker for home purchases, and so on. Each professional would attempt to solve the consumer's financial problem with his or her own products.
>
> As a result, many consumers felt financially disorganized. Responding to the consumer's need for more centralized financial

services, some specialists began offering 'financial planning,' while still basically selling only their own products.

Recognizing that confusion, a number of colleges and universities across the country began offering courses in financial planning, at the bachelor's and the master's level. For example, Golden Gate University offered the following courses in its 1985-86 graduate program:

Real Estate Investment offers financial advisers the knowledge and tools to help clients select and evaluate appropriate investments. Topics covered include real estate valuing, strategies, ownership issues and vehicles such as limited partnerships and REITs, conventional and creative financing, investment return and risk analysis, decision models, leveraging, tax considerations, and economic factors.

Personal Financial Planning introduces the broad scope of financial planning, relating it to personal goals and values, as well as its role in the financial services industry. Topics covered in this course include careers in financial services, management of personal financial statements, time-value-of-money analysis, calculator and computer applications, insurance, Social Security, house-buying strategies, investments, retirement planning, income and estate planning.

Estate Planning offers students essential tools and techniques to assist a client in developing, maintaining, and transferring his or her wealth. This course emphasizes understanding gift and estate tax laws as a framework for advising individuals, partnerships, and closely held corporations on appropriate estate planning options.

Pension and Retirement Planning covers strategies a financial adviser can use to assist the client in reducing the tax burden while planning for retirement. Topics include the applicability of incorporation, ERISA, defined benefit and contribution plans, profit sharing, ESOP, SEP, Deogh, IRA, TSA, Social Security integration, vesting, funding vehicles, plan installation and administration, asset balancing, buy-sell agreements, stock redemption, and cross-purchase plans.

Financial Planning Case Analysis is designed as a strategic personal wealth management seminar for students who plan to advise clients in comprehensive financial and estate planning. The course emphasizes case analysis and independent research, etc.

These are merely samples of the courses being offered by Golden State University, along with many other colleges and universities across the country. For those skeptical of the emergence of financial planning, those courses represent challenging proof that financial planning as a profession has arrived.

One of the most interesting developments in the academic branch of financial planning is the formation of the Association for Financial Counseling and Financial Education. Led by Jerry Mason of Brigham Young University and Tahira K. Hira of Iowa State University, it already has members in colleges and universities across the country.

The AFCFE was established to promote research in personal financial management, to help educate financial counselors and planners, and to "actively participate in educating individuals in all areas of finance."

In addition to the increasing emphasis that established institutions are placing on financial education, other education organizations are also entering the field.

One example is the California University for Advanced Studies, located in Novato, California. The University recently announced that, in conjunction with its management program, it will develop new degree programs in financial education and financial planning.

These developments, and others, are indicative of the increasing interest in financial planning and education among leaders in the academic community.

PART SEVEN:

PERSPECTIVES, DANGERS AND A LOOK AHEAD

The history of financial planning includes some skeletons in the closet, much as the medical profession does. However, no one can deny the tremendous strides doctors of medicine have made in the last 100 years, particularly in gaining respect.

Financial planners are the general practitioners of the financial services industry. They give as much thought and care to the financial health and well-being of their clients as doctors do for their patients. Like the medical profession, the profession of financial planning is evolving to the point that, for many clients, specialists are also needed. However, while clients may need specialists for one or more aspects of their personal financial plans, they rely on the general expertise of their primary financial planner first. He or she can then recommend when a specialist is required, just as the family doctor can advise when the services of a surgeon or other medical specialist are needed.

Another important factor in the development of a profession is the availability of literature geared to its practitioners.

If I weren't so proud of having started it, I would be embarrassed at how much *Financial Planning* magazine has improved since I left. From its small beginnings as a four-page newsletter, designed to play a key role in the transformation of the insurance/mutual fund marketer into today's financial planner, it has grown into a well-respected and sophisticated international monthly magazine, complete with full-color graphics and excellently researched and written articles. The magazine and its role are discussed in Chapter 19.

Chapter 18 discusses regulation, an issue that will affect financial planners and the way they are preceived by the public. I do not strongly support a Self-Regulatory Organization (SRO), which IAFP began arguing for in late 1985, or state regulation, which the ICFP favored. If I thought that individual states could band together on similar regulations that did not greatly increase the cost of doing business, I would be in favor of ICFP's position. However, I think the nature of states is such that each would have clauses and sections added to satisfy its constituency specifically, regardless of their application to other states.

Unless the states gather together for common objectives, as Midwestern governors did recently in order to encourage business ventures in their area of the country, the result will likely be a lengthy regulation with more modifications than similarities for each state. Witness, for example, the differences between even contiguous states when it comes to governing insurance policies and premiums. Unfortunately, if additional costs are tacked onto conducting business, it is the consumers, who will pay those costs.

If the ICFP position can be negotiated without adding substantially to the cost of doing business, I would support it. If that's an impossible task, then I would prefer an SRO patterned after the National Association of Securities Dealers (NASD), although that may be more expensive for the financial planner and may be insured with skepticism by the media.

17 An Analogy to Physical Health

"The way people abuse their bodies, you wouldn't think physical health was something to which they attached much importance."

Those were the words of my personal physician in 1960. A few years later, his thorough interviews and insistence in finding out all he could about his patients—*before* making any recommendations— kept coming into my consciousness, as I was trying to articulate how I felt a financial counselor to the middle classes should operate. Later, other analogies between the physician's concern for physical health and the financial planner's concern for financial health would be drawn. In 1984, NCFE conducted its first "Financial Fitness Festival" in Chicago.

For years, many of us have talked about the similarities between the medical and financial counseling professions. No one, however, has worded it as succinctly as Harold W. Gourges, Jr., of Atlanta. As he put it:

> A medical analogy—as opposed to the retailing analogy so frequently used—points up the true future of financial services. The management of wealth is much more like the management of health than the selling of stocks and socks. The financial services industry is already dividing itself into financial Eli Lillys (manufacturing), Eckerd Drugstores (selling) and Mayo Clinics/Money Doctors (financial planning), rather than into boutiques and department stores. Clearly the separation is according to function rather than size.

All Professions Evolve

As we spoke of the IAFP and who would belong to it, Jim Johnston and I had a much simpler analogy to the medical profession. We used to say:

> You might liken the financial planner to the general practitioner of the medical profession. The general practitioner, or family doctor, is highly qualified, but doesn't hesitate to call in a specialist, if additional input is needed.

Within 10 years, many financial planners were viewing themselves as general practitioners in personal financial health and well-being. Fifteen years later, the profession had evolved to the point where many financial planners were specialists themselves.

Different observers see evolutions from differing perspectives, of course, but there is little disagreement that one's physical health and one's financial health have a great many similarities.

Professions Receive Criticism

Financial planners recall 1984 as the year when their profession garnered a tremendous amount of publicity. A number of magazine and newspaper writers focused on the negative elements. Even articles that concluded there are many benefits to financial planning often began with a horror story. It was the first time many conscientious and dedicated financial planners found their profession under media attack and analysis.

My early research into the development of other professions had prepared me for the criticism. In fact, I had collected, over the years, criticisms of other professions, to help maintain a healthy perspective. But to the actual financial planners the negative media lights were painful.

Actually, one of the healthiest signs of a profession's maturation is the growing willingness of one segment to criticize another segment of practitioners. Before he died, Dr. Nathan Pritikin took his profession to task for its slowness to recognize the importance of diet, particularly for heart patients. Criticism can work to hold back a new profession, or it can help to strengthen it, as the medical profession has already proved.

Like physicians of earlier times, the first financial planners may have lacked knowledge that we now know to be important. The advertisements used during the first 10 or 20 years of financial planning may seem ludicrous today. However, no less than the *Journal of the American Medical Association* once proclaimed that cigarettes were good for the nerves and the general well-being of both doctor and patient, according to syndicated columnist Nicholas Von Hoffman.

Fact Finding: Mark of the Professional

Morey Sahr, CFP, of the Washington D.C. area, recently recounted what information he obtains in his interviews with prospects before making any recommendations or preparing any portion of the financial plan. He explained that he always asks about "obligations to elderly parents and other relationships" and even touches on "the possibilities of divorce" with his married clients. I couldn't help thinking that he needed to know as many details as a family doctor does, to ensure his clients' well-being and financial health.

Financial planner Karl Byrd of Jackson, Mississippi, serves as a business consultant to doctors and medical clinics. He notices certain parallels between what he does and what his clients do—

> I think there are several corollaries that can be observed. First, neither profession in the early stages of its respective developments was recognized by society as a respectable, value-contributing profession. Only with time did society begin to realize the value and importance of the medical profession and also the financial planning profession.
>
> Second, physicians tend to be highly trained in clinical medicine, but have very little training and experience in managing the business applications of their practice. Correspondingly, the American public tends to be highly trained and specialized in various segments, such as engineering, accounting, law, etc., but has very little education in the management of personal financial affairs.
>
> As a result, I think there has been a growing recognition by society of the need for comprehensive financial planning, and a growing recognition by the medical community of the need for education and training in business management.
>
> The trend in modern medicine is to hire a clinic manager who is responsible for the business operations; the same can be said for society. People are realizing that they are inadequately prepared educationally to properly manage their personal financial affairs and so are turning to financial planning professionals for much needed advice.
>
> Other similarities between the medical profession and the financial planning profession include the following:
>
> - Both professions are subject to the risk of malpractice liability.
> - Both are rendering professional services on a fee basis.
> - Both are subject to a high degree of government regulation.
> - Both professions are promoting consumer education.
> - Both have the capability of being self-serving or serving the needs of society.

Comparing financial planners with physicians, many people ignore a very important difference between physical health and financial health. As adults, we all have about the same amount of blood, the same general physical structure, the same sets of muscles, and the same digestive system. However, the difference between a couple earning $30,000 a year and a couple with $200,000 to spend, shelter or save is as great as the difference between a bicycle and an airplane.

Comparing Oaths and Codes

In attempting to get a better perspective of the financial planning profession by looking at the medical profession, it might be interesting to compare a financial planner's code of ethics with the Hippocratic Oath of the medical profession. A physician takes the following oath:

> I swear by Apollo the physician, by Aesculapius, Hygeia, and Panacea, and I take to witness all the gods, all the goddesses, to keep according to my ability and my judgement the following Oath:
>
> To consider dear to me as my parents him who taught me this art, to live in common with him and if necessary to share my goods with him; to look upon his children as my own brothers, to teach them this art if they so desire without fee or written promise; to impart to my sons and the sons of the master who taught me and the disciples who have enrolled themselves and have agreed to the rules of the profession, but to these alone, the precepts and the instruction. I will prescribe regimen for the good of my patients according to my ability and my judgement and never do harm to anyone. To please no one will I prescribe a deadly drug, nor give advice which may cause his death. Nor will I give a woman a pessary to procure abortion. But I will preserve the purity of my life and my art. I will not cut for stone, even for patients in whom the disease is manifest; I will leave this operation to be performed by practitioners (specialists in this art). In every house where I come I will enter only for the good of my patients, keeping myself far from all intentional ill-doing and all seduction, and especially from the pleasures of love with women or with men, be they free or slaves. All that may come to my knowledge in the exercise of my profession or outside of my profession or in daily commerce with men, which ought not to be spread abroad, I will keep secret and will never reveal. If I keep this oath faithfully, may I enjoy my life and practice my art, respected by all men and in all times; but if I swerve from it or violate it, may the reverse by my lot.

The Certified Financial Planner's Code of Ethics has recently been greatly expanded. The original version is concise and to-the-point, and is well-worth reprinting here:

> These principles are intended to aid the Certified Financial Planner individually and collectively in maintaining a high level of ethical conduct. They are not laws but standards by which a CFP may determine the propriety of conduct in relationships with clients, with colleagues, with members of allied professions, and with the public.
>
> The honored ideals of the Institute of Certified Financial Planners state that the responsibility of the CFP extends not only to the individual, but also to society. The CFP will participate in

activities which improve the financial well-being of the client and the community.

CFPs should strive continually to improve skill and knowledge, and make available to their clients and colleagues the benefits of their professional attainments.

A CFP should practice a method of planning founded on a legal and practical basis and should not voluntarily associate with anyone who violates this principle.

A CFP may choose whom the CFP will serve. Having undertaken a client, the CFP may not neglect the client unless discharged. The CFP must discontinue service only after giving due notice.

A CFP should seek consultation in doubtful or difficult cases, and whenever it appears that the services of members of other professions would tend to provide a more complete and better quality or degree of advice.

A CFP may not reveal the confidences entrusted in the course of consultations, or the deficiencies the CFP may observe in a client or any client's affairs, unless the CFP is required to do so by law.

The members of the Institute of Certified Financial Planners should guard the public and themselves against any planner deficient in moral character or professional competence. CFPs should obey all laws, uphold the dignity and honor of the profession and accept its self-imposed disciplines. They should oppose, without hesitation, illegal or unethical conduct of fellow members.

Shouldn't Your Financial Planner Be Certified?

The American College of Surgeons advertises the expertise of surgeons who are certified by a surgical board approved by the American Board of Medical Specialties. The college points out that board-certified surgeons have after medical school satisfactorily completed years in approved surgical residency programs and have passed a rigorous specialty examination. The ads conclude, "When you need an operation, make sure you have a competent physician whose specialty is surgery. It could be the most important decision you make."

Don't be surprised if the College for Financial Planning sometime in the future starts running a similar advertisement, asking, "Shouldn't your financial planner be certified?" Then, possibly, there would be a comparison made between entrusting your financial health to a certified financial planner and someone who isn't. This future ad might point out that the average CFP spends the better portion of two years studying the subjects he or she needs to know to operate successfully.

18 Regulation: Coming and Needed

The interest in regulating financial planners reached new heights in 1985. Some think that "due diligence," or the obligation of the financial planning professional to research any recommended investments, should be the focus of regulation. According to Stuart Ober of Security Investigations, Inc. (SII) in Woodstock, New York, due diligence goes well beyond mere full disclosure. Undoubtedly, this aspect of regulation will be analyzed by state officials, as they begin proposing regulations for financial planners.

"Will financial planners have to be licensed?"

Invariably, that question is posed by someone in the audiences of financial planners to whom I speak. They aren't concerned by any great danger that the concept might suggest. Generally, when the question is asked, I get the feeling that any concern over the possible complications of regulation or licensing is outweighed by appreciation for the good it could do. In fact, I've heard many financial planners say, "It will be worth it, if it gets the charlatans out of the business, or at least keeps them from offering financial planning services, if all they want to do is sell securities or insurance."

Financial planners welcome regulations that will further enhance their image as professionals and think that even licensing would be a small price to pay. However, because many of them have clients in more than one state, some are apprehensive about state regulations that might vary greatly or require an inordinate amount of time-consuming paperwork.

As California Goes?

While not the first state to take steps toward regulating financial planners, California is proceeding and being closely monitored because many observers believe a number of other states may follow its lead. In December 1984, a number of us went to Sacramento and appeared before Senator Joseph Montoya's Committee on Business and Professions. I represented the NCFE and the consumer; the ICFP was represented by Kemp Fain of Knoxville, Tennessee, and Richard Smith of Washington, D.C. Dr. William Anthes represented the College in Denver. Hubert Harris and Alexandra Armstrong of

Washington, D.C., were impressive as the national voice of the IAFP.
Harris's testimony at the committee hearing follows:

> TESTIMONY OF HUBERT L. HARRIS, EXECUTIVE DIRECTOR, IAFP, BEFORE THE SENATE COMMITTEE ON BUSINESS AND PROFESSIONS, DECEMBER 11, 1984, SACRAMENTO, CALIFORNIA
>
> Financial planning is a process-oriented service that helps consumers successfully plan for and accomplish security and independence. In the process, the financial planner gathers financial data from the client, helps the client establish goals, analyzes the client's risk tolerance level, develops a written financial plan, implements that plan, and periodically follows up and reviews the plan.
>
> The financial planning process has changed and improved over time. Originally, financial planning was done by a professional using a calculator or some rudimentary data processing capability. Today, there are highly sophisticated software programs available for financial planners to use on mini- and microcomputers that allow for modeling and matrix design. These offer the client the opportunity to evaluate a number of planning scenarios based on different numerical assumptions. Furthermore, there are companies which offer, through the mail, to the public, computer-generated financial plans which are useful even though there is very little personal contact between the planner and the client.
>
> The cost of financial planning advice varies greatly. Computer-generated financial plans drawn from questionnaires filled out by a client are available for prices ranging from $50 to $300. A financial plan developed by a financial planning professional who also offers professional advice on an ongoing basis usually will cost at least $500 and may range as high as $3,000 to $4,000. Fees charged for individually tailored plans usually are determined by the length of time required to develop the plan, the complexity of the plan, and the sophistication of the financial planner. Financial planning firms usually charge hourly fees for the advice given, and many firms have retainer relationships with their clients.
>
> Financial planning clearly has been accepted by the public as an important consumer service. Many large financial services companies are moving into financial planning. The reasons for this shift in marketing strategy are numerous, but essentially they are consumer driven. Early this year a principal officer of a national financial services firm made the following statement:
>
>> We think we can manage this [selling financial services] with one major strategy—total financial planning. That's

> nothing more than working as a partner with our clients to create a personal financial plan for achieving these specific goals. It's a simple, straightforward, and immensely appealing offer. It unites dreams and realities, aspirations and achievements. Total financial planning emphasizes tomorrow and its pleasure, not today and its problems. It lends itself to motherhood and apple pie and more practically ties in all of our diverse and somewhat sophisticated products into neat care packages. From the standpoint of our sales force, a financial planner is certainly a more professional calling than being a trader or a stock jockey.

This attitude, expressed by a senior officer of a major financial services firm, presents a dilemma for the industry. Many feel that there should be standards for those calling themselves financial planners, and that the term should not be used by salesmen who are merely trying to gain an advantage to help them sell a product.

Most of those currently practicing financial planning have come to the field from experience in other financial services specialties, and usually from the retail side. At the present time most financial planners have backgrounds in the insurance industry or stock brokerage. However, more and more bankers, CPAs and lawyers are coming into the field, as are a growing number of individuals who are educated and trained specifically for financial planning prior to establishing a practice.

In a consumer research study done for the IAFP by an independent research firm, we were able to determine that the public's primary apprehension about financial planning is based on the perception that it is "just another sales technique." At the same time, those surveyed indicated that if they chose to have a financial plan done, the two factors of most importance in selecting a financial planner would be: (1) the planner's objective knowledge of a variety of investment tools and (2) their track record with other clients. It seems clear that there is a willingness and desire on the part of the public to deal with financial planners who are knowledgeable about product alternatives and who have experience in financial services. The growth and success of the industry attest to that. There was no consensus among those surveyed as to appropriate methods of compensation for financial planners. The sample breaks fairly evenly among a flat-rate fee, commission compensation only, and a combination of the two.

The IAFP is the oldest and largest financial planning association. Our membership of over 21,000 is made up of individuals who come from a variety of backgrounds and disciplines within the financial services industry. The IAFP does have a corporate program which offers to companies that meet minimum qualifications (related to the quality of the companies, their principals, and their products or services) the opportunity to promote those products and services to our membership.

The IAFP provides a wide range of services for its members. These are designed to provide educational and professional enhancement opportunities. The IAFP annual convention has become the annual meeting of the financial planning industry. Over 6,000 attended our 1984 convention. We offered 120 educational workshops along with four general sessions. We were honored to have Vice President George Bush address our attendees. We feel the success of this event highlights the growing impact of financial planning on the financial services industry.

The IAFP also sponsors a practice management conference which offers members insights into effective management of their businesses. We also offer an advanced planning conference which is designed to provide educational meetings of a more technical nature designed for more experienced financial planners who are oftentimes dealing with more sophisticated clients. Our world congress meeting is an effort on our part to educate our members on international investment opportunities and financial market trends in other countries. There are 117 local chapters of the IAFP. Each of these has monthly meetings which feature both educational and informational speakers.

The IAFP Code of Professional Ethics is a key element in our efforts at industry professionalism. It is more than a document. Our staff general counsel receives and processes reports on potential ethics cases on a regular basis. He solicits further reports from a variety of sources to determine if there are circumstances that warrant review by our ethics committee. This committee is made up of nine members who serve staggered terms to ensure continuity of effort and uniform application of standards. In 1984 we have reviewed and disposed of 18 cases which resulted in nine disciplinary actions. Each IAFP chapter has an ethics officer whose job it is to promote our ethics policy at the local level and provide informational and other support and liaison to the national office.

Financial Planning magazine has become the leading publication in the financial planning industry. It is published by the IAFP and its principal purpose is to be just that—a publication for the industry. We have a staff of highly qualified editors and writers who actively report on issues, products, services, and companies and individuals that are of particular interest to financial services professionals. Obviously the orientation is to the financial planning sector of the financial services industry, and we try very much to educate all readers on emerging trends, current industry events and regulatory and legislative matters.

The Registry of Financial Planning Practitioners was established by the IAFP in 1983. Its purpose is to set minimum standards for the practice of total financial planning and to identify those who are in fact delivering quality financial planning services to their clients. Since its beginning in September of that year, 361 individuals have been admitted to The Registry. A practice knowledge examination was developed during 1984 to clearly and objectively analyze the skills of those seeking admittance to The Registry. The examination takes $5^1/_2$ hours to complete and is designed to thoroughly analyze the professional competence of those applying for The Registry. While there are other requirements for The Registry, this examination is clearly the most comprehensive in the financial planning industry. The requirements for The Registry are more difficult to meet than those for any financial services designation.

The IAFP membership believes that regulatory issues are very important. The regulatory committee of our board reviews various regulatory and legislative issues and recommends policy positions to the board. Once policy is adopted it is the responsibility of our staff and our regulatory department to communicate these views to the appropriate regulatory officials. We actively and regularly provide information to securities regulators in all states and NASAA. We also meet on a regular basis with officials of the Securities and Exchange Commission and the NASD in Washington. We also have established and maintain liaison with various other financial service industry associations to maintain an open information flow on regulatory issues.

As mentioned before, the popularity of and acceptance by the public of financial planning is growing at the most rapid rate in the history of this industry. Along with this growth there has been a proliferation of individuals and companies who declare themselves to be financial planners when in reality they are primarily interested in selling a specific product. The IAFP membership believes strongly that the public should receive the full value of competent, professional service when they purchase something called financial planning. Therefore, the IAFP public awareness campaign has been developed. It is our effort, through print media advertisements, to educate the public on what financial planning is and what it is not, who really should seek financial planning advice, and how to find a qualified financial planner.

In conclusion, then, financial planning is a very rapidly growing sector of the financial services industry. Public demand for objective advice on alternatives for developing financial security and independence has certainly increased recently, and it is expected to continue to grow at a similar rate. As the principal industry organization, the IAFP has likewise experienced tremendous growth in its membership from all sectors of the financial services industry. As an organization that is heavily involved in developing professional standards for this entire industry group, we are deeply interested in regulatory and licensing alternatives that might be considered at the state or federal level. Our membership wants financial planning to be perceived by the public as a profession and has taken initial steps to enhance that perception. The development, implementation, and operation of an ethics policy is an important step in that direction, as are our efforts to ensure that the public receives fair and equitable treatment from those financial planners who are members of the IAFP. The formation of The Registry of Financial Planning Practitioners is another important step. The recently developed practice knowledge exam as a requirement for admission to The Registry is clearly the most positive step this industry has ever taken toward evaluating the competence of those in our industry. Financial Planning magazine and our continuing education programs are designed to enhance the professional development of our members and thus to benefit their clients. We are an active and dynamic organization operating in one of the most interesting and complicated industry environments. We seek to do what is good for our membership by developing policies that are truly oriented toward serving the best interests of the consumer. We believe that by ensuring that the consumer receives valuable service from a competent, qualified professional who conducts his business in accordance with the highest ethical standards we will best serve the needs of our members, our industry and the public.

A Great Obligation

As I tell my audiences and others who argue for self-regulation, and as the new profession of financial planning grows, it's wise to remember that the self-policing of other professions has led to problems and consumer resentment. Because a "profession" ranks higher in the public consciousness than does an "occupation," it also carries with it a greater obligation and the need to meet higher standards.

19 Chronicling A New Profession

Earlier chapters made reference to the first issues of *The Financial Planner* magazine, as it was called then. Looking at *Financial Planning* magazine today, it's hard for me to believe that the small, amateurish magazine I created could ever have evolved into the slick, professional, and very helpful publication that is currently published by Hubert L. (Herky) Harris, edited by Jack W. Lange, and creatively presented by Guy Styles. That magazine, more than any other publication, played a major, vital role in chronicling the development of financial planning as a profession and the financial planner as a professional, thanks to the efforts of its publishers and editors.

Lending Class

Richard T. White was editor of the magazine from 1977 to 1980. Under his direction, the magazine developed class, better writing, and a style that set the tone for subsequent editors. It wasn't long before the regular reader recognized the professionalism and high standards he was injecting into the magazine. White also played a dynamic role in the success of the IAFP's national conferences in Dallas, Chicago and Boston. According to White, however, much of the credit for the magazine's success is also due to the hard work and genius of Fred Harris, IAFP executive director.

In September and October of 1979, two issues of the magazine were devoted to "Ten Years of History," tracking the creation of the profession, the Society, the IAFP, the College, and the ICFP. The report was a monumental task and did an outstanding job of chronicling those first 10 years. By looking back, the magazine made it easier for its readers also to look ahead with confidence.

When Richard White left, executive director and publisher Vernon Gwynne, CFP, had the unenviable task of replacing him. He found Forrest Wallace Cato, a bundle of talent and hard work and just what *The Financial Planner* needed to catapult it to new heights of achievement.

Under Gwynne and Cato, the magazine gained greater stature and profitability. Cato's national reputation as an editor and public relations genius soon resulted in the magazine running interviews with national figures, including U.S. presidents. Looking back at those 1981 and 1982 issues, with associate editor Bill Gregory, art director Guy Styles and editorial assistant Gary Goettling, it's amazing that such a high caliber magazine was produced by such a small internal staff, backed by two columnists and four foreign correspondents.

Advertising Contributes

Along with the magazine's editorial content, advertising also played a key role, rapidly increasing in both volume and scope. More highly respected companies were either getting into financial planning and/or dealing with financial planners; each issue of the magazine reflected that trend. Joyce Brigman, advertising manager, and Robert Abrams, advertising representative in New York, took advantage of the profession's growing importance and the magazine's leading role and brought in new advertisers by the score.

The October 1981 issue, "Welcome to San Francisco," featured 168 pages and was the talk of the national convention. That issue also featured a powerful letter of review by Lee Pennington that disturbed a number of insurance people and organizations. "I Resent the Years" not only pointed out the difference between selling insurance and providing financial planning services, but it also read as a real challenge to the old way of doing business:

I Resent the Years

The American College of Chartered Life Underwriters' new professional designation for the Financial Planning Industry is at last a positive statement from this group. They have for the last fifteen years acted as though they hoped the concept of financial planning (where a broad range of products commingled to solve multiple economic problems for the American public) would go away.

In 1968 and 1969, when the industry needed guidance and training, the American College sat on the sideline waiting for us to fail and, in some cases, being openly critical of what was occurring in the market place.

As a result of their attitude and lack of caring and guidance for the financial planning industry, the Certified Financial Planner program was born in Denver, Colorado. Many of us were delighted to have a systematic study program which dealt with all products as part of the American economic process and not just life insurance as the panacea for all economic ills.

The life insurance industry and the American College consistently down-played the significance of the total financial planning concept.

Now they (the American College) have decided to have their own designation which would be a result of a well-designed and well-thought-out program. They can provide us with quality education in lots of areas. They serve a valuable purpose to the life insurance industry.

I do not believe their designation can have any more value than the present CFP program or IAFP study programs can have as far as the industry is concerned. Don't misunderstand, I think they can put together study programs which will be more difficult, more thorough and more time consuming than what we have experienced with the College for Financial Planning and the IAFP, yet I do not believe they can be as objective about what serves the public best in the area of financial planning because of their total and complete brainwashed attitude about life insurance being the number one solution to most economic problems.

I, for one, would prefer the American College and the IAFP to work in conjunction with the College for Financial Planning to further develop what has been the forerunner to this industry called financial planning.

The CFP program is a long way from being where the CLU programs are at this stage, but it will and can be there in a few years and could be there much quicker with help and guidance from the American College.

I have sold millions of dollars of insurance, I am a life member of the MDRT, I made a $1,000 contribution to the MDRT Building and I completed four parts of CLU. My background is insurance and I am grateful for the product and its function in our society, but I resent the years when the life insurance companies and the American College made absolutely no contribution to the concept of total financial planning. I personally will not take the American College study courses unless they become a part of us. I hope they will not be so presumptuous as to insist we become a part of them. The best way for them to become a part of us is to join with the IAFP and the College for Financial Planning study program to enhance the financial planning industry, not the life insurance industry. This will do the most benefit for the intended recipient—the consumer who needs help in forging and implementing a total financial plan consistent with his/her goals, objectives, and temperament.

"I Resent the Years," from *Financial Planning* magazine.
Copyright © 1981 by Lee Pennington. Reprinted by Permission.

Serving the Winners

The October 1982 New Orleans convention issue under Vernon Gwynne and Wally Cato had 208 pages and began with a particularly revealing editorial, "Explaining About Winning."

Explaining About Winning

You must be a winner! Recent in-depth readership studies by Epsilon Data Management of Burlington, Massachusetts, revealed the following new findings about those who use *The Financial Planner* magazine.
- 78% of our readers make $50,000 to $100,000
- 19% make over $100,000
- The longer a person has subscribed to *The Financial Planner* the more designations he is likely to have.
- 68% of our five-plus year readers have more than one designation.
- 97% have multiple sources (four or more) of income.
- 96% say *The Financial Planner* is "very useful."
- 75% have attended local chapters.
- 54% have attended the IAFP national convention.
- 97% indicate *The Financial Planner* is the most used regular service provided by the IAFP.

Obviously, winners in the world of financial products and services have made this publication "the Bible of the financial planning industry."

The first issue of our magazine was in January of 1972, the total number of pages was 48, there were 36 pages of editorial, 12 pages of ads, and the print run totalled 5,000, most of which was not paid circulation.

This October edition of the official journal of the International Association for Financial Planning is the largest issue in our publishing history, with a record 212 pages. This edition has 91 editorial pages and 121 ad pages, with a paid circulation of 13,500, plus an additional bonus distribution of 3,500, for a total of 17,000.

How powerful those 17,000 winners are! They actually constitute a mini Wall Street. Because of their influence, *The Financial Planner* is the only magazine in the world which can make the above claims and promises.

This edition is a tribute to our reader loyalty and advertising support. Thank you for your strong involvement over the years. Advertising investments in *The Financial Planner* produce results. We have documented examples of outstanding results.

Today our editorial quality reflects this winning edge; we feature

> practical content for financial planning professionals and those in the related financial service disciplines. Editorial content is always exclusive and original, and includes responsible controversy, in accordance with the IAFP's "open forum" concept. Our publication, written by professionals and for professionals, reflects these developments in our editorial content and graphics. We strive to present information that is of immediate interest or lasting value.
>
> Financial planning today is a complicated, highly technical and very detailed undertaking. More than ever before, this involves a wider variety of complex tasks and requires a team of professional skills.
>
> The changing and evolving financial planning profession is vibrant and growing. It is also very demanding of financial planners.
>
> President Ronald Reagan told your editor, "The American people require timely and accurate information about financial planning to prepare for their futures. The success of my Administration's program for economic recovery depends vitally upon the soundness of planning decisions."
>
> Financial planners help their clients win the battles against inflation, taxes, and other factors which negatively affect their quality of life.
>
> This magazine serves winners. Those winners attend the annual IAFP convention. If you were not among the more than 3,000 participants in the 1982 IAFP's annual convention held at the New Orleans Marriott, you missed many valuable opportunities. The 1983 IAFP Expanding Horizons Convention and Exposition will be held in Las Vegas. Plan now to attend and be counted among the winners.
>
> The staff and management of this magazine promises continued adherence to our first standard and foremost goal, that of serving our readers and advertisers by helping them win.
>
> "Explaining About Winning," Copyright © 1982, *Financial Planning* magazine. Reprinted by permission.

At this time, the magazine also gave a preview of Richard "Dick" Wollack's *Digest of Financial Planning Ideas,* which, under Jim Miller, was to become a powerful force for the marketing of financial planning products and services.

Changing the Reins

By the 1983 convention in Las Vegas, Nevada, John Cahill of San Francisco became chairman of IAFP and Bill Carter became president. They brought with them some fresh and talented faces to run the growing IAFP and to edit and publish the magazine.

Hubert L. Harris became publisher, and John W. Lange became editor, quickly making their progress apparent in the magazine's 236-page October 1983 issue. With them also came a growing professional staff, introduced in the October 1983 issue in a memorandum that also gave a good picture of what was to come.

> **Memo From the editors**
>
> In many ways, this issue of *The Financial Planner* might be best described as an "introductory" issue—introductory in the sense that we would like to acquaint readers with our new staff members, with some of the latest ideas about financial planning, and with a new approach to putting out this magazine, the official journal of the IAFP.
>
> For the first time in many months, *The Financial Planner* has a full complement of editorial, art and sales staff.
>
> Robert N. "Bob" Veres, a native New Yorker, joins *The Financial Planner* after many years as a free-lance journalist and advertising copy writer. Bob holds a BA and an MA in English from the University of Georgia, and most recently was editor of *Air Cargo World* magazine.
>
> Our new associate editor, Lisa Lawley, recently received a BA/MA degree in English from Emory University. Lisa, who grew up in Atlanta, has done public relations work for local government and interned with *ATLANTA* magazine before becoming assistant editor of *Air Cargo World*.
>
> Art Assistant Regina Schwartz will be helping *The Financial Planner's* art director with all aspects of designing and pasting up the magazine. While completing training at the Art Institute of Atlanta, Regina, who calls Nashville home, served an internship with *Southern Homes* magazine.
>
> In addition to her credit and collections duties as the magazine's advertising productions manager, Kirsten Gastley will lend her assistance in advertising sales support. Besides running her own consulting business, this native of Toccoa, Georgia, previously worked as credit and collections manager for Male Sportswear, a division of Genesco, and as a collections clerk with Dun & Bradstreet.
>
> Dean L. Aldrich, *The Financial Planner's* new advertising manager, comes to the magazine directly from Communication Channels, where he served as publisher and advertising director for two international magazines, *Airline Executive* and *Commuter Air,*

and as associate publisher and advertising manager for *Business Atlanta*. He also has many years experience in radio advertising sales. Dean grew up in Kansas, attended Wichita University, and came to Atlanta by way of Chicago and Michigan 21 years ago.

The entire staff is pleased to bring you, in this convention issue, two sections devoted entirely to the IAFP convention held at the end of September. Though we've included the usual departments and columns—along with feature articles on the computerization of financial planning practices and the economic outlook as of mid-year—at the heart of the magazine you'll also find a series of articles by the experts invited to speak at the convention. Some of these articles condense material presented during the four-day gathering of financial planners in Las Vegas; others expound upon the speakers' knowledge of related financial planning topics.

Whether you attended the convention or not, in the days ahead these articles should be a useful reference on new trends and ideas which could help make your financial planning practice even more effective.

The special convention section, with its history of Las Vegas, sightseeing guide, restaurant synopses, and seminar and presentations listings was designed to make convention-goers' stay in Las Vegas as productive and hassle-free as possible.

If you didn't attend the convention, we hope a review of these sections will encourage you to make plans to attend next year's convention in Atlanta.

As you read, we also hope you notice a change in the look and style of the magazine.

The new layouts and improved articles are just the first in a number of adjustments in format and editorial content *The Financial Planner* will be making in the coming months. We will be taking a more active position in reporting activities and trends within the financial services industry, focusing on those issues which affect the financial planning professional and the way he runs his business.

We hope you enjoy the October issue. Just remember, more improvements are coming!

"Memo from the Editors," Copyright © 1983, *Financial Planning* magazine. Reprinted by permission.

From *Financial Planner* to *Financial Planning*

In January 1984, *The Financial Planner* magazine became *Financial Planning,* and another mountain had been scaled. Now, the IAFP and the magazine were both listened to by the professionals and the entire financial services industry.

With more funds to employ, Jack Lange increased the magazine's staff considerably. By October 1984, the magazine's masthead contained not only a publisher, an editor, and a few others, it had an executive editor, a managing editor, a senior editor, two associate editors, an assistant editor, two editorial interns, 11 contributing editors, an art director and assistant, a business manager, an advertising director, an advertising sales manager, a production manager, a circulation manager, two advertising salespeople, and an advertising sales assistant.

The contents of the magazine also were growing. The October 1984 issue contained 11 major features, 19 departments, and three columns, in 236 pages, with a separate "convention issue" of 182 pages. By 1985, the magazine had become the strongest answer to those who were still reluctant to look upon financial planning as a new profession and the financial planner as a new professional.

A Peek Backward

Once in a while I cannot help looking back and being grateful for the help we had in starting that magazine. It came from a variety of sources and sometimes strange places. One of the earliest supporters of the magazine was Frank Eckles of Costa Mesa, California. He not only served on several boards, he also helped in selling ads and getting the printing done.

I hope the large staff at *Financial Planning* magazine today is finding some of the same satisfaction we found in the beginning.

PART EIGHT

Building on the Foundation
Constructing the Base

The eventual success of most building efforts depends largely on the soundness of the initial foundation. Those of us who were involved in laying the foundation for the financial planning profession were fortunate enough to attract crusading personalities, willing to put in long hours and often selfless devotion.

Offering their time, money and reputation, a number of the early champions of financial planning were insurance agents who marketed mutual funds out of a conviction that combining insurance and investments was important to the financial well-being of their clients. Many of them tolerated scorn and sometimes costly antagonism from less visionary agents and management. Hundreds of other early supporters were essentially mutual fund salespeople who also sold insurance; they helped us in establishing the first 30 chapters of the IAFP.

A large percentage of these two groups were our natural pioneers. But even with their support, we could not have brought about the acceptance of the financial planning profession had we not also found businesspeople with professional attitudes and the willingness to do what needed doing. Fortunately, these leaders and powerhouses also supported our movement.

Educators and academicians who witnessed our society's evolution also played an increasingly important role in building the financial planning profession that was gradually rising atop a carefully thought out, but somewhat shaky and terribly underfinanced foundation.

The 1960s belonged to the pioneers. The 1970s must give credit to the dreamers willing to be doers. The 1980s are paying homage to both.

20 Today's International Association for Financial Planning

In 1985, the International Association for Financial Planning had approximately 22,000 members. Of these, 62 percent indicated they were practicing financial planners, while the other 38 percent were in financial services specialties, such as accountants and attorneys. The total number of clients served by practicing financial planners was estimated in 1985 to be 2.4 million and growing rapidly.

In 1980, the IAFP under president Ron Melanson and chairman Robert Spenser changed the association's name to the International Association for Financial Planning, as opposed to "...of Financial Planners." In 1976, a year after I left, the board decided to replace George Ratterman as executive director and to move the IAFP's office from Denver to Atlanta. The board also decided to get *The Financial Planner* magazine back from the Chicago Savings and Loan Association to which Ratterman had sold it.

With lawsuits and negotiations, the next few months were trying. Eventually, however, the move and the magazine's reclamation were achieved, thanks to a conscientious board of directors. The main heroes—at least from my outside observation—were Chandler Peterson, Dick Venezia, and Jim Lang, who invested courage, time and money in the profession. Fred Harris, from Chandler Peterson's office, became executive director in Atlanta. After Fred Harris, Bob Strader became the national president of IAFP and then served a period as executive director. He was followed by Vernon Gwynne, one of the earliest CFPs, who became the association's executive director and served for five years during its first major growth and development period. He left in 1982, and Hubert "Herky" Harris, also of Atlanta, became IAFP's executive director.

Herky Harris has an impressive background in both association management and politics and lost no time in instituting an even more efficient and businesslike operation. The influx of new members, plus the ever-growing popularity and profitability of the magazine and the conventions, soon allowed Harris to beef up the staff with experienced personnel. Here is executive director and national board member Herky Harris's view of the current IAFP.

Professional financial planners come from a variety of backgrounds and offer a diverse array of services. Yet together, they share a number of mutual concerns with their estimated 50,000 colleagues around the world. They face issues of professional ethics and definitions of standards for a profession literally nonexistent 15 years ago. They face the possibility that state regulators in each of 50 state jurisdictions will create slightly different standards and requirements. Where do they find continuing education opportunities and updates on new tax laws and NASD or SEC requirements? More importantly, how can they share common concerns, experience and expertise with their peers?

To address all these issues at once is more than any one planner can do. That is why they join the financial planning industry's leading professional association, one of the fastest growing organizations in the country: the International Association for Financial Planning.

The Heart of the IAFP

To detail the full range and scope the IAFP's activities would require a small book of its own. Structurally, it encompasses the industry's leading financial planners, executives with NASD-licensed broker-dealers and syndicators, accountants, lawyers and other professionals interested in promoting financial planning standards and its success in the marketplace. The heart of this organization is the local chapter. In the 18 months between July 1983 and January 1985, these chapters grew in number from 86 to 117, ranging from the giant Metro New York Chapter with 1,020 members to Middle Georgia with 21.

Each chapter is governed by a president, vice president and a board of directors. The officers and board are elected yearly. The chapter's most important function is to host monthly meetings and offer a forum for financial services professionals to share views and develop a sense of community, the key to any professional organization. Chapters also publish newsletters sent out to each member and sponsor—sometimes in conjunction with other chapters in the immediate vicinity—and host one or more regional seminars or conferences.

In addition, the chapters' officers and members serve as the IAFP's liaison with educational institutions in their area, state and local regulators, and members of the local media. In these activities, they are assisted by the national association, headquartered in Atlanta. The national association is governed by a board of directors made up of financial planners and financial services professionals from across the country.

National Activities

On a national level, the IAFP's activities are designed to include and in some way benefit the members of the local chapters. Perhaps the most basic service is an extension of the local and regional conferences. Every year, the IAFP hosts the largest multidisciplinary gathering of financial services professionals anywhere. The IAFP convention offers educational seminars on topics ranging from the proper evaluation of syndication investments to post-mortem tax planning, from professional marketing of financial services to trends in information systems technology. Among the 315 or so companies represented on the exhibit floor at the recent convention in Atlanta were the New York Futures Exchange, the Travelers Insurance Company, Apple Computer, the Investment Company Institute and the College for Financial Planning.

The IAFP also hosts two more specialized gatherings. The Practice Management Conference is an intense three-day workshop covering ways to manage growth and help control the added business responsibilities that often plague the successful entrepreneur. The Advanced Planners Conference offers the most rigorous educational opportunities in the financial services industry. It is designed for those financial planners whose educational requirements go beyond those of their younger or less experienced peers.

The IAFP is active in setting meaningful standards for the new profession. All members must subscribe to the IAFP Code of Professional Ethics—which specifies different aspects of professional integrity—and to a six-step process that defines comprehensive financial planning. The six steps are: (1) collecting and assessing data; (2) identifying financial goals and objectives; (3) identifying problems; (4) writing recommendations and alternative solutions; (5) coordinating implementation of recommendations; and (6) periodically reviewing and updating the client's financial plan.

The Registry

These standards also are embodied in a more ambitious program administered by the IAFP on behalf of the profession. The Registry of Financial Planning Practitioners—The Registry—defines standards and qualifications for professionals in the financial planning industry. Criteria include education, experience and practice skills, plus passage of a three-section test, the Practice Knowledge Exam.

On a broader scale, the IAFP is working toward a definition of ethical standards across the traditional boundaries of the financial services marketplace. Three years ago, the IAFP board of directors invited representatives from other professional associations to participate in a cross-industry dialogue about issues of professional ethics. The most recent meeting—hosted by the IAFP in Washington, D.C. in June 1984—attracted representatives from, among others, the American Bar Association, the American Bankers Association, the Million Dollar Roundtable, the American Savings and Loan Institute, the College for Financial Planning and the American College.

Getting Out the Word

The financial planning profession also has won increased visibility, thanks in part to a national public relations program. The national headquarters' public relations office works with consumer and trade magazines and other media outlets; providing statistics, interview sources and background materials about the IAFP, members, activities and the profession at large. As a result, feature-length articles have appeared in publications as diverse as *Working Woman, Money, The Kiplinger Washington Letter, Vogue, The New York Times* and *Inc.* magazine.

On a grass-roots level, the Atlanta office coordinates the Speakers Bureau, a listing of available speakers throughout the country. Made up of more than 200 IAFP members, this service is designed to help local civic groups and other organizations locate persons in their area who are conversant with investment opportunities, current or proposed tax law changes, or the financial planning process itself.

Recently, the national leadership has become concerned about the level of consumer awareness in the still-young marketplace and about salespeople or outright charlatans posing as financial planners with less than ethical motives. In 1984, the IAFP board of directors commissioned a broad-based market survey by one of the nation's leading advertising firms to determine consumer attitudes toward financial planners and the profession at large. This, in turn, led to the Public Awareness Campaign. This multi-million dollar advertising effort was designed to help the consumer better understand what financial planning is and is not, what a financial planner does, and how to choose an ethical financial planner.

This increased visibility has led to new interest among state regulators and state and federal legislative bodies. In an effort to help develop meaningful standards to benefit the public and the financial planning profession, the IAFP has moved into another key area of activity in recent years. On the state level, the association's regulatory coordinator, executive director and members of the board have begun a new dialogue with members of the North American Securities Administrators Association, who have formed a special committee to evaluate the need for regulation of financial planners.

Watching Regulations

The members of the individual chapters—particularly those located in state capital cities—also serve as a "regulatory alert" network. This provides two important functions for the membership at large. First, it keeps members abreast of all the various state and local regulatory requirements their practice entails. Second, it alerts the national office to initiatives proposed in the state legislature. Thus, the national office can help local planners in educating their elected officials and in developing meaningful guidelines for a safe and ethical marketplace.

Because national regulations tend to be slower to develop and more far-reaching in scope, the national effort has moved at a more deliberate pace. The IAFP has formed a small political action committee on behalf of members and opened discussions with the Securities and Exchange Commission concerning the possibility of developing an industry-sponsored self-regulatory organization at some future date. Perhaps more important, both the IAFP's Washington counsel and me, as executive director, and a former executive with the Office of Management and Budget, have met on a regular basis with leaders of the relevant committees in the House and Senate, as well as key administration officials.

Other Benefits

The overall idea of the International Association for Financial Planning is to offer members the opportunity to take advantage of the strength gained from numbers without sacrificing the individual input so often lost in large organizations. There are other benefits as well. Probably the most tangible do not fit easily into the categories previously described. The IAFP has coordinated the only errors and omissions insurance policy currently offered to members of the financial planning profession. The home office publishes *Financial Planning* magazine, the industry's leading monthly publication and an increasingly valuable tool for the individual financial planning practitioner. Each month, it evaluates new trends and developments in the marketplace at large and profiles individual planners from all segments of the profession, including NASD-registered broker-dealers, product manufacturers, and the industry's larger securities, insurance and banking firms as they introduce their own version of planning services. *Financial Planning* also serves as a clearinghouse for more technical information on financial and tax-related strategies and includes regular features on practice marketing ideas and services, portfolio management concepts, computer software, and educational resources.

Serving the New Professional

Taken together, these and other IAFP activities are designed to have a positive impact on every aspect of a financial planner's business life. The IAFP has experienced one of the most impressive growth spurts of any professional association in recent times. It serves as an important educational, informational and experiential resource for financial planners. When we talk about the "new professional" in the financial services marketplace, we can also talk about the IAFP—a new kind of professional association, one that is member-driven, much as the financial planner is client-driven.

21 The College for Financial Planning

While I was doing research for another book, the idea of a college for financial planning began germinating. I realized that what the public needed was not another book but rather a more objective professional, supported by an association and educated by a college.

The two men I approached first were Bob Leary, then executive vice president of WESTAMERICA Securities in Denver, Colorado, and Dr. Daniel Kedzie, a Chicago-area insurance and management consultant, who for several years had been educational director of the American College of Life Underwriters. Bob Leary provided guidance for the IAFP, which was the professional division of the Society for Financial Counselling, while Dan Kedzie advised me on the college.

Getting Under Way

Jim Johnston Shapes the College

Hiring Jim Johnston truly made it possible to get the college courses designed. Working for much less than he could have elsewhere—sometimes deferring even that—he enabled us eventually to get together the 13 men in Chicago who helped really launch us.

Jim Johnston had a flair for applying educational process as an aid to developing the new profession. While he didn't sell companies on supplying corporate sponsor money for the Society, his sincerity and congeniality attracted other men and women to help in formulating the educational courses that would lead to a professional designation.

Jim also agreed with and supported our conviction that there should be no "grandfather clause" to allow experienced professionals to become CFPs automatically without proper education.

Help from Lewis Kearns

Lewis G. Kearns, senior vice president of Wellington Group of mutual funds in Philadelphia, was intrigued with our concept. After he became acquainted with Jim Johnston, he decided to play a helpful and dominant role.

For several years, Lew Kearns and others kept Jim Johnston going. Without their support, he might have given up. As a matter of fact, one time he did quit when we got too far behind in paying the small salary he needed to live. My sister Eileen had already helped financially on a number of occasions, when our financial straits finally became too desperate. Then my wife Jane cosigned a crucial $5,000 note that helped us get Jim Johnston back to work on the College's course development.

Dr. Anthes Becomes President

A key influence for the 1980s began in 1978 when a search committee from the college's board of trustees, headed by Robert Oberst, Sr., hired Dr. William L. Anthes, who has been president of the College for Financial Planning since 1980. Highly respected prior to this assignment, Bill Anthes is now the most prominent educational figure in the financial planning profession.

The College Program

The college offers three major financial planning education programs: the Certified Financial Planner Professional Education Program, the Associate Financial Planner Program, and the Financial Paraplanner Program. The Certified Financial Planner Professional Education Program is a six-part program leading to the professional designation of Certified Financial Planner (CFP). The program is designed for individuals who are currently working within the financial services industry. The Certified Financial Planner Professional Education Program gives enrollees the opportunity to acquire technical expertise in the six areas vital to personal financial planning. Each part of the CFP program includes a case analysis, which is designed to help apply the technical knowledge gained from studying a specific area of finance to the situational needs of clients.

Enrollees may choose one of three ways to take the CFP program: through self-study, through classes taught by adjunct faculty members of the college, or through an affiliated college or university. There are more than 400 adjunct faculty members and more than 60 college and university affiliates located across the country. To successfully complete the CFP program, one must pass an examination on each of the six parts. The exams are administered across the country annually during April, August and December. They include multiple-choice questions and a short-answer case analysis.

The program consists of six courses:

- **CFP I—Introduction to Financial Planning.** This course is designed to give an overview of the financial planning process.

- **CFP II—Risk Management.** CFP II covers the principles of risk management, how to identify a client's risk exposures, and how to select appropriate risk management techniques for clients.

- **CFP III—Investments.** This part of the program is designed to acquaint enrollees with a variety of investment vehicles, the environmental influences affecting investment vehicles, and the fundamentals of investing, including financial markets, sources of investment information, sources of investment risks, tax considerations, and securities regulation.

- **CFP IV—Tax Planning and Management.** CFP IV provides the student with an understanding of the fundamental methods of individual income tax management.

- **CFP V—Employee Benefits and Retirement Planning.** This course is designed to familiarize students with various individual and employer-sponsored retirement plans. It examines IRAs, tax-sheltered arrangements (TSAs), qualified retirement plans, and health and welfare plans.

- **CFP VI—Estate Planning.** This part of the program teaches the various components of the estate planning process, and about the fundamentals of federal estate and gift taxation.

There are now more than 20,000 individuals enrolled in and about 10,000 graduates of the College for Financial Planning, which is located at: 9724 East Hampton Avenue, Denver, Colorado 80231, (303) 755-7101.

The Need for Cooperation

As time passed, the society, the IAFP, and the College each went its own way, as was intended. Unfortunately, competition, territorial encroachment, duplication of effort, and empire building worked against the close cooperation and synergy we had visualized. While conscientious officers and directors of all three organizations worked hard at doing what they thought best for their constituency, they often seemed to be losing sight of what was best for the profession and the members they were representing.

In December 1983, Kemp Fain, Graydon Calder and Dianna Rampy invited college representative Bill Anthes and IAFP representatives Hubert Harris and Bill Carter to a small "summit" meeting in Denver. Three items dominated their agenda:

1. calendar of events coordination;
2. agreements on "turf";
3. financial planner supervision.

Apparently, the concept needed time to germinate. Other meetings were held in the spring of 1985, no doubt as a response to Donald Pitti's stirring call, at the 1984 IAFP national convention, for cooperation and a concerted effort to promote the financial planning profession. Those of us vitally involved looked forward to this coordinated effort again.

As the talks between the IAFP, the college and the ICFP progressed, the IAFP came up with a proposal that a new organization be formed called the Financial Planning Industry Association.

It would be divided into several sections and the ICFP would become the practitioners' section of the membership.

The IAFP, under this new umbrella organization, would continue to run the chapters, its annual convention and its corporate program.

The college, and the academic section of this new association, would provide CFP courses and continuing education. It would however, give up its exclusive granting of the CFP designation.

It is my understanding that the ICFP's reaction and their objections were summed-up in the following uncredited quote:

"Our members would never approve becoming a part of an organization that included product purveyors."

This proposal apparently fell by the wayside in 1985 and the IBCFP, it would seem, arose out of the ashes of these non-productive joint meetings.

In November 1985, the new president of the IAFP, Alexandra Armstrong, sent out a letter to all members, that explained the IAFP Board's decision not to accept the invitation of the IBCFP to nominate two of its officers to sit on the IBCFP's Board.

It began to seem that if the IAFP and the ICFP were going to work together it would not be under this new organization.

So much for synergism.

We still visualize an integrated nucleus of financial planning organizations, around which all other segments of the financial services community would rally. In turn, this could lead to expanded cooperation among the banks, securities firms, and insurance organizations. Such a united effort might even be able to compete with the terribly strong forces in our society that are trying to get people to *spend* their money.

It still might come about...but unfortunately it hasn't yet.

22 The Institute of Certified Financial Planners

Dianna Rampy became the executive director of the Institute for Certified Financial Planners in 1981. In fact, she was its first full-time executive director, though ICFP was founded in 1973 in Denver by the 42 graduates of the first class of the College for Financial Planning. Here is Dianna Rampy's perception of ICFP, from where it began to where it is heading.

This is a time of growing personal financial uncertainty. Not only the affluent with thick financial portfolios, but average middle-class families, too, are faced with increasingly complex tax laws, high interest rates, eroding savings and social security, a proliferation of financial products and services, and the need to invest wisely for the future.

Consequently, more and more individuals, families, business owners, and investors are turning to the financial planner—a professional who, ideally, has a solid working knowledge of the complex financial picture that enables him or her to recommend sound investment strategies. These planners have brought much-needed financial services to the public. Unfortunately, the heavy public demand has also drawn in people who call themselves financial planners but who, in fact, do not practice financial planning. Little wonder regulators and potential clients too often skeptically view financial planning as a hodgepodge of activities in the securities, insurance, tax and real estate fields.

The mission of the Institute of Certified Financial Planners (ICFP) is the committed effort at the national and grassroots level to integrate and upgrade these financial services. We are doing this in several ways: by establishing and maintaining integrity and high professional standards for the burgeoning financial planning industry; by raising the visibility of financial planners; by educating the public; and by keeping our members abreast of the latest developments in this rapidly changing field.

The result is that the financial planning industry and the public it serves are coming to recognize that CFP is a leading designation denoting professional excellence in the field. It should also be noted that many of the institute's members are already qualified career professionals in other financial disciplines. Within its membership, the ICFP serves CFPs who are also

CPAs, CLUs, trust officers, attorneys, stock brokers, insurance specialists and bankers. Having passed examinations covering the broad financial planning curriculum offered by the College for Financial Planning, members who have earned the CFP designation have been able to greatly expand their careers.

The positive response to the ICFP's efforts is reflected in our astonishing growth. The institute was founded in 1973 in Denver by 42 CFPs comprising the first graduating class of the College for Financial Planning. When I joined the ICFP in 1981 as its first full-time executive director, we had a part-time secretary, a rented typewriter, and a few tangible benefits for our 1,200 members. Today, we have a professional staff of 21 people and an impressive array of services for our over 18,000 members.

None of this phenomenal growth and maturation could have been accomplished without the dedication, innovation and skills of the members themselves who, voluntarily and often at substantial personal and professional sacrifice, serve as officers, board members, and committee members. Institute members are well represented by a 20-member board of directors from a diversity of geographical regions in the U.S. as well as different orientations in the financial planning field. The ICFP's various standing committees, including education, regulatory, public awareness, and membership, have responded quickly and effectively to the expanding needs of our membership.

What does it mean to obtain the coveted CFP designation? CFP candidates take part in an intensive six-course study program (usually spanning two years from the College for Financial Planning, the academic arm of the financial planning industry. The curriculum, which covers risk management, employee benefits, retirement and estate planning, taxation and investments, is available through over 60 colleges and universities. Following their studies, candidates must pass a rigorous set of written exams and meet prior experience requirements in at least one financial services area as set by the college. Utilizing his or her experience and education, a CFP is able to analyze a client's financial position, identify the client's financial goals, prepare a comprehensive plan, and recommend precise financial strategies.

Membership in the ICFP is limited to those who have been conferred the CFP designation or who are actively working toward it. But the education of a CFP does not end with graduation. We require that each member obtain 30 hours of continuing education related to financial planning each year. This commitment to professionalism within financial planning has spurred the formation of grassroots societies of the institute, as well as continuing education groups, which are instrumental in offering educational opportunities and providing public awareness exposure at the local and regional levels. To date, there are 30 societies located throughout the U.S.

The ICFP also conducts a variety of seminars, retreats and conferences designed to assist members with continuing education and developing peer relationships. Our summer retreat last year at Colby College in Waterville,

Maine, for example, included such timely and practical topics as the review of actual case histories on different client markets, investment evaluation, and various practice management subjects. Our first annual international conference, held last October in London, focused on international investment strategies. In Boston, we recently held our second annual conference, in which over 400 members attended. The ICFP is continually searching for educational opportunities that will enhance the quality and educational background of our members.

Another membership benefit is our national referral service, which last year responded to over 22,000 requests for information on how to select a Certified Financial Planner. With additional media attention and an increasingly sophisticated public, we expect our efforts in this area to grow even more. Members also receive monthly newsletters and can subscribe to our quarterly scholarly publication, the *Journal of the Institute of Certified Financial Planners.*

In another innovative move, the ICFP created the Financial Products Standards Board in late 1983 to develop independent guidelines for evaluating and sorting out the bewildering proliferation of financial products that CFPs must select for their clients. Products in several specific financial areas will be examined, and standards will be developed to measure their risk, suitability, quality and appropriateness in meeting an investor's goals and objectives.

Providing services and benefits for our members is only one part of the ICFP, however. As the voice for a preeminent group of financial planners, the institute is dedicated to keeping abreast of the fluctuating policies of legislative and regulatory bodies. This includes our participation on an advisory committee of the North American Securities Administrators Association. We have worked closely with a number of state legislative bodies to help them create suitable legislation for financial planners. Although the ICFP already has a strict Code of Ethics and a rigorous review and censure procedure, we believe that state licensing similar to that of physicians and attorneys would bring us much closer to professional recognition.

Closely linked to these efforts is our goal of raising the visibility of the profession. This means educating the public on why they need and how to select a qualified financial planner. We provide to the public such information free upon request. As part of this public awareness effort, we annually select four regional CFPs and a national CFP of the Year. The awards recognize these individual contributions to the financial planning industry, while at the same time enhancing the professional image of all CFPs. The ICFP has also developed effective institutional advertising programs to bring local and national exposure to our members.

While the financial planning industry has gained momentum, its credibility has come under close scrutiny, particularly from the news media. The ICFP is working hard to clear up any misconceptions of the financial planning profession.

The years ahead for the financial planning industry are sure to be exciting and explosive. With financial planning becoming a regular occurrence for many Americans, it is critical to present the best possible image of financial planners. CFPs represent financial planning at its best. The Institute of Certified Financial Planners will continue to promote the Certified Financial Planner as the consummate professional in the field.

Publishers Note: Chapter 16 includes information about one of the newest developments of the ICFP and the College for Financial Planning: the International Board of Standards and Practices for Certified Financial Planners (IBCFP).

23 Networks, Services, and Other Associations

A large number of elements had to fall in place so that financial planning would be recognized as a profession and financial planners as professionals. Three of those elements—networks, services and other associations—are covered in this chapter.

Networks

There are a number of financial networks, and only a few can be covered in this chapter. One of them is Money Concepts International, Inc., of Miami, Florida. It is a widespread operation that franchises its financial services and organizes professionals in their own "Community Financial Centers." The holding company is headed by a young old-timer in the financial services industry, Jack Walsh. His vice chairman is the well-known golfer and businessman Jack Nicklaus.

Associated Planners, Inc., of Los Angeles, is an entirely different type of operation. Directed by one of the country's leading planners, Phil Gainsborough, it is a network of top financial planning firms in a number of states. They receive their own intra-firm publication, published by Associated Planners Securities Corporation, one of API's subsidiaries. According to some observers, this type of joint venture in the financial planning field will most effectively compete with the giant firms now beginning to offer financial planning services.

Using still a different approach is Bob Dart, president of American Financial Planning Centers, headquartered in Oklahoma City. Now affiliated with Travelers' financial planning operations, Bob Dart also has large and different building plans for American Financial Planning Centers.

Services and Other Associations

No look at this new profession could be considered complete without also looking at what Confidential Planning Services (CPS) of Middletown, Ohio, has done to expand the profession and to increase the chances for the success of those who want to enter it. CPS's unique approach is that it does not engage in product sales. Each affiliate may handle insurance and investments with the vendors of his or her choosing; many operate on a fee-only basis.

CPS began in 1976 and by 1984 had more than 140 affiliates using its multiple services. (For more details on this company and its approach, please refer to "An interview with Edwin P. Morrow," beginning on page 113.)

Making Up for Size with Services

Financial planning boutiques, as some observers call small firms, are compensating for their size by knowing when and where they can receive outside services for their clients. For example, trust company services often are given major credit for the professionalism with which some of the independent financial planning pioneers operated in the early days of the profession.

One of the earliest, beginning some 15 years ago, is Hugh McCafferry's firm, Trust Company of America (TCA), located in Boulder, Colorado. TCA not only provides trust services, but it also provides leads for financial planners who request them. It's not unusual for a planner to be furnished as many as 200 names of people with existing plans, who might be interested in a rollover. The names on the lists are all defined by zip code.

Consolidated Capital of Emeryville, California, uses another method—publishing. Its *Digest of Financial Planning Ideas,* under publisher Dick Wollack and editor Jim Miller, ended 1984 (its second full year) with more than 7,000 subscribers. The *Digest* provides field sales, marketing and public relations advice that can make the difference between success an failure.

The Planner and the Outside Experts

A number of insurance-oriented financial planners have expanded their practice by recognizing the potential of using outside experts and their services. One of the most interesting is Certified Planning Consultants, Inc., of Raleigh, North Carolina. This firm specializes in developing employee benefit plans for financial planner clients. It already has completed hundreds, but according to Tom Pate, CPC's vice president and marketing director, there are in the U.S. 20,000 medical groups alone to which financial planners could offer employee benefit plans.

An entirely different outside expert is Becky Barker of Corpus Christi, Texas. Her firm, "answers period, inc." (P.O. Box 72666, Corpus Christi Texas 78472), publishes the *answers* workbook, which had sold more than 15,000 copies by 1984. Here is her story, which does point to the need for financial planning services:

> When my husband was killed by a drunken driver three years

ago, doctors, insurance agents and funeral directors asked questions I could not answer. What insurance policy covered my two daughters who were injured in the crash? Where was the key to the safe-deposit box? Where were my husband's business records? Did he have a burial plot?

The result is a blue-and white looseleaf workbook called "answers." It contains forms that families can fill out, listing everything a relative or neighbor should know in an emergency.

There is a section for filing household necessities, including a consent form for emergency surgery for a minor child, a list of burial instructions, the location of the extra house key and alarm system box, and the names and phone numbers of the family doctor, veterinarian, electrician, pharmacist and clergyman. Pockets are provided for copies of such things as wills and birth and marriage certificates.

The section on finances has pages for lists of bank accounts, credit cards, stocks and bonds and loans, and pockets for copies of loan agreements and income tax returns. There are also chapters that keep track of real estate, insurance and business records.

I produced the first copies of my book the Christmas after my husband's death. I typed the pages myself and reproduced them at the Insta-print store in my hometown of Corpus Christi, Texas.

These are just a sampling of the wide variety of outside experts and services available to the financial planner.

The National Association of Personal Financial Advisers

The National Association of Personal Financial Advisers, based in Indianapolis, Indiana, is for fee-only financial planners. John Sestina, CFP, is the organization's president and an impressive spokesperson for NAPFA. (However, I will take issue with some of his viewpoints after I share his comments with you.)

Financial planning is the most exciting growth industry there is in the country today; it is a growth industry from several perspectives.

Studies point out that the service industry has the brightest future, and, of course, financial planning is a service. We also know financial planning is a growth industry because of the thousands of people who are becoming involved in it. According to IAFP statisticians, there are some 200,000 people who call themselves financial planners today.

It's also a growth industry as the public is becoming more aware and sensitized to the need and the workings of financial planning. As a result, the most important goal to the survival of this industry is to create a definition for 'financial planner.'

Personally, after 20 years in practice, I would like to one day stand before a group of people, identify myself as a financial planner, and have them know what that is. For the first 15 years of my practice, my wife and I struggled with identifying labels other than financial planner, for fear of being identified with what some people were doing at the time. I used such titles as 'entrepreneur,' 'financier,' and 'financial counselor'—anything to avoid the label 'financial planner,' for I didn't want to be guilty by association.

Today, things are gradually changing. I think we critically need to develop a profession; I am very excited by some of the recognition we are getting as fee-only planners from the commission industry. For example, IAFP seems more willing to have fee-only planners speak on the topic at national conventions, and the attendance at those speeches is dramatic.

I also see changes occurring with the public. I personally receive hundreds of letters each year from people asking, 'Where do I find someone like you?' or 'How do I become involved as a fee-only planner?'

To respond to the latter question, the National Association of Personal Financial Advisers was founded. In the past, fee-only financial planners often were in an outcast position and needed to discover that there were literally hundreds of other fee-only planners out there.

Hopefully, this division between commission and fee-only planners will disappear over the years, for it can only cause harm on a long-term basis. It is important that financial planning no longer be used as a means to an end, but rather as the end itself. The product, if there is one, is really financial planning.

Over the years, several myths have developed concerning the fee-only planner. For example, some people maintained that as a fee-only planner you could not earn a substantial income. Another myth was that fee-only planners could work only with the high-income individual. Still another claimed the fee-only planner could not implement.

These myths are being dispelled. Based on IAFP studies, the successful fee-only financial planners are in the top one percent of earnings. It may be that only the fee-only planners can truly implement; it is now clear that the small-income client can be served profitably on a fee-only basis.

Overall, we have the opportunity to establish a credible profession that doesn't call for baboons on the cover of *Forbes* magazine and attacks by financial journalists. Unfortunately, to date, our image has created such impressions; it is up to us to fix it."

Most of John Sestina's reasoning is right on target, of course. Unfortunately, few people can and will pay a nice fee to have a financial plan prepared for them. None of us believe that medical care should be limited to people who can afford to pay for it; neither should financial planning be limited to a few people in an up-scale income category.

For this reason, I take issue with those who disparage the role of the commission-based planner, whose services are often more readily available to those in lower income groups. Harold Gourgues, for example, gave two outstanding talks to large audiences at the IAFP national convention in October, 1985. He is an astute observer of the financial planning industry, and much of what he had to say was right on target. But he ignores the fact that many fee-based planners were able to begin charging fees only after some high-commission years, and his conclusions, recommendations, and predictions seem to be based on only the top two of his three consumer/prospect groups. While his analysis is probably right for these two groups, it ignores the third group of consumers—the "bottom group," which he characterizes as earning less than $50,000 a year, having assets of less than $100,000, and not being able to spell "informed society." Every chance I get, I like to remind him, and others, that this is the largest group of all and the one that will be the most important for the thousands of financial planners now coming into the field. And this group contains the very people who most need a financial planner to help them accumulate money by changing their spending and saving habits.

Satisfying as it is to reduce taxes and to increase and conserve wealth for the already wealthy client, it is even more satisfying to help someone become well-off. My response to Harold, and to those who share his opinions, is to remind them that it is this third (and largest) group whose lives can be changed for the better and whose futures can be made brighter by a professional and conscientious financial planner. These are the clients who make financial planners proud and unique members of the service professions.

I also take exception to John Sestina's statement that, "It is important that financial planning no longer be used as a means to an end, but as an end itself." How can the financial plan be an end? What good is a financial plan by itself? A financial plan isn't very valuable if it sits in an executive's office drawer or atop a bureau at home. It is to be hoped that fee-only planners will promote the plan not as an end, but as an important means to the end: financial security.

My definition of financial planning is a follows:

> Financial planning is the continuous process that forward-looking people go through, usually with professional help, to record on paper where they are financially, what short- and long-range goals they want to achieve, and what they might best do to achieve these goals.

To be fair, fee-only planners often do tell me, "Of course, implementation is important, and we help them do it." That I like to hear, which is why fee-only planners are adding gratitude to the respect they've always had. John Sestina and his organization deserve much of the credit for that.

To provide a more comprehensive picture of NAPFA, this chapter includes a copy of the letter NAPFA sends in response to inquiries, as well as a set of four questions and answers it mails.

National Association of Personal Financial Advisors
8140 Knue Road, Suite 110 • Indianapolis, Indiana 46250

Dear Financial Planner,

Enclosed is an application for membership in the National Association for Personal Financial Advisors (NAPFA), the first professional organization for fee-only personal financial planners.

In general, membership in NAPFA requires that your primary business activity be the practice of comprehensive personal financial planning on strictly a fee-only basis. Planners who have been practicing for less than a year on a fee-only basis are accepted and listed as provisional members.

NAPFA represents to the public that its members are independent of conflicts of interest in serving the client's financial planning needs. Therefore, a key qualification for membership in NAPFA is that you may not have a direct or indirect affiliation with product vendors such that you (or your employer) would stand to benefit from the implementation of product recommendations to the client.

If you feel that you qualify, we hope you will consider membership in NAPFA. To date, NAPFA has provided a referral service for more than 8,000 requests for a fee-only financial planner. NAPFA sponsors an annual educational conference for fee-only planners. As a member you will become part of a network of the top financial planners in the country. And finally, NAPFA will continue to support the development of no-load investment products.

We believe that membership in NAPFA will play an important role in your development as a fee-only planner and in the emergence of the fee-only planner as a leading client-advocate in the financial services industry.

QUESTIONS AND ANSWERS CONCERNING NATIONAL ASSOCIATION OF PERSONAL FINANCIAL ADVISORS, INC.

Q: When and why was NAPFA organized?

A: NAPFA was organized in February 1983, because of the need among fee-only financial planners to communicate with one another in the areas of practice management, client services, and investment selection. Since there are very few fee-only financial planners disbursed throughout the country, it had been difficult to communicate with one another without an organization.

Q: How many members are in the organization now?

A: The current membership is approximately 200 members.

Q: What are the goals of NAPFA?

A: The goals of NAPFA are to help fee-only financial planners to communicate with one another and to share ideas in the areas of investments, practice mangement, client services and all other phases of the financial planning process. A mailing list will be provided to all members to facilitate this exchange of ideas. We encourage all NAPFA members to talk to one another, to share ideas, and also to have regional meetings in order to help one another.

Q: Who will qualify for membership in NAPFA?

A: Applications for membership will be accepted from individuals who spend the majority of their time practicing comprehensive financial planning with clients on a fee-only basis. The application is rather lengthy and all information requested will be subject to verification.

Newsletters, Journals and Computer Software

Once a business has evolved into a profession, newsletters, journals and computer software become available for it. Computer software for the financial planner was covered in Chapter 15 and *Financial Planning* magazine was featured in Chapter 19.

In addition, there are a number of highly professional newsletters available for the financial planner. For example, Longman Financial Services Publishing Inc., publisher of this book, also issues the *Longman Report,* a monthly newsletter for financial planning professionals.

In addition, Tax Management Institute, Inc., has a new program on *Financial Planning & Tax Management,* according to TMI president Sandra Degler. The program is incorporated into three manuals covering the entire financial planning process. The first manual serves as a comprehensive guide for the financial planner; the second includes client memos for actual use; and the third is constructed around TMI's monthly journal-newsletter.

There are many others as well, which are often advertised in *Financial Planning* magazine. Many of them can be personalized for the planner.

In 1985 two new and important organizations started attracting attention. One was the national *Financial Service Times,* headed by John Meyer as Publisher and Liz Chapman as Editor. It billed itself as "the newspaper for financial planners" and quickly earned a surprisingly influential niche in the financial planning community.

The other, The ADVISOR Group, headed by Charles J. Whitaker, a highly successful fee-only planner in Washington, D.C., announced itself as a firm of "Specialists in Marketing for Financial Planners." Whitaker apparently enticed Joyce Henry away from Confidential Planning Services; she became a partner and Executive Vice President.

Both organizations serve to add confidence to those considering going into financial planning. To some they also added greatly to the image of a financial planner as a true professional.

Product or Process

People in financial planning continually debate whether financial planning is a product or a process. It seems to me that we can trust the dictionary for this semantic battle.

A *plan,* as such, is a noun; therefore, a financial plan can be a product. However, financial planning is an action taken or not taken, and it isn't an object or product. When a firm or individual "goes into financial planning," it is actually going into *providing* financial services or financial plans.

PART NINE

The Financial Planning Career Is It Too Late?

"Is it too late to decide on a financial planning career? Should I have gotten into it five years ago?"

I often hear those questions after my talks around the country. In fact, I recall one young man wondering if the field was already overcrowded because of the number of Certified Financial Planners being accredited by the College for Financial Planning. I sincerely assured him that the field is far from overpopulated and that anyone entering the field during the 1980s would still be in a new and developing career field.

In the last 10 years, and particularly in the last two or three years, financial planning has become one of the most popular "perks" available to executives. Beginning at the upper management level, now it is working its way down to middle management. In fact, financial planning is becoming so popular that a number of companies are now wondering if there isn't something similar that they can offer their average employee. Unfortunately, before that happens, employees will have to be made receptive to financial planning, for most people still do not view financial planning as a method of accumulating money, but rather as a way to manage money once it is acquired.

This attitude can change, however; one catalyst for that change is financial education. The other factor that will play a role in this change is the growing recognition that "information about money is becoming almost as important as money itself," according to Paul Richard, director of education for NCFE.

While the average employee may not be ready for financial planning, he or she is receptive to learning more about managing money. That means, of course, that we should begin with an objective financial education approach rather than an initial financial planning approach.

However, the result—assuming that financial planners are the ones to undertake that educational job—will be millions of financial planning prospects for tomorrow who aren't potential customers today. I believe there are enough of these people to keep thousands of financial planners profitably employed. The final result could be millions of consumers not reliant upon Social Security when they retire.

24 The Career Counselor's Dilemma

How can a career counselor decide to recommend financial planning as a career choice? After all, the attributes that make a successful financial planner are yet to be clearly defined. Obviously, the financial planner is part entreprenuer, part counselor, part teacher, part professional, and perhaps even a bit of a crusader.

Even after a modest interview, ascertaining whether or not a person has the basic attributes to be able to learn the field is easy. But, does he or she have the self-discipline, character, and inward drive necessary for the follow through? Measuring "can do" is easy; measuring "will do" is a different matter.

Can "Will Do" Be Tested?

As a sales consultant 20 years ago, I became intrigued with the idea of devising a successful testing procedure for measuring "will do" factors for prospective field salespeople. As a sales supervisor and sales manager, I found it comparatively easy to chart the "can do" factors. Education, personality, verbal fluency, mental agility, and appearance were easy to assess and enabled us to say with confidence that this person or that person *could* succeed in sales. However, it was nearly impossible to develop any interviewing technique or combination of tests that would determine whether people *would* do the things necessary to succeed. Would they do the research necessary for the next day's calls, for example, or watch television in the evening?

Even though I tried several combinations of tests—Wonderlic, the Kuder Preference, the Stanford test, graphology, body language, eye contact and others—I failed the challenge. We tried them all, but I never felt we achieved a successful method for determining those inner qualities that increased the chances of someone succeeding as a salesperson.

Salesperson-Planner-Accountant—Lawyer

The career counselor faces the same challenges with the financial planning profession. In a new profession such as this, young people can save years by entering the field right out of school. On the other hand, youth and obvious inexperience can be real handicaps in giving advice on financial matters.

Indeed, one of the needs that created the profession is the need to convince young people especially to put aside a larger segment of their discretionary dollars for the future. Essential also is the ability to convince executives and others to implement the plan immediately. You might not call that selling, but it certainly is important.

Possibly, the career counselor would be wise to suggest a few years of entry-level work positions and professional courses of study that would increase an individual's chance of succeeding as a financial planner later.

The Young College Graduate

Dr. Robert Bohn of Golden Gate University is not a career counselor. However, while at Brigham Young University, he created the first college program for training financial planners. He and some of his 12 young men and women were honored in Dallas during the 1977 IAFP annual convention.

Today, career counselors both in the universities and elsewhere are on the lookout for young men and women who might have that balance of talents necessary to become successful financial planners. However, they do have a dilemma. While 22-year-olds may be better at absorbing the techniques and information necessary for creating intelligent financial plans, they also have to impress and convince the client. It is not easy for a 25-year-old with few assets to convince $50,000- or $100,000-a-year prospective clients that he or she knows what should be done with those assets.

Internship the Answer?

So, what advice can the career counselor give? As Edwin Morrow of CPS has described in earlier chapters, one answer is internship. In fact, Morrow thinks an internship of at least 12 weeks should be the entry point for new financial planners. He observes that this solution has a historical base in times when the entry into any trade or professional career began with an apprenticeship. This is how Morrow puts it:

> The financial planning firm has a dilemma. Employers must ask themselves how they can afford to hire a totally inexperienced person and fund that person's training, until he or she becomes profitable.
>
> An employer is seeking several characteristics in a new employee: good work habits, pleasant personality, intellectual skills, the ability to

tackle and overcome tasks, and, in some cases, even marketing skills.

A would-be employee needs specific job experience, a chance to move from classroom theory to real-world achievement, a frame of reference from which to judge a prospective employer, and a chance to produce tangible evidence that new learning is now a marketable skill.

For career counselors, recommending a 12-week internship could be the answer. For the individual considering a financial planning career, it could be an ideal first step as well.

Professionals Ask the Question

"I have a pretty good practice as a CPA, but one of my associates thinks we ought to get into financial planning. What do you think?"

After asking several probing questions and getting better acquainted with my questioner at a cocktail party, I had reservations and suggested that he analyze it further before making any decision.

A career counselor generally must make more definite recommendations. For accountants, for example, you will want to know what research they've been doing in the last five years. If they cannot define financial planning, haven't been doing substantial reading about it and haven't taken advantage of information from the College or the IAFP, you may wish to be cautious about recommending financial planning as a career.

Financial planning is not merely adding tax advice and IRA recommendations to accounting services. It is so much more that anyone thinking like that won't have a chance in the real world of financial planning. Much the same advice, in my opinion, applies to lawyers wondering whether or not they should "start doing financial planning."

Will Tomorrow's Planners Be Accountants or Lawyers?

Everyone seems to agree that accountants and lawyers are going into financial planning. Who will dominate? Attorney Bruce Winter in Boca Raton, Florida, makes a case for lawyers eventually entering more into financial planning. Here's how he puts it:

> As an attorney and Certified Financial Planner, I think that over the next 10 years there will be many attorneys who will become Certified Financial Planners in order to provide their clients greater services in the area of financial planning. This transition from being an attorney to an attorney/financial planner, is really not that dramatic. Obviously, the attorney will register with the Securities and Exchange Commission as a Registered Investment Advisor. This requirement is necessary because the rendering of financial advice will

no longer be incidental to the practice of law and, thus, not fall within one of the exceptions to the Investment Advisor Act. Furthermore, because most attorneys/financial planners will want to charge fees for their services, registration as an investment advisor is necessary.

Although, historically, the legal and accounting professions have created artificial barriers as to their services, the role of a competent tax or estate planning attorney and accountant is similar to the role of a Certified Financial Planner. The training and education of a tax and estate planning attorney, such as myself, having received a Masters in Tax Law from New York University, involves courses, that although more comprehensive, are similar to the Certified Financial Planner program, dealing with the areas of taxation, retirement planning, and estate planning. Nevertheless, attorneys/financial planners must take additional courses or have additional experience in the areas of insurance and investments, in order to provide their clients competent advice concerning comprehensive financial planning.

Furthermore, these future attorneys/financial planners may find it desirable to implement their clients' financial plans by also becoming licensed in the areas of securities, insurance and real estate. The ethical considerations concerning the independence of the attorney will still remain a major concern once an attorney becomes licensed in these other areas. However, with full disclosure to their clients as to their fee and commission income, attorneys can satisfy this ethical problem.

In conclusion, because of the attorney's legal training and background in financial planning concepts, the attorney/financial planner is likely to become the dominant professional in rendering financial planning services to clients in the future.

Bruce Winter presents a short but convincing case to buttress his conviction.

Another Contributing Force

Another development in our society may also mean that lawyers will give accountants a competitive run for the largest corner of the financial planning profession. Chief Justice Warren Burger capsulized it when he referred to the lawyers graduating from law schools by the phrase "hordes of lawyers, hungry as locusts." By the late 1970s, this country had almost 2,000 lawyers for every million residents, almost double the ratio of any other industrialized nation. The ratio is still increasing.

That hunger to which Chief Justice Burger referred has led some lawyers to pursue nitpicking and frivolous lawsuits, which is not a good testimonial to the legal profession. Instead of clogging the dockets with such lawsuits, self-respecting lawyers may look elsewhere for employment of their skills. That elsewhere may be financial planning, so career counselors may want to take into account this interest in financial planning, when advising people about legal, accounting *or* financial planning careers.

Several Ways of Putting It

For career counselors, it often helps to read what a financial planner says about the profession. Here's how Allen Hamilton, CFP and western regional vice president of WZW Financial Services, Inc., in Walnut Creek, California, puts it:

> Financial planning is no longer only for millionaires. It is for all those seriously concerned about their future financial stability.
>
> We continually hear the statement, 'It's not how much money you make, but how much you retain for the future and how those dollars are positioned.'
>
> Today, we all face problems with inflation; tax bracket creep, alternative minimum tax (flat-rate tax); insurance; college education costs; savings dollar choices; numerous and confusing investment alternatives; personal business decisions; and distribution of assets to surviving family members at death.
>
> So, financial planning today is a must. A new breed of professional advisor has been developing during the past 15 years—the financial planner or advisor. Securities, insurance, real estate, accounting, law and teaching are a few of the allied professions from which a financial planner may develop.

The Retiree and the Retired

What about the 50-year-old who plans to retire in another year but doesn't want to stop working? Should career counselors recommend financial planning as a second career during the golden years?

For the right individuals, I think it's a viable career choice. For example, during the 1960s, a number of 40- and 50-year-old military personnel were retiring and learning how to sell mutual funds; many of the early-retirees who started their second career selling funds graduated to doing financial planning in the 1970s. Some who are now in their 60s are leaders in the profession.

As the new career opened to these people, a new prospect group is opening to others. The retired or about-to-be retired also need financial planning, but many experienced planners are ignoring them. That means there are more opportunities for the new financial planner, perhaps newly retired him-or herself.

In fact, some financial planners already are finding that niche for their services. Shirley A. Cairns, CFP, of Roseburg, Oregon, addressed this area in an article she wrote for a local paper, entitled, "Retire as a Couple: Plan as a Single." She describes John, 59, and Mary, 52, who have a fairly solid resource base, but without thoughtful planning could find themselves in an impossible situation. As Cairns points out, "There are many ideas that should be explored for asset repositioning for a better and safer retirement."

In Deltona, Florida, financial planner Genevieve "Jenny" Hansen has built almost her entire practice around the retired people who make up the majority of that town. She now has more than 600 clients.

Can This Person Do the Research?

Not too long ago, anyone helping people toward a better financial future could know almost all the answers. But that is certainly no longer true in the financial planning field. Insurance, savings, investments and taxes have all become so complicated, particularly in the last decade, that one individual simply cannot know it all.

Therefore, career counselors need to make sure the person asking for advice has the ability and capacity to do research. The information and help are available to do solid financial planning.

For example, taxes may be the most complicated area of all for a financial planner. However, the financial planner does not *have* to be an expert, though he or she does need to know who and where the experts are.

Tax Management, Inc., is a Washington, D.C. subsidiary of the Bureau of National Affairs. TMI recognizes the needs of the financial planner and offers assistance, including a wealth of prepared material. "When you're faced with a new or unfamiliar tax problem, or specialized compensation planning matter, tap the experience of an expert with your Tax Management portfolio," TMI recommends in its material. "It could mean the difference between finding the solution—or losing the business."

Having tax information and advice available is, however, only part of the answer. Financial planners must take advantage of that information and advice, which simply means *financial planners have to do their homework*.

Potential Positions Still Developing

Bob MacDonald, president of ITT has some interesting predictions that prospective financial planners may find of interest. Here's how he views it:

> For the vast majority of people, the future will mean getting their financial products from the same place they look to for financial help and advice today.
>
> I believe that possibly by the end of this decade, and certainly by

the end of this century, banks, S&Ls and credit unions can become the dominant distributors of life insurance and related financial products. People are used to talking with these institutions about their financial affairs; the sale of insurance and related financial products is a natural.

The financial institutions have two things the insurance industry doesn't have: credibility with the consumer and a customer base.

If Bob MacDonald is correct, there may be many salaried positions for financial planners under the auspices of these financial institutions. For future financial planners with some sales ability, this could offer an excellent career choice, for, as Bob MacDonald points out:

Bankers are absolutely the worst sales and marketing people in existence today. They even rank well behind actuaries and underwriters. Most bankers think marketing means putting a full-page ad in a newspaper, putting some tent cards in the lobby and maybe a few statement stuffers in the mail, and then sitting back and waiting for the phone to ring.

We all know that this won't work for insurance and most other financial products. The distribution of financial service products can become a major profit center for banks, but not without a lot of salespeople helping them.

MacDonald's remarks confirm many people's feeling that the individual trained as a financial planner and possessing selling ability can have a good future in this new profession.

A Story and a Question

I am still grateful to a senior executive who played a helpful part in my own career change. Having studied speech and psychology in college, I was working in personnel and seriously considering entering sales. He invited me to his golf club to play a round and to give me some advice along the fairways:

My first suggestion is that you get into straight-commission selling. If you are any good, you can make more money than you would otherwise; if you aren't any good, you should get out of selling.

Don't go with a firm where you have to sell your friends, but never go with a firm where you have to sell something that isn't good enough for your friends.

That obviously was solid advice for me. But, how does the career counselor, or any of us, tell just what a financial planner is? How much is the financial planner a researcher, a salesperson, a psychologist, and an executive?

Personally, I don't think the financial planner is one person or one particular type of person. Still, one of the most important functions of a financial planner is to motivate people, so some sales ability is essential.

Conscientious financial planners are successful at helping people learn to live within their income. They use their powers of persuasion to get their clients to put aside a larger share of their discretionary income for the future. Advising clients properly as to where to put those funds is, of course, valuable and one way the financial planner justifies his or her fees or commissions.

But the real service done for the client, even when a $100,000-a-year individual is living beyond his or her means, is straightening out that person's financial life, not merely helping him or her make good investments. That is what, for some financial planners, is the most rewarding reason for choosing their career.

Many Exciting Choices

Besides full financial planning, the College for Financial Planning offers a "para-planner" course of study, which is one possibility that career counselors may wish to recommend.

Some large firms offer other avenues that might lead to a financial planning career. Many successful financial planners started as insurance agents or stock brokers. More accountants are entering financial planning; banks and savings and loans have recently been receptive to giving people experience that will help them succeed later as financial planners.

Is Financial Planning Truly a Growing Profession?

This book was written to point out that, of the exciting new professions evolving in our society today, financial planning is certainly an emerging growth profession of the 1980s and beyond. According to Robert Kley, chairman of Granite Capital in San Marcos, California, financial planning has a bright future. He explains it this way:

> While people are making more money, they're also being forced into higher tax brackets. They face a bewildering array of investments offered by an evergrowing list of financial institutions. More than anything else, they need advice, guidance, and a plan for the future.

I asked Kley two questions that a career counselor might want answered. First, I asked him to tell me how he saw financial planning growing corporately. He responded, "It will continue to be a cottage industry—in fact, more so with more private practitioners."

My second question was his opinion of financial planning as a career. I received the following answer:

> Financial planning is an excellent career choice. In the book, *The 90 Highest Paying Careers for the 80s,* of the top 10, four are in the financial services business. Financial planning is ranked eighth, and we concur.

25 Is This A Career for Me?

If you're considering financial planning as a career, you should first make sure that you would be comfortable as a professional, any professional. To understand what constitutes a profession and a professional, let's look at a professional outside the financial planning profession but inside the financial services industry.

Dr. Edwin S. Overman, CPCU, is president of the American Institute for Property and Liability Underwriters and the Insurance Institute of America. Here is how he describes a new profession:

> When any business strives to emerge as a profession, at least six requisites are necessary to earn and maintain the respect and trust on the part of the public it serves. When growing numbers of practitioners meet and adhere to these requisite, the public's recognition of that business as a profession is almost certain to follow. Accounting, with its professional CPA designation, and architecture, with its professional AIA designation, are recent examples of businesses which have been accepted as professions by their respective publics.

Here are Dr. Overman's six thought-out requirements:

1. *Commitment to Serve Others.* This first requisite of a profession may be summed up in a single word—*altruism*. Altruistic behavior involves the sublimation of one's selfish and acquisitive tendencies through a commitment to serve the welfare of others.

2. *Adherence to a Published Code of Ethics.* One of the distinguishing marks of human beings is their possession of a conscience. This sense of right and wrong enables people to choose between what they *should* and what they *should not* do under various circumstances. The philosopher John Dewey defined mankind's responsibilities this way: 'In this theatre of man's life, it is reserved for God and the angels to be lookers on. Man must act; and he must act well or ill, rightly or wrongly.'

A published code of ethics can help men and women judge whether they are acting well or ill, rightly or wrongly, in their business dealings with the public. Each of the established professions—the clergy, medicine, law, accounting and architecture—has formulated and published a code of ethics as guiding principles for its respective professional practitioners.

3. *Mastery of Specialized Knowledge.* Individual practitioners in each established profession are distinguished by their possession of a unique, highly specialized body of knowledge related directly to their profession and unknown to others outside the profession. This body of knowledge has been gathered from the experience accumulated over the years by numerous practitioners. This knowledge, documented in textbooks, research findings, monographs and technical articles, forms the body of literature for each field of endeavor.

4. *Generalized Knowledge of Other Related Fields.* In our increasingly complex society, it is no longer sufficient to be a specialist only; a true professional must also be a generalist. The total intellectual equipment of a professional practitioner must be interdisciplinary in nature. In the field of medicine, for example, total concentration in the disciplines of physiology, anatomy and biology alone to the exclusion of other related disciplines would result in a narrow, less-than-qualified physician. A generalized understanding of the fields of chemistry, bacteriology, sociology, psychology, philosophy and ethics would serve to produce a fully qualified and professional physician.

5. *Standards for Measuring Knowledge.* Imagine the chaos and confusion in creating a profession if there were no standards by which to measure the levels of knowledge of persons seeking admission to the profession. A method for testing an individual's knowledge of the field itself, as well as a general understanding of related fields, is essential in distinguishing those persons who acquire the proper knowledge.

6. *Active Participation in a Professional Society.* A closely knit professional society, through which individuals can collectively update their skills and contribute to the welfare of the public they serve, is essential for professional recognition and status. To speak with authority, a professional society must maintain a set of high standards for membership, follow a strict code of personal ethics laid down by the society, and work continuously to improve its profession.

Its Future and Your Future

Before you proceed further, please answer this question honestly. Would you, with your personality, be comfortable as a professional in a profession? If not, stop right here. If yes, then consider these five key questions:

- Is the financial planning profession likely to grow?
- Am I a persuader or one persuaded?
- Would I rather work with numbers or with people?
- Do I have more than an average amount of self-discipline?
- Do I have enough money to live on until I am established?

You should answer these before deciding whether financial planning is the career choice for you.

Will It Grow?

Naturally, I think financial planning will grow. But, admittedly, asking a father (even of a profession) whether or not his offspring "show great potential" is going to lead to a prejudiced response. So, you may wish to consider the view of Stuart P. Gassel of First Financial Planners Services, one of the Travelers Companies, instead. Here's his analysis:

> A survey of the market indicates that the affluent customer who requires financial planning services wants a comprehensive plan from a professional, independent, and trusted advisor. Our study found that approximately eight million families are at or above the $40,000 annual income level, which constitutes a major potential for financial planning services during the 1980s.
>
> We expect the market to grow to 12 million households by 1987. Meanwhile, there is a growing trend toward families in the $25,000 to $40,000 bracket, who are also seeking guidance. Clearly, the potential for financial planning is enormous.

Now, if you happen to be in your 30s or 40s, financial planning still is a viable alternative for you. The College for Financial Planning reports that many retired military personnel are currently studying for their CFPs and looking forward to the 1990s and their second careers.

To Persuade or to Be Persuaded

Are you good at persuading people to do something? Or, to put it another way, are you a good salesperson? As in most other professions, much of a financial planner's success depends on the power to motivate, not manipulate, people.

If you don't have any sales ability, and particularly if you don't like selling, think about financial planning as a career or even a second career very cautiously. Even the fee-only financial planner who never sells a financial product usually doesn't get a client to choose him or her and agree to pay the fee without being pretty good at selling, whether or not the planner will admit it.

People or Numbers

Financial planning is a people business. While the practice does require much figuring and number crunching to prepare the comprehensive financial plan, the financial planner must be good at working with people. That usually means the financial planner enjoys and prefers working with people.

On Self-Discipline

To succeed as a financial planner, you will need a large amount of self-discipline. You need to get the studying done, you need to make the contacts, you need to make the calls, you must propose the plans, you must follow up to make sure the plans are being implemented, you must stay current on regulations that may affect your clients, and so on.

Also, as a financial planner, you have to be the one who makes things happen. A barber may be able to hang his pole and have enough customers just walk in to provide an income, but few financial planning offices work like a barbershop.

Eating Until You're Established

The doctor, dentist and some other professionals usually need to make a considerable investment in equipment. While the financial planner's initial investment for equipment is often much less, the time it takes to become established can be even longer. So, you must know how you will survive the lean years, until your financial planning practice is firmly founded.

Many Other Variables

As part of your soul searching, you'll want to consider numerous other questions. For example, do you already have the knowledge and experience in some segment of the financial services industry that would be helpful to you as a financial planner? Are you knowledgeable about:

- insurance?
- taxes?
- interviewing?
- money management?
- tax shelters?
- sales and marketing?
- accounting?

If not, you'll want to learn these first, of course.

Other Routes

There are numerous ways to begin preparing for a career in financial planning, and one chapter can hardly cover all the routes available. However, you may wish to consider beginning as a para-planner with an established financial planning firm. Or, you could also consider an internship. You might choose to become employed by a large company, as more of them in the financial services industry are getting into financial planning.

Before you enter the field, you may wish to find information about financial planning and a local chapter where you can attend a meeting or two. (Write to the International Association for Financial Planning, Inc., Two Concourse Parkway, Suite 800, Atlanta, Georgia 30328.)

You'll also want to investigate the Certified Financial Planner program discussed in more detail in Chapters 16 and 21. You may decide to enroll and begin the courses as a way to decide whether or not the profession is for you. Or, you may wish to make your decision first, then enroll.

Not an Easy Decision

By now, you realize that whether financial planning is good for you is no longer a simple question. Part Ten provides a variety of self-profiles of financial planners, and there are half a dozen interviews with financial planning executives in earlier portions of this book. When you read the interviews and the self-profiles you will see that financial planning offers a variety of career paths.

Some Guidelines

Only you can say if the financial planning profession is for you. But my research, though somewhat biased, would lead me to suggest you say yes to financial planning if:

1. You would like to help people change or modify their spending habits so as to have a better retirement or a better chance of reaching other financial goals.

2. You like dealing with other people's finances and find you have no trouble getting people to confide in you.

3. You like to work with management people or professionals in other fields.

4. You like the idea of taking financial planning courses, knowing that they are only the beginning of a continuing academic search.

If you like these four areas, chances are you will like being a financial planner.

Are You Good at Prospecting?

I admit that I am sold on financial planning as a profession, but I do not recommend that everyone become a financial planner. For instance, I won't recommend the profession if you lack the ability to prospect. The single most common reason that financial planning companies fail—there are some that fail—is an inability to prospect.

In 1984, some well-educated individuals in California put together an extremely qualified financial planning group. The group included all the professionals necessary to provide outstanding financial planning services to even the wealthiest of clients or largest of businesses. Their office gave assurance that they certainly could handle that business. They even had a reputation that was encouraging to any client who wanted to investigate.

But they suffered from a fatal flaw. They didn't have enough clients to support the team or the overhead, nor did they know how to prospect for new clients. They didn't recognize how to have one client lead to another or how to get referrals. Possibly, they were too proud in their individual professions to prospect for new clients. Like others that have failed, they probably thought that merely doing a sterling job for one client would automatically lead to other jobs and other clients.

Doing a sterling job certainly can lead to new clients and new jobs, but *not unless you ask* and *not automatically.* What that firm needed was salespeople or sales experience. Had you asked when they opened their office doors where their salespeople were located, they might have laughed.

Whether you are thinking of opening your own office or becoming one of the financial planners in an already established financial planning firm, you will want to explore your ability to prospect. However, if you have no desire to learn prospecting, you can join a large company or office and perform one of the many specialized functions that don't require that you personally find prospects and clients. If, however, you already have successful sales experience and know how to prospect, you will be starting out in this profession with a distinct advantage.

Some of my contemporaries in financial planning circles believe I attach too much importance to the selling requirements of the business, because of my sales background. Many of them, however, don't realize what good salespeople they are and how influential that selling ability has been to the development of their practice.

Don't dismiss financial planning as a career choice just because you haven't had direct sales experience. Most people can learn to sell, to prospect, to make solid presentations of themselves and their abilities. You can learn to close sales and get appointments and referrals; you can also learn to motivate your clients to implement the financial plan you've prepared for them, which might earn you some commissions if that is the way you're working.

You have to decide for yourself, of course, if you can, or if you are one of the exceptions. To assess objectively your day-to-day relationships with people, you may wish to think about these questions. Are you an influencer? Can you motivate people to do the things you want them to do, or must you rely on commands to get things done? Can you get people to serve on a committee and work toward a common goal?

When you were growing up, did you ever deliver newspapers, sell Girl Scout cookies, etc.? Were you any good at it?

Ask the Pros

You will want to talk with more than one financial planner before deciding whether or not financial planning is a career you should seriously consider. You'll also need to determine how important it is to have, or to develop, the ability to sell.

You Will Have to Register

"Will I have to register as an investment advisor?" is a question often posed by individuals considering a financial planning career. Here's how Ron Bufe of Confidential Planning Services in Middletown, Ohio responds to that question:

> In 1981, the Securities and Exchange Commission (SEC) cleared this issue up by publishing an article that said in effect: 'Financial planners must be registered.'
>
> There are three areas to consider in determining who must be a Registered Investment Advisor:
>
> *Advice.* Do you provide advice regarding securities? (Remember that bank instruments are securities, as are stocks, bonds, limited partnerships, etc.) Do you advise regarding specifics? Do you advise generically, such as, 'I believe bonds would be good for you,' or 'I believe the market will continue to rise and you should retain your stocks'? There is no way a financial planner can avoid this type of question, and nearly all written plans consider either the retention or acquisition of securities.
>
> *Business.* Is the advice part of your normal business activity? An attorney who occasionally suggests that executors establish an interest-bearing account or certificate for cash funds would not require an RIA designation, since these suggestions are incidental to an attorney's normal practice. However, an attorney who prepares financial plans and provides specific advice regarding the acquisition or disposal of investments would need to be an RIA.
>
> There are five exemptions for professionals who may from time

to time give advice regarding securities that may be incidental to their primary practice or business—bankers, attorneys, accountants, engineers and teachers. However, an accounting firm which advertises financial counseling that includes review of documents will need to be registered.

Compensation. Do you earn income or other benefits in this process? Fees, commissions, even free trips count in this category. A minister who provides free counseling to young couples and who might discuss securities would be exempt, but not a financial planner.

Proliferating Financial Planners

With 20,000 CFPs soon to be practicing, some of you may be concerned about making a living in the field. If the client/prospect group were a limited market, there would be some cause for concern. But it isn't. In fact, the market is just beginning real growth.

In the 1960s and 1970s, with Congress increasing the benefits of Social Security, millions of people were unreceptive to the concept of preparing for their own retirement, financially. Many were counting on Social Security to take care of them, so financial planning was something they could put off.

Now, however, the rapidly decreasing confidence of employed people in the Social Security program has led to a growing awareness of the need to plan ahead. If Social Security is still around, it will be nice, today's 30- and 40-year-olds reason, but they aren't banking on it for their retirements, as many of their parents did. Here are millions of prospects for financial planners; some authorities point to the acceptance of IRAs as proof of the changed attitude.

Even those of us who think the Social Security program could be overhauled and made fiscally viable are willing to concede that if the cynicism of the younger generations causes them to plan for their retirement years now, it will put less of a burden on the federal government later.

I think the pool of financial planning prospects will not only grow, but also will become, on an average, much younger. For more than 10 years, the bulk of the experienced financial planner's business came from clients primarily interested in tax shelters. But I think that emphasis will shift back to the way financial planning was conceived. The dually licensed mutual fund/insurance salespeople in the 1950s and 1960s helped their clients prepare for their financial futures with investment vehicles that accumulated money, rather than with investments that merely sheltered wealth from taxes or guarded against inflation.

Other Questions to Ponder

"How do I learn more about the profession itself?"

You should read *Financial Planning* magazine, if you are seriously interested in considering financial planning as a career.

"Who would I call on as a financial planner?"

Joseph Gemma, one of the dually licensed pioneers and now director of the Money School of Boston advises, "Concentrate on prospect groups approximately your own age, and with financial problems similar to your own."

One question you should ask yourself is whether or not you are comfortable dealing with intangibles, which make up a significant portion of the average person's assets. Some people are effective only at selling tangibles such as automobiles, computers or clothing. To discuss and sell an intangible, such as an insurance policy, can be difficult for them.

However, even if you are uncomfortable with intangible selling, you might still succeed in financial planning by marketing tangible investments. According to Harold F. Chorney, president of Cumberland Investments in Boston, Massachusetts, a number of tangibles have outperformed almost all other investments in the last few years. And, they are much easier to present.

Choosing a Company

If you are considering a career as a financial planner, you will want to look at several companies and carefully determine where there is a fit for you. Important aspects to look at, in no particular order, are the following:

- local management;
- commissions, draws, expense allowances;
- available training programs;
- home office support;
- local office support;
- company reputation;
- financial products and their quality;
- company image;
- the *future,* possibly the most important of all.

Is the company growing, and is management positive about the future? Is the company in a growth posture? Is it cutting back or expanding? Is the company actually in the financial planning profession?

To give you some idea of a company that is doing all of the above, in a unique manner, you may wish to learn more about Anchor National Life Insurance Company of Phoenix, Arizona, headed by Ben Burr. Anchor has apparently decided to make itself a financial planning company, rather than another insurance company.

According to Charles Shafer, president of Anchor National Financial Services, the company now has 1,200 financial planners in the field, but expects to have 2,000 within five years. The company has a noncaptive sales force, with respectable commissions, and prefers hiring experienced financial planners. To quote Charlie Shafer:

> Our projected growth rate, which is to almost double our present field force, is also the growth rate we expect to see for the financial planning profession.

26 Questions, Answers, Predictions and Warnings

As the 1980s arrive, many people predicted what this decade might contain for the financial services industry. Two who were on target were Richard W. Arnold, then chief financial officer for Charles Schwab Corporation in San Francisco, and Robert W. MacDonald, CLU, president of ITT Life Insurance.

When Arnold wrote a chapter for *Your Book of Financial Planning,* published by Reston/Prentice-Hall in 1983, he provided some clear insights into the banking and securities industry. He accurately predicted how the banks would interact with brokerage firms and how the consumer could benefit by becoming more familiar with the computerized services becoming available.

Zeroing in on the future of the insurance industry, Bob MacDonald proved an effective forecaster on the changes to occur in the insurance industry. He predicted that whole life insurance would go through some tough marketing problems and that term insurance and the newer interest-sensitive insurance, marketed largely by financial planners, would earn for the planners a larger segment of the consumer's insurance dollar. He described the new consumer this way:

> Before plunking down their money, they're asking tougher questions and demanding better value. Gone are the days when the life insurance industry was in the enviable position of being able to sell the products it wanted to sell, rather than the products the consumer wanted to buy. Gone are the days when marketing strategies could be based upon the concept that the consumer was dumb and would remain dumb.

Relationships resembling the ones ITT and other companies are arranging with banks strike fear in the hearts of some agents, according to MacDonald. However, he views the entry of banks into insurance as an opportunity rather than a threat, predicting that:

The new way of selling life insurance will create three separate kinds of agents—the traditional agent, the agent who works with the financial institution, and the financial planner.

In order for agents to survive—and they must survive if the industry is to survive—we must find a way to have the agent spend most of his time doing what he and only he can do—sell!"

That means that the only independent purveyor of financial products, including life insurance outside the income market, will be professional financial planners.

I'm talking now about the *true* financial planner. There are garbage collectors who call themselves sanitation engineers, and there are politicians who call themselves statesmen...and there are life insurance agents who put "Financial Planner" on their cards so they can hide the fact that they're really trying to sell life insurance. Or maybe they just don't want to be embarrassed at parties.

I see tremendous opportunity for the true financial planner—the person who is honest, competent, and is attempting to develop a balanced financial plan. If he's simply trying to sell insurance, the consumer will catch on.

Most true professional planners will come from law, accounting or banking, but there are a good number of professional life agents and stock brokers who should, could and will move into this field. These financial planners have an opportunity to become the true 'third professional' in personal planning, along with the lawyer and the accountant.

New Ball Game Today

In the 1970s, inflation seriously hurt cash value life insurance, making it difficult to refute Bob MacDonald, though many tried. Now, with inflation perhaps under control, it will be interesting to see if he turns out to be right about where the professional financial planner will come from in the future.

Another question some financial planners are contemplating is how far the interaction of financial planner and client should go. "Should we, as financial planners, involve ourselves with car insurance, home insurance, medical and dental coverage, etc.?"

A Software Executive Worth Listening To

One thought-leader in the growing financial planning software field is David Grace, chairman of Interactive Financial Services (IFS) in Marietta, Georgia. He believes the successful financial planner quarterback should recognize the following practicality: "We believe that the average financial planning client only wants to undress financially once."

Roger Johnson, IFS president, believes the computer will play an increasing role as a tool for the professional financial planner. He reasons, "The continuing diversification of financial products and the tax law changes will ensure that the market for financial planning services will continue to grow and change; the tidal wave of information and paperwork will continue to mount."

Property/Liability Insurance

New Emphasis

Lawrence G. Brandon, CPU, is senior vice president of the American Institute for Property and Liability Underwriters. He sees an increased emphasis on property/liability needs in the future. Here's how he sees the shift occurring:

> As I look to the future, I believe much more emphasis will be given to risk retention and risk management programs as ways of handling pure or static (as opposed to speculative or dynamic) risks. These are risks that previously were handled solely by insurance. The primary reasons for the shift from insurance to other techniques are as follows:
>
> 1. Cost savings—as the insurance market "hardens," premiums are increasing and there will be stronger incentives to turn toward risk retention or self-insurance.
> 2. Declining image of private insurance companies—there is a growing mistrust of insurance organizations by businesses.
> 3. Self-insurance fits well with the changing management style of the 1980s—the development of 'quality of work life programs' has resulted in firms hiring experts in this area. Given that level of expertise, companies will be capable of handling their own self-insurance.
> 4. Self-insurance has grown in stature—many self-insurance associations have developed and are providing more service and education to firms electing to self-insure.
>
> As businesses with low to moderate loss exposures shift to these programs, only the more volatile risks will remain in insurance programs. This will push the cost of the insurance product up, giving motivation to additional large commercial clients to seek noninsurance alternatives, and leaving insurance companies with a far less stable pool of insured exposures.
>
> Those property and liability insurance organizations that include

financial planning services as part of their total operations will be in a position to retain their customers by providing them with either insurance protection or financial planning advice to guarantee their survival in the event of substantial loss. Without financial planners, insurance organizations have nothing but insurance to offer their customers, and when that is not the option chosen, the customer is forced to look elsewhere for assistance.

It seems to me that every insurance organization today should be asking, 'What business are we really in?' If they define their function so narrowly as to limit operations solely to insurance, they will face a shrinking share of the market. On the other hand, if they see themselves as providers of financial protection, then they will position themselves to offer a variety of financial services—not the least of which will be financial planning.

Property/Casualty Expertise

Some financial planners are recognizing the wisdom of having a property/casualty expert closely available to make their financial planning practice more complete. Still, many financial planners are paying too little attention to this side of a client's financial situation, according to property/casualty consultant Dave Goodwin of Miami, Florida.

But, for the continued emergence of financial planning as a profession, Dave Goodwin is quite optimistic; here's how he sees it:

> This is a growth industry with tremendous potential. We believe there are more people in the world who need financial planning than there are people who need, for instance, a real estate broker. Of all the related professions, financial planners, as generalists, will grow larger, more quickly, and serve more people than the other financial service industry specialties.

Some Other Growth Areas

Jay Lewis of Nathan and Lewis in New York is an insurance securities executive and financial planner. He says, "For the last few years, financial planners, rather than selling, have been allocating a portion of their clients' capital to tax shelters. This will have to change, and it will be healthy when it does."

Meanwhile, Elizabeth Sims, former vice president of Delaware Funds in Philadelphia, predicts, "By the 1990s, funds will be an even more realistic investment medium, because the public is being educated with respect to mutual funds and investments in general. Anyone doing true financial planning in the 1980s will rise to the top and be grateful for starting early."

More Predictions

John Watts of Washington National thinks forward-looking financial planners should have the following uppermost in their long-range thinking:

> I think it will be essential that independent financial planners or even financial planning offices belong to a network of some sort:
> 1. to have some buying clout in purchasing financial products;
> 2. to have access to various data banks;
> 3. to have access to electronic marketing facilities.

That's how he saw things changing 10 years from now.

The Future Starting Now

During all of 1985, one question on many financial planners' minds was what effect the tax regulations proposed by the Reagan Administration would have on clients in tax sheltered investments. Before anything was decided on Capitol Hill, I asked Ben Baldwin what he thought the effect might be. He responded:

> The proposed tax regulations should continue the trend of the past couple of years, driving out tax shelters that merely reduce taxes and don't create tax liabilities. For the most part, they are economic losers or frauds.
>
> The gradual elimination of these from the market-place will make more room for the economically sound tax shelters: those that eventually create tax liabilities because they are economic winners. The long-range effect should be a flight toward quality by the consumer and more confidence in the economic quality of tax shelter products by both the consumer and the salesperson.
>
> In time, more sales of better quality tax shelters will result in positive income effects for both consumers and salespersons. I, for one, cheer this trend.
>
> There was concern over the proposed change dealing with elimination of the long-term capital gains exclusion from taxation of 60 percent of such gains, with total taxation of these gains *except* that portion of the gain attributable to inflation. This proposal has the potential of greater taxation in good times (low-inflation periods) by taxing more of the gains, or in bad times (high-inflation periods) taxing less of the gains. However, most people are willing, if not eager, to face and plan for eventual high taxation caused by wise investments that make them economic winners.

The Future from Another Perspective

While the major concern in 1985 was what effect the proposed tax changes and the growing antagonism to tax loopholes would have on the financial futures of financial planners' clients' portfolios, there was also another concern regarding real estate investment trusts.

Mitchell Hochberg, senior vice president of VMS Realty, Inc., of Chicago, addressed the issue of REITs for tax shelters or for accumulating wealth as follows:

> It is important that financial planners distinguish between 'syndicators of real estate' and real estate firms which acquire, develop, finance and manage properties, while sharing the risk and reward through syndication. Conceptually, VMS and the few firms like us are real estate concerns, not packagers of tax shelters.
>
> The favorable economic aspects of an investment—not the tax benefits—are paramount in our appraisals and purchases of real estate. A property's economic viability is the motivating factor to buy and has been determined prior to the decision to syndicate.
>
> A real estate firm like VMS buys property with three elements having to be satisfied:
>
> 1. cash flow;
> 2. appreciation potential; and lastly
> 3. tax benefits.

Financial planners should measure these elements and place their clients into those real estate partnerships which are good long-term investments, not solely tax shelters. As long as the planners conduct extensive due diligence on the sponsor and each specific product, they and their clients will come out better than less informed investors have made out in the past.

Organizations and Profession at Crossroads

In 1984 and 1985, Harold W. Gourgues, Jr., a nationally recognized financial planner in Atlanta, devoted a portion of his newsletters to observing the real dangers facing the financial planning organizations. He contended that the proliferation of organizations, the overlapping of functions, and the extra calls upon financial planners' time and money were becoming counterproductive.

From their conception, the IAFP and the college were designed to split off from the Society to guard against duplication of efforts. A great deal of synergy and division of effort was designed into what was intended as the final structure. However, in the late 1970s much of that was lost, as organization leaders, often very conscientiously, focused their efforts and decisions on doing what they perceived as best for their individual organizations, rather than what might be best for financial planners or the financial planning profession as a whole.

The National Center for Financial Education, Inc.

In 1982, the Society was reactivated as the National Center for Financial Education, Inc. (NCFE), a "nonprofit educational corporation for public education, dedicated to helping consumers do a better job of spending, saving, insuring, investing, and *planning* for their financial future, so as not to be so dependent upon social security and other government programs."

Since organizing their own foundations, the IAFP and the ICFP also are spending money in advertisements to the consumer. Now, they are even talking about educating the public, despite the fact that the NCFE already can do that more effectively, objectively and believably.

Financial Planners Shouldn't Have to Educate the Masses

To use their time effectively, financial planners should not have to educate individual prospects. They should be free to spend more of their time helping people, particularly young people, accumulate money by better financial planning and self-discipline. They also need to spend time helping their clients implement their plans; of course, they have an obligation to *explain,* but not to *educate.*

Few financial planners can afford to educate one on one. The "Dollarplan (Financial Education 101)" course, designed by Paul Richard, is ideal for groups and as such is useful as a prospecting tool. The NCFE was organized to be not only educational but also openly motivational. (For more information about its programs, write to the National Center for Financial Education, 25 Van Ness Avenue, San Francisco, California 94102.)

At NCFE, we believe it is vital that people in this country start putting a larger segment of their discretionary dollars aside for the future. Motivating and educating them to do that is our major goal. We don't advise consumers where specifically those dollars should go, suggesting that be decided by working with a financial planner. As a consumer-membership organization, NCFE has an educational posture that positions us ideally to motivate objectively and effectively—far more so than professional or trade associations, whose efforts are too often viewed as prospecting for their members.

Headed by directors Christopher Hegarty, Donald Simon, Lawrence Krause, Paul Richard and myself, the NCFE also has a 22-member board of governors, originally comprising people from the financial services industry but now diversifying into other industries. NCFE was designed to also serve as an umbrella organization to assist various segments of the financial services industry in competing more successfully with the powerful forces in our country that are trying to convince people to *spend* their money.

The ICFP, the College for Financial Planning, and more than 80 companies are already supporting our efforts to educate and motivate the consumer, but we do need more support from other segments of the financial services industry as well. They all have much to gain.

Some Positive Notes

I hope the initial synergy we designed into the financial planning organizations will be recovered. If that happens and all of the financial planning organizations work together once again, they can lead the way in bringing about real cooperation within the entire financial services industry. The banking, securities and insurance segments will be able to compete more successfully for the consumer's discretionary dollars and will no longer need to divide up the six or seven cents of each dollar, which is all that most people are currently setting aside for their future. Instead, they may be sharing 10 or 12 cents out of each dollar; what a wonderful future and retirement that could mean for millions of people.

Best of all, what a tribute that change would be to our free enterprise system, now being criticized on so many sides. Imagine millions of people approaching their retirement independent of Social Security and other governmental welfare programs. When that day arrives, financial planners will have come into their own; they will deserve much of the credit for making it happen.

PART TEN

Who's Who in Financial Planning
Financial Planners Coast to Coast

Thousands of people deserve to be included in this special section, and unfortunately, space precludes listing them all. Throughout this book, we have tried to present a picture of financial planning and its practitioners through descriptions of interviews with, and quotations from many of the financial planners who have had an impact on the development of this new profession. In addition, 31 planners, representing a broad spectrum of practitioners throughout the country, have written self-profiles in which they discuss their practices and how they view their profession. But there are still others who are well-known and competent, who were not included because of space limitations.

The Pioneers

Two groups of financial planners deserve special note. The first includes those early rebels, pioneer insurance agents blazing a trail to a new profession by becoming dually licensed in mutual funds and insurance or securities and insurance. Many of these agents were willing to accept being ostracized by their associates and even termination by their companies in order to better help their clients achieve financial goals. They weren't fortunate enough to work with the enlightened insurance executives of today. To them, I give head-table status on my list of who's who.

The other major group that deserves praise includes the early supporters of the Society for Financial Counselling, the International Association of Financial Planners and the College for Financial Planning. Fortunately, enough of them saw that a new profession was needed...and were willing to help.

Who Is and Who Was

As discussed earlier, *The Financial Planner* magazine devoted two issues in 1979 to chronicling the pioneers. The September issue focused on Jim Johnston, Lew Kearns and me. It also contained a "Who's Who in Financial Planning (1969-1979)," which included 14 others under the headline: "They Came Early...and Stayed Late". They were:

<pre>
John J. Gray   Donald R. Pitti
Lewis G. Kearns   Paul M. Shatz
John B. Keeble   Jay A. Smith
Charles D. Lowenstein   Robert W. Spenser
William F. McMurry   C. Robert Strader
Richard A. Ollen   Larry G. Wills
J. Chandler Peterson   Herman W. Yurman
</pre>

The October issue, entitled "Expanding Horizons '79," focused on the new leadership, specifically on J. Chandler Peterson as one of the outstanding leaders I recruited into the movement. Assisted by impressive educational and professional qualifications and a superior intellect, Chandler and Christopher Hegarty were frequently voted the outstanding speakers at the early IAFP national conferences.

However, I would like to note that while Chandler was president, he, Richard Venezia and Jim Lang headed a group that actually saved IAFP, financially and otherwise.

My Choices

In 1981, I was given the privilege of writing an article for *Financial Planning* magazine, entitled "Special Early Heroes of the IAFP." It was my opportunity to feature 12 people who had in my opinion done even more than they were ever credited with accomplishing. In alphabetical order, they were:

<pre>
Julius Cahn   Robert M. Leary
Richard W.A. Davis   Donald R. Pitti
P. Kemp Fain, Jr.   Val Lodholm
</pre>

H.L. "Jamie" Jamieson
Jim Johnston
John Keeble

Donald A. Simon
Jay A. Smith
Austin B. Speed, Jr.

ICFP and IAFP Officers and Committee Heads

Another segment that deserves noting comprises past and present officers in the various professional associations highlighted earlier in this book. It takes time, effort and often some expense to do a conscientious job of being an officer or committee head in a professional or trade association. Unfortunately, or perhaps fortunately, there are too many of them to list.

The First Accredited Financial Planners

The first class of CFPs was confirmed October 13, 1973; 35 of the 41 attended the first annual conferment at the University of Denver. In looking over the following names, it's not surprising that so many are still quite active in the movement and have contributed so greatly to making the CFP the coveted mark of professionalism it is today.

David L. Allard
Kay H. Baird
John M. Bulbrook
Graydon K. Calder
Charles F. Church, Jr.
Colin B. Coombs
Lavell G. Craig
W. Paul Crum, Jr.
Harold W. Dance
Joseph F. Dillman
Walter A. Durham, Jr.
P. Kemp Fain, Jr.
John C. Gebura
Jerrold Glass
Ruthe P. Gomez
Richard E. Hanson
John L. Hawkins
W. Robert Hightower
Billy Joe Johnson
Robert C. Keple
Bernard J. Kessler

Jordan M. Kokjer
Herman A. Kramer
Jerome M. Ledzinski
Ronald A. Melanson
William E. Moore
E. Claude Morgan
Bernice E. Newmark
J. Chandler Peterson
Shannon Pratt
George W. Ratterman
Joseph Ross
Gordon A. Shephard
Richard A. Stone
John Strutt
Anton van der Valk
Richard F. Venezia
Lawrence M. Vukelich
Dennis Wielech
Larry G. Wills
H. W. Yurman

The second annual conferment ceremony took place on November 6, 1974. Those who had been previously skeptical about the College staying alive seemed to relax after Jim Johnston and the College's board of trustees, headed by Fred Nauheim and Lew Kearns, had done it again. In the second class to receive the CFP designation, a high percentage played and continue to play an increasingly important role in both the profession and the organization.

Kathleen S. Albert
Diana P. Blakeslee
John C. Bloom
Thomas F. Borst
Donald A. Carlson
Raymond W. Ceton
William C. Cleveland
James C. Cusack
Daniel W. Deloney
Frank W. Eckles
George A. Gilbert, Jr.
Vernon D. Gwynne
Robert Hallum
J. C. Harris, III
James R. Hight
C. William Hoilman
George C. Huff
Charles G. Hughes
Lewis G. Kearns
David M. King
George M. Knapp
Paul D. Kreminski
Richard B. Lentz
Harry D. Mandelbaum
Leon V. Mason
Nicholas C. McDaniel
William F. McMurry
Eric H. Medrow
Charles A. Mitchell
George W. Morris
Gary N. Newquist
Donald N. Pierce
Albert S. Pitts
Philip L. Ramsdell
William H. Shaw, Jr.
L. E. Swayze
Beverly F. Tanner
Robert J. Underwood
Robert L. Ward
Gary Webster
James R. Wilcox
Aivars Ziedins

It isn't easy to take five or six courses and then pass proctored examinations in any profession. It takes a high degree of dedication and study to get a CFP; those who have or will acquire it all belong in my who's who—but none more than Jim Johnston.

The Top Four Financial Planners

As the founder of financial planning, I'm frequently asked to pick those I consider to be the nation's outstanding financial planners. Now, I would qualify the four I've chosen by noting that I really am not passing judgment on their way of preparing individual financial plans for their clients. Instead, I recognize these four people for what they've done to further the professionalism of the financial planning business.

Two for the 1970s

For the 1970s, I put J. Chandler Peterson's name at the head of the list for reasons you've already read. With him, for different reasons, I put Venita

Van Caspel. While she didn't begin as soon in helping establish the profession directly, once she started, in many ways she passed us all. Her books, her television program, her speeches and interviews made her, by 1980, one of the best-known financial planners in the nation. Undoubtedly, the people she has motivated to do financial planning must number in the thousands.

Two for the First Half of the 1980s

It's impossible to predict who will be the best-known financial planners during the latter part of the 1980s. But for the first half, I give the nod to Alexandra Armstrong on the East Coast and Lawrence A. Krause on the West Coast.

You will get to know Alexandra Armstrong of Washington, D.C., through her self-profile, beginning on page 224. I'm pleased that her credits and accomplishments make such an impressive list, as I'm sure you'll also discover when you read her self-profile.

Lawrence A. Krause has been a financial planner for 15 years. He has a broad background in investment banking, securities, tax shelters, real estate, and business management and is president of the San Francisco–based Lawrence A. Krause & Associates, Inc., a professional financial advisory/financial planning firm.

Krause frequently participates in radio and television interviews and writes a monthly column, "Krause on Financial Planning," in *California Business* magazine. He is a founding director and secretary-treasurer of the National Center for Financial Education, Inc., and was voted Financial Planner of the Year for 1982–83 by the San Francisco chapter of the International Association for Financial Planning, Inc. In 1983, he wrote a chapter in *Your Book of Financial Planning,* entitled "Financial Planning for the Professional," and in 1985, he wrote *The Money-Go-Round*. His latest effort is a book on marketing for the financial planner (Longman, 1986).

A popular speaker all over the country, particularly at financial planning functions, Larry has elevated the financial planning profession several notches. His self-profile begins on page 259.

Adjunct Faculty: Members and Educators All

"One never really learns to do until one starts to teach." I've used that saying for about 40 years, and I believe it as strongly today as I did when I first said it. I also believe, "With most people, the greatest day-to-day satisfaction comes from a life that is balanced between learning, earning and teaching," which may be why I reserve a special place in my who's who for those financial planners who serve, have served, or will serve in some instructional capacity with the College for Financial Planning or its accredited affiliates.

ALEXANDRA ARMSTRONG ADVISORS, INC.
PERSONAL FINANCIAL PLANNERS

Alexandra Armstrong, CFP
President

1140 Connecticut Avenue, NW   Washington, DC 20036   (202) 887-8<!-- cut -->

Profile of Alexandra Armstrong, CFP

I am a financial planner with two firms based in downtown Washington, D.C. The first, Alexandra Armstrong Advisors, is a registered investment advisory firm that charges a fee for financial planning and investment advice. The second firm is Alexandra Armstrong Associates, a broker-dealer registered with the National Association of Securities Dealers. Through this firm we can implement the plan the client wishes. This implementation could include investment in stocks, bonds, mutual funds, public and private partnerships, as well as the purchase of life and disability insurance.

We have 17 people in our firm including five planners besides myself. The rest provide support to produce the plan and to help implementation.

We think computers are an important financial planning tool and have invested in what we consider a state-of-the-art system with four terminals. We use the computers for sophisticated number crunching, but more importantly for client records so that we can immediately access a client's situation.

Prior to starting my own firms, from 1977 to 1983 I ran the financial planning division, and was senior vice president and principal, of a New York Stock Exchange firm based in Washington, D.C. I have a college degree, am a CFP, and worked with the New York Stock Exchange for 22 years.

We started our firms in April of 1983. Our planners, with college degrees, also have their CFPs or are CFP candidates, as are our case writers (assistants to the planners). Two of our planners have MBAs. We believe strongly in continuing education, particularly through the International Associates for Financial Planning and Institutes of Certified Financial Planners meetings, but also through books, magazines and local courses. We also believe in education for our clients, offering them an annual day-long seminar as well as a monthly newsletter.

Almost without exception, our clients come to us by referrals and are typically in the higher tax brackets. Usually they have earned, rather than inherited, whatever wealth they have accumulated. Most of our clients live on the East Coast, with the majority, predictably enough, from New York City and Washington, DC. We work particularly with corporate executives, partners in law firms and dual-income couples primarily in the 45-to-65 age range. Our fees are charged annually and are based on the complexity of a client's situation. They range from $1,000 to $5,000 and are tax deductible.

When potential clients call our firm for information, a planner explains our services. They are sent a 10-page questionnaire to fill out as well as a list of information we will need to produce a financial plan. If they prefer to meet one of us prior to providing the information, we would be glad to do so; however, most people return their information before the first meeting. When we receive the data, we review it to make sure it is complete, then we call for an appointment.

At that meeting, we review the information provided as well as ask clients their qualitative goals. This interview usually lasts about $1^1/_2$ hours. At this point, a plan is prepared. It will be sent to clients in a month, not because it takes a month to prepare, but because there are others to prepare for also.

After the client reads the plan, we get together for a follow-up meeting to explain it and answer any questions. At that point, we start implementing—that is, taking the steps to improve the client's current situation so goals are better achieved. This process is a lifelong one! We charge a renewal fee at the end of the year that is two-thirds the original fee and meet again during the year as often as necessary.

We strive to provide the best service, produce the best plan, and select the best investments possible. Our goal is to have our clients achieve financial independence as soon as they can without taking unnecessary risks.

THE EQUITABLE
FINANCIAL SERVICES

THE EQUITABLE LIFE ASSURANCE SOCIETY OF THE UNITED STATES
5 Revere Drive, Suite 500, Northbrook, IL 60062
Agent/Registered Representative

BEN G. BALDWIN, CLU, CFP
Chartered Financial Consultant

(312) 498-7111
(312) 398-1063

Profile of Ben Baldwin, CLU, MS, CFP, ChFC

How does an English major who spent seven years flying for the United States Navy become first an insurance salesman and then a financial planner?

My path to "Financial Planner/Registered Representative" has been strange and winding, as is the case with most people who call themselves financial planners. This is a result of the newness of the profession and the fact that most of us did not set out to be financial planners; we evolved into them.

I was born in Syracuse, New York, in 1936, and raised in Oak Park, Illinois, the son of an expert insurance agent in employee benefits. I received an NROTC scholarship and attended the University of Rochester in Rochester, New York, graduating with a B.A. in English in 1958. Upon graduation, I had a commitment to the U.S. Navy and extended that commitment by going to flight school. I was married to Maureen M. McGuigan in 1959 and, as is typical of every good U.S. Navy aviator family, we began having children—1960, 1961, 1962 and 1965.

In 1964, I resigned my commission and put away my wings. Over the years, Dad began to look wiser and wiser to me, in addition to being happy and successful. I joined him in the life insurance business as an agent for the Equitable Life Assurance Society of the United States in October of 1964. We bought a home in a suburb of Chicago, and I went to work with long hours, many evening appointments and phone calls. Dad's charge to me was first, "Do it on your own," so no matter what happens, you know that you can do it and can start over again; second, "Concentrate your efforts and education on helping the individual with life insurance and estate planning." Dad needed help in those areas. He would teach me and be the back-up in the employee benefit field, since that was his area of expertise. The idea was that if I could assist the corporate officers of his corporate clients with their personal affairs, and he could manage the firms' employee benefits, we could be a valuable team to a client and retain good business. We did.

From six months before entering the insurance business right up to today, my financial education has been directed toward providing greater value to clients. The education began as an interesting chore, progressed to being essential in keeping up with the needs of my clients, and has matured into a happy and rewarding obsession. It has progressed as follows:

Chartered Life Underwriter (CLU)	1964–1970
Master of Science in Financial Services	1970–1979
Certified Financial Planner (CFP)	1979–1981
Chartered Financial Consultant (ChFC)	1981–1982
Master of Science in Management	1982–

To make more of my education, in 1981 I began teaching courses leading to the CFP designation and had one class stay with me through all five courses. It was an extremely rewarding experience. The participants in that class gave me what amounted to a two and one-half hour oral exam every Thursday evening for two years, which reinforced my financial education. The students gave me the courage to teach one of the best and most challenging courses leading to the ChFC designation, Wealth Accumulation Planning, when it was first offered. For that class, I was both student and teacher.

I tried to use and organize everything that I learned and taught in these courses to benefit my clients. In the spring of 1980, my wife and I copyrighted and published the first edition of *A Baldwin System Financial Plan*.

In the spring of 1982, Delphi Industries, Inc., reviewed the Baldwin System Financial Plan, and decided that it was a good starting point for what they wanted to create: a credible, objective financial planning system that could be delivered efficiently and profitably for $1,000 per plan. Delphi Industries, Inc., hired Baldwin Financial Systems, Inc., in November 1982 to build such a plan utilizing the IBM Personal Computer. This contract was substantially complete in July 1984 with the copyrighting of Delphi's Omni-Guide Financial Plan. Efforts to market Omni-Guide to a major company are continuing.

Can you see the pattern developing from an insurance agent to a financial planner? A salesperson wishes to sell to a client. The well-informed client demands more information to make sure the products are appropriate. The salesperson seeks out answers for the client through education. Education builds confidence and, eventually, an urge to teach. Teaching educates the teacher more than the student and forces the teacher to communicate with clarity. Each small success in communication encourages the teacher to go on, the written result of which, in my case, is the Baldwin System Financial Plan. The ability to teach resulted in preretirement seminars for employees and spouses of the IBM Corporation and other organizations, and special education talks for the AICPA and the Executive Financial Planners of Price Waterhouse.

What has the business meant to me? Let me tell you the bad part first. There is never enough time to do as much as you would like to do for each client. Because you have to be self-motivated, it is easy to become obsessed and somewhat of a workaholic. The good part is that you are doing satisfying work for appreciative clients, which results in a six-figure income.

I currently am a Registered Representative of EVLICO Securities, a life insurance agent, and an insurance broker, in addition to being a financial planner and the owner of Baldwin Financial Systems, Inc., a registered investment advisory firm. I earn commissions on the sale of products purchased from me, and I earn fees for consulting work, seminars and speeches.

I try to give financial planning clients a flat fee prior to starting the creation of a financial plan. I try to be efficient enough to keep the normal fee down to $2,000 and still make a profit. My clientele is limited since my wife, Maureen, and I are the only employees; we have a real Ma and Pa business. As a result, obtaining prospects and clients has not been a problem; they come by way of referrals. The problem has been giving each one the time and attention he or she deserves for the compensation we are paid. We work with clients from all income groups. For some I am the insurance agent, for some the educator, and for others the financial planner. I am happy to work in any of these capacities. I would prefer that each of my clients have a quality financial planner, but the financial planner does not have to be me. I am perfectly happy to be a member of a client's financial planning team and to work with other planners in the client's best interest.

What does it mean to those of you interested in the financial planning profession? To me it means that if you deal in any financial product, you must have a real concern for the well-being of your client. To be interested in financial planning, you must recognize that what a client buys from you is only a part of his or her total financial situation. It must be an appropriate and productive part. It takes a great deal of education and understanding to know it all fits together and to make sure that it all works together. If you care that much and are willing to make a lifetime commitment to the education needed in order to give your clients the service they deserve, then we want and need you in the financial planning business.

THE BARRY FINANCIAL GROUP, INC.

James A. Barry, Jr. CFP
Chief Executive Officer
Admitted to the Registry
of Financial Planning
Practitioners

1499 W. Palmetto Park Road, Suite 220
Boca Raton, Florida 33432

Boca Raton (305) 368-9120   In Florida 1-800-432-3029

Securities through Asset Management Securities, Member NASD, SIPC

Profile of James A. Barry, Jr., CFP

After graduating from Burdette College in Boston, I followed my father's footsteps, selling life insurance in the Boston area for Hartford Life Insurance Company. I liked the work and was good at it, rising to the position of general agent within a few short years. But something was missing. By this time I had developed the old K.I.—killer instinct—but the opportunities for the high-level advancement I sought still eluded me.

I joined the Putnam Management Group (which oversees some $12 billion of other people's money) and developed a national financial planning program. At Putnam, while dealing with some of the nation's top corporate executives, I discovered that most people—even the most successful executives—lack the time and expertise to manage their personal finances properly. They could talk for hours about their businesses, but bring up their own personal finances and 99 percent of them would throw up their hands. They just didn't know how to handle that area of their lives, and most were too busy to learn on their own.

In 1975, I founded Asset Management Corporation in Boca Raton, Florida. The clients were there, ready and willing to listen and learn how they could achieve greater "Money Power" by using OPB (other people's brains).

I became a Certified Financial Planner and an advisory member of the National Committee of the College for Financial Planning in Denver. As a member of the IAFP, I founded the Gold Coast Chapter in Florida, and was listed in *Who's Who in Finance and Industry.*

I believe you have to promote your practice right from the beginning. You must let people know what you do and who you are. Year after year, I continuously travel from coast to coast speaking at conventions, meetings and associations in order to motivate and educate the individual to take charge of his or her financial future. Hopefully, I've done a pretty good job of getting my message across: "The American dream is alive and thriving." After all, there is no other place on this earth that offers a piece of the pie to anyone who knows how to slice it!

The perfect platform for "spreading the word" has been promotion through my frequent guest appearances on national radio and television shows as the author of the best seller, *Financial Freedom: A Positive Strategy for Putting Your Money to Work,* which is a comprehensive layperson's guide to personal financial planning.

I also host a lively financial radio talk show aired over WGBS, 710 AM, an ABC and Mutual Network affiliate, which allows me to spotlight my seminars while offering professional financial advice to a captive audience of middle- to upper-income groups who seem to feel comfortable asking me questions about their personal finances on the air without the fear I'll send them a bill. Our offices have been deluged with appointments from listeners seeking solutions to their financial problems.

I have been interviewed or quoted in *The New York Times, Barrons, Money,* and *U.S. News & World Report.* The end result has been respect and recognition i.e., a recent appearance on Latenight America, and a "live" call-in TV show from Detroit with a viewing audience covering 22 states resulted in more than 7,000 letters to our Boca Raton offices from viewers who wanted to know how they could start putting their money to work for them. Many Americans have learned how to make money, but they still need to know what to do with the money once they have made it.

After years of promoting Jim Barry and financial planning, I made the decision to change our name to the Barry Financial Group, Inc. From an office of one in 1975, we have grown rapidly to a team of 22 highly qualified financial planners, lawyers and accountants who work together. My secret for success lies in surrounding myself with other people's brains—hiring competent individuals with expertise in my areas of weakness—which allows me to work on perfecting my strong points.

We do not try to compete with the mass market approach of Sears, Prudential-Bache or Merrill Lynch, which offer limited computer advice for the small investor. We provide each client with professional in-house services and personalized attention. Computers cannot develop sensitivity for the individual's objectives, needs and goals.

Every quarter we review each client's progress, while keeping him or her informed of the latest opportunities available. This personal service is included in our fees, which are based upon the complexity of each individual's portfolio. However, in some cases there is no charge for our services.

We believe the best computer ever created is the computer that you have in your head—your brain. Our "software" package consists of past experiences being continuously updated. We cannot make today's decisions based on yesterday's software. We listen to the individual and communicate with the experts in order to achieve a successful financial plan.

It is not a matter of selling products. We guide and direct each client toward the best investment plan available for his or her needs.

My dream came true when my son, Jim, joined the group as a financial planner; we are anticipating the expansion of our company into a major south Florida financial force. The Barry Plaza is under way to serve as permanent home in Boca Raton. Meanwhile, plans for the national syndication of a cable television show is in the works. Our newsletter, *The Barry Report,* is not a "doom and gloom" report. Rather, it takes an incisive look at the market with objective, optimistic predictions and useful inside information.

I decided a long time ago that I would be successful (and I do not measure success in terms of money). My goal is to let the world know that America has something really great going for it. We are not going to fall apart and float out into the oceans. I want to make sure that every American ignores the doom sayers in the media and acknowledges the fact that our opportunity is here, in America. I firmly believe this. Further, that belief and support from my wife, Rosemarie, is why I am in the position I am today.

JOHN T. BLANKINSHIP, JR.
CERTIFIED FINANCIAL PLANNER

(619) 755-5166/455-1930

2775 VIA DE LA VALLE, SUITE 201
DEL MAR, CALIFORNIA 92014-1981

BLANKINSHIP
& ASSOCIATES
FINANCIAL PLANNING ADVISERS

ASSOCIATED PLANNERS SECURITIES CORPORATION

Profile of John T. Blankinship, Jr., CFP

I look back at the 1960s and three years as a Naval officer as preparation for what was to become my calling: advising people and businesses concerning financial obstacles in meeting attainable goals and objectives. I left Caterpillar Tractor Company in 1969 to work for a major New York Stock exchange firm, Hornblower & Weeks-Hemphill, Noyes, Inc., as a stock broker. After two years and a few months, I was called to Wall Street by Hornblower, to help develop, organize and coordinate the firm's training school for stock brokers and branch managers. Two and a half years later, I was assigned my own branch and named resident manager, vice president of Hornblower's San Diego office.

In the fall of 1974 I started my own firm and began my career as a financial planner. During the early 1970s more and more investment tools were being developed—alternatives to just stocks and bonds—that could be used in investment portfolios to help people realize their objectives of capital preservation and buying power maintenance. Investments became available, affording clients the opportunity to have interests in real estate, oil and gas, equipment leasing, research and development, and others. As inflation heated up in those years, and as interest rates became so historically high, hedges against the loss of after-tax purchasing power became a chief concern. Finding those hedges and developing a portfolio incorporating those that were also designed to preserve capital became the job of the comprehensive financial planner.

As were many other financial planners in the 1970s and even the first year or so of the 1980s, I was a one-man office with a secretary. I built my business by conducting seminars, teaching adult education classes, giving speeches to service organizations, and receiving referrals from existing clients. Tax analyses were made using a relatively simple calculator. Financial plans, anywhere from 10 to 30 pages in length, were manually typed. We did good work. But I sometimes wonder what we would do today without the computer to help us with our investment alternative analyses and our word processing requirements, and to assist us with spreadsheet software.

My practice is now 10 years old. My firm consists of five other planners plus a staff of two. Four of us have been conferred the designation Certified Financial Planner; the other two expect to complete their course of study with the College of Financial Planning within the next six months. Of the five other planners, two are graduates of Brigham Young University with degrees in financial planning; one is a graduate of the University of California, San Diego, with degrees in economics and computer science; and the other two are graduates of Cornell University and the University of Iowa, respectively. All of us are active members of the IAFP and the ICFP. I am a past president of the San Diego Chapter of the IAFP and am currently on the national Board of Directors of the ICFP. In July 1984 I was named the CFP of the Year for the West Region by the Institute. In 1985, I will be retreat dean for the Institute's Fifth Annual Retreat, its in-depth education project for members. I was one of the first financial planners in the United States admitted to the Registry of Financial Planning Practitioners in the fall of 1983; I am a Registered Representative and a Registered Principal of the National Association of Securities Dealers. My firm is licensed as a registered investment adviser with the Securities and Exchange Commission and the Department of Corporations of the State of California under the Investment Advisers Act of 1940.

My firm is completely computerized. All work except the occasional typing of envelopes is accomplished on personal computers. We have developed our own financial planning computer software, which we market to other planners throughout the country. Tax analysis and tax planning, more complicated today than ever, are performed on our computers, allowing highly sophisticated scenarios to be developed to help clients choose an investment strategy in meeting defined financial objectives.

We do total comprehensive financial planning for individuals and businesses. We have structured our practice to encompass the complete process of financial planning—plan creation, plan implementation, plan review, and updating. We do not circumvent any one phase; we never exclude any one phase. Most of our clients are referred to us by other professionals, attorneys, accountants and other clients. When a person calls, we send our company brochure, our Statement of Understanding and a four-page questionnaire. Our first interview, at no charge, is an exploratory meeting.

During that meeting and a second interview if a client relationship is established, a thorough examination of facts, goals and objectives is undertaken. During our analysis, we identify barriers to meeting goals and place in writing recommendation of alternative investment strategies. We call this examination, diagnosis and therapy, the ingredients of a comprehensive financial plan.

Implementation of the written work is possibly the most important phase of our financial planning process. A plan isn't worth the paper it's written on if it just sits on a shelf gathering dust. Implementation is taking action on the written work; the action might be only the decision to do nothing for the time being in one or more areas of the plan.

Working with our clients throughout the year, conducting reviews and updates at least semi-annually, preferably more often, is the phase in which we help our clients track the implementation of the plan, to make sure this or that investment is on schedule, and to make sure that what is being done meets current goals and objectives. People change. Our environment changes. We must remain flexible and adaptable.

My firm receives a fee for its written work. And, should the client choose to use us to implement the pan, members of my firm would earn the commissions inherent in the particular vehicles used. We attempt to mitigate the commissions whenever possible. We firmly believe that, in the not-too-distant future, most, if not all, of the firm's income will be generated by fees. Today, however, because there are relatively few investment tools that are low-load or no-load, we find it necessary to charge both fees and commissions in order not to have the client be "double billed." In any case, the client has complete freedom to choose to pay only a fee for our written plan work, implementation guidance, ongoing update, and review.

All in all, I cannot imagine a line of work incorporating so many of the disciplines I find so challenging and interesting nor a line of work generating so much satisfaction for a job well done. The financial planning process is hard work, both for the planner and the client. Making sure that every little detail of a person's financial life has been garnered is rather tedious, and divulging one's total financial life can be traumatic. But the financial planning process is also fun. It is eminently satisfying. And it lets you sleep at night.

Profile of Graydon K. Calder, CLU, CFP

When I entered the mutual fund and life insurance business back in May 1961, there really was no such thing as a financial planning profession. Many of us made a very sincere effort, however, to ferret out clients' objectives; we tried to help them develop an organized program for funding certain goals, such as family security in the event of a premature death, college education for children, and financial security at retirement. We were the pioneers in what has become one of the fastest growing professions in the country.

I worked for one of the first regional financial planning firms in the country and, in 1963, became its director of advanced training and head of what is called the Estate Planning Department. Salespeople from the company's offices throughout the 11 Western states sent me their challenging cases; then I would send them back a written report with recommendations for their client. This was the crude beginning of my writing financial plans.

I had taken some course in investments and insurance as a business major at San Diego State University but felt the need for more education in that area. Therefore, I enrolled in extension courses at San Diego State in 1964 and completed the requirements for the CLU designation in 1966.

I met Loren Dunton in 1969 and, with his urging, helped organize the San Diego chapter of the IAFP, the second such chapter in the country. After serving two years as vice president, I became chapter president the third year. I also enrolled in the first courses offered by the College for Financial Planning and was a member of the first graduating class in 1973.

There were 42 CFPs in that first class and, after the conferment exercises were over at Denver University, 35 of us met to organize a new professional association—the Institute of Certified Financial Planners. I was elected western vice president and served in that capacity for two years. That same year, I was also elected to the national board of directors of the IAFP, where I served for five years.

In 1975, the College for Financial Planning presented a national CFP of the Year award, which I shared with Jerrold Glass of Florida. The award is now presented each year by the institute; I was honored to receive it again in 1982. I rejoined the national board of the institute in 1978, was elected president in 1982, and became chairman of the board in 1983. The ICFP has grown from that small 35-member nucleus to more than 17,000 members today. I have also been privileged to serve as a member of the adjunct faculty of the College for Financial Planning for the past 11 years and am now helping the College as a member of its curriculum review committee.

I have done a great deal of writing about every phase of the financial planning process and have served as a consultant to several periodicals such as *Money, Medical Economics, U.S. News and World Report* and *USA Today*. I also write a monthly financial column for a local newspaper.

Three good friends and I formed our own company, Financial Planning Consultants, in 1973. We were the first fee-only financial planning firm in the San Diego area. However, after about a year of operating strictly on a fee basis, we reached the conclusion that most of our clients preferred to implement their plans through us as well, so we became a branch office of a full-service brokerage firm.

We keep the two companies completely separate; clients who use our financial planning services are under no obligation to place securities or other financial product orders through us in our other capacity, but the service is there for their convenience. We charge a flat one-time fee for the design of a financial plan, but will also do consulting on an hourly fee basis.

I consider myself a general practitioner, but have developed a specialty of working primarily with widows and retired people as well as those approaching retirement. My clients come entirely from referrals or call-ins.

In my experience, most people's financial plans become somewhat of a hodgepodge over the years. With the increasing complexity of our tax laws and the bewildering array of investment alternatives available today, I am convinced that a well-qualified and objective CFP can be of great service in helping the people develop a better organized and more efficient financial plan.

Bill E. Carter, CFP
President

CARTER FINANCIAL MANAGEMENT

5956 Sherry Lane, Suite 1100
Dallas, Texas 75225   214/363-4200

Admitted to The Registry of Financial Planning Practitioners.

Profile of Bill E. Carter, CFP

When I founded my own financial planning firm in 1976, I had one clear goal in mind: to create wealth, financial independence and peace of mind for clients.

In this age of tax reform, that goal is even more important. Many financial planners prepare their financial plans with the tax code in mind. While the reduction of income tax liabilities is vital, I think overall growth of a client's portfolio is more important.

Investments should have a sound basis in business sense. Simply developing a financial plan around avoiding income taxes is not enough. A good financial plan should create wealth and financial independence.

There is another side as well. Investing in strong, healthy businesses helps those businesses grow and fuels the economy, an aspect from which everyone benefits.

Growing up in rural Texas, my background stressed this common-sense approach. My parents were dairy farmers, and every decision my father made directly impacted the success of the farm. As a young man, I learned to make decisions based on facts quickly.

This tenet served me well during my college career at Texas A&M University. I was president of the student body my senior year and graduated in 1969 as a distinguished military graduate with a degree in agricultural economics.

My college days taught me more than simple economics. By working with my fellow students to accomplish things for the betterment of the student body, I learned there was more to life than monetary rewards. Helping others achieve their goals through student activities showed me that people must work together to become successful. The insight I gained from this experience has been the basis for my career since.

I feel that it is vital for the financial planning profession to take an active role in our industry and the communities we serve. We must constantly work to improve the profession, not only to help us as professionals to serve our clients better, but also to keep our communities growing. Our standard of living is directly related to how well our communities do, and it is vital that we put back more than we receive.

With this in mind, I have devoted a major portion of my career to serving the financial planning profession and the Dallas/Fort Worth community. I feel so strongly about community service that it is a requirement of all Carter Financial Management and FPS Advisory employees to take part in at least two community activities per year. Our semi-annual public service projects have included such worthy causes as the Mothers' March of Dimes, American Heart Association, and KERA Channel 13, the local public broadcasting station. While this is a requirement, the employees enthusiastically embrace this concept because they feel, as I do, that community activity is vitally important.

Personally, I have served as past president of the Dallas County American Diabetes Association and the Big "D" Toastmasters Club. I was Dallas area representative for the Texas A&M Association of Former Students and am currently on the Board of Directors of the Aggie Club. I am also a past president of the Dallas A&M club.

I enjoy a special satisfaction from my professional involvement. I am currently Chairman of the Board of the IAFP and served as president for the 1983-84 term. I have previously served on the National Board of Directors for the Institute of Certified Financial Planners and am past president of the North Texas Chapter of the IAFP. I am also a member of the National Speakers Association.

Through this involvement with the financial planning profession, I have become convinced that the Registry of Financial Planning Practitioners is critical to the growth of the profession.

Public perception of our profession will determine its future, and there have been times when this perception has not been what it should be. There have been too many people calling themselves financial planners who are really insurance or securities salespeople. There is nothing wrong with these professions, but they have clouded the financial planning profession.

The Registry brings this into sharp focus. Through strict standards of admission, the Registry enables our business to enhance its professionalism and give our clients guidelines by which they can utilize our services.

Carter Financial Management and FPS Advisory, Inc., have benefited from this strict sense of standards. I founded the firm in 1976 after working for three years as a financial planner upon my discharge as an Army officer.

Our approach has been to act as financial counselors to our clients, and many times we work on a fee-only basis. We also conduct quarterly learning seminars in which our clients may listen to experts in major investment fields such as real estate, securities and the stock market.

Financial Panning Day is the highlight of our year. Our attendance is an average of 250 clients and guests that attend a day-long Saturday session at a Dallas hotel to hear a variety of national speakers discuss topics ranging from the weather's effect on the economy and national tax policy to economic forecasts and investment alternatives.

Our clients come from all occupations and usually obtain their prosperity through their businesses and investments rather than inherited wealth. They all have one goal in common. They want to increase their net worth and create financial independence.

Carter Financial Management's planners look at each individual's situation and develop a plan that reflects a persons short- and long-term needs. Whether those needs are a secure retirement, educating their children, or maintaining their current standard of living during retirement, we keep this in mind and constantly review our client's progress, utilizing a comprehensive written annual review.

The financial planning profession is a new and exciting field that will continue to grow and prosper. Through setting standards and adhering to them, I feel our profession will continue to play an essential role in the ever-changing financial services industry.

Carter & Carter
Independent Personal Financial Planners
696 Country Club Rd.   Eugene, Or. 97401   747-2900 • 683-2900

Profile of Kenneth Carter, MBA, and Donna Carter, CFP

We both worked as savings officers and insurance specialists in local savings and loan associations prior to opening our practice in mid-1982. Kenneth, a Registered Investment Adviser with an MBA, is currently being certified to practice before the IRS. Donna is an educational consultant for the National Center for Financial Education, and a Certified Financial Planner. We are both NASD-registered for general securities and brokerage services and have our Oregon life, health, and variable annuity licenses.

Kenneth's background in education at the university level, and Donna's in financial and retirement sales and service, brought us to realize the need to have total financial planning available to all persons, at all income levels, who are serious about their own and their families' financial futures. We emphasize a tax planning approach, exploring goals, repositioning assets and/ or motivating savings, initiating living and death estate planning, and providing ongoing review and service.

Donna does some fee-basis planning, separation and divorce financial counseling, as well as counseling for companies with employees who are experiencing financial crises brought about by death, divorce or other life trauma. Our primary income is from commissions on investments and is fully disclosed. Extensive financial data gathering, projections, estate and retirement analysis, and recommendations are available if clients need and desire such services. After visiting clients, initially or over a period of time, we may together determine if a written financial plan is needed. We give clients a firm price initially. If clients are doing investments with us, we often waive these fees. Financial projections and updating portfolio presentation seldom result in a cost.

When working with clients, we stress education—sharing information and concept so clients become better informed consumers. Educational client seminars are given twice a year to help clients stay up-to-date. We also sponsor financial-related public education seminars and currently teach various short adult education classes at the local community college: "Packaging Your Student for Success" assists students and parents in securing scholarships, gaining entrance to colleges of their choice, and obtaining financial aid through various grants; "Annual Tax Update" is a community education service; "Financial Concerns of Separation and Divorce" is provided as a community college class; "Income Transferring Techniques" assists clients in funding special needs; Roundtable Lunch Sessions at local libraries are led by a variety of our associates. "Financial Planning—Especially for Women" is jointly sponsored periodically by Carter & Carter Financial, along with a women's organization, and a tax consulting firm. In addition, we write and publish a quarterly newsletter. Working with our clients' attorneys, CPAs or tax preparers further assists us in staying in touch with clients and providing them up-to-date information.

Through professional associations we stay updated and connect with other professionals such as CPAs, attorneys, tax preparers, trust officers, real estate agents, investment advisors, and timing service persons, as well as marketing and management specialists. We think that a team approach to financial planning is important; we have associates who can be called upon to provide clients with accounting and tax preparation, legal services, casualty an health insurance programs, and real estate counseling. These professionals are either in or adjacent to our office area.

Diverse, quality product availability is very important to us and gives our clients access to a large range of security and insurance products. Since our clients are generally conservative investors, we have established associations with Investment Management & Research Inc.:

1. equity and debt instruments (stocks, bonds, etc.);
2. insured certificates of deposit, money funds, and loan needs;
3. mutual fund groups (load and no-load);
4. quality partnership investment programs; and
5. quality insurance programs and annuity products, and disability insurance programs, offered through our own insurance agency.

When you go to a travel agent, you want the best buy for your money, the best route to your destination, and travel at your desired comfort level.

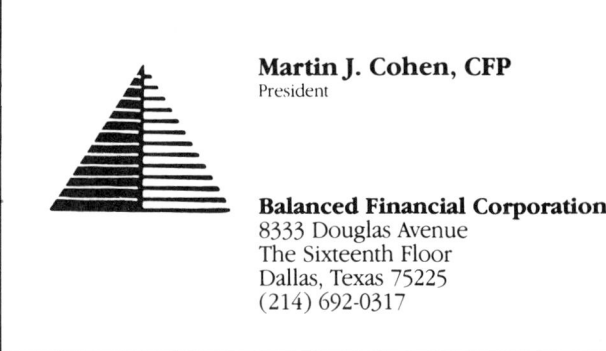

Martin J. Cohen, CFP
President

Balanced Financial Corporation
8333 Douglas Avenue
The Sixteenth Floor
Dallas, Texas 75225
(214) 692-0317

Profile of Martin J. Cohen, CFP

Major changes in our lives occur because of dissatisfaction or adversity: My entry into the financial planning profession resulted from both.

In 1960, I retired from military service and joined a Dallas-based New York Stock Exchange firm, Eppler, Guerin and Turner. For 18 years, I was associated with a fine group of stock brokerage professionals before I began my career change to financial planning. Those years of good and bad market periods, serving a broadly based clientele, were critical to the development of my investment judgment and to my learning how to deal with people.

The disastrous market period of the early 1970s hurt both me and my clients financially and led to my disillusionment with the undisciplined Wall Street approach to serving clients. I felt a the personal need for professional recognition, yet was frustrated by a broker-client relationship that did not make that kind of recognition possible.

The concept of financial planning was introduced to me in 1973, and I quickly became involved with the movement as a co-founder of the North Texas Chapter of the IAFP. I served in most offices in the chapter—twice as director of successful regional financial planning meetings, as chapter president, and then as director. This led me to a certification program with the College for Financial Planning; I received my CFP in September 1977.

I spent a year attempting to convince my brokerage firm to initiate a financial planning service, but to no avail. So, it was a critical and fruitful change in my career when I became associated with Balanced Financial Corporation in 1978. Kent Bicknell, CFP, established Balanced Financial in the early 1970s and dedicated it to serving clients in the accumulation and preservation of wealth, utilizing a disciplined financial planning process. The missing element in his fee-oriented planning approach was the timely evaluation and implementation of high-quality investments and services to assure the execution of the client's plan. What Kent learned in years of practice was that a sophisticated, comprehensive financial plan was worthless if the client did not implement the plan. Thus, Balanced Financial evolved as a custom-design financial services company, including stock brokerage, insurance, real estate, and advisory services, with a continued mission to serve clients in the areas of disciplined planning and financial management. The ultimate purpose of these services is to help clients achieve their prioritized financial objectives and personal goals.

No human being can keep up with the explosion of information involved in financial management—personal finances, taxation, estate planning, pensions, investments, insurance and law—especially when serving a diverse clientele. Balanced Financial was structured in a highly disciplined corporate fashion, utilizing team approach to leverage the client's time in the financial management process. We have built an operating staff of 30 people, including five outside members on our board of directors.

The chairman and chief executive officer, the president, and the executive vice president guide the management of the company, with each division required to have an operating plan, and each individual, a job description. The director of our financial services division supervises a cadre of account executives who coordinate the client's needs with our advisory staff and product specialists to assure the timely completion and implementation of each plan.

The client base of our company is composed of business owners, professionals, corporate executives, and affluent individuals with annual incomes ranging from $100,000 to $1 million, and with net worths of $250,000 to $30 million. We deal with an affluent, busy, and financially sophisticated clientele, who require dependable, discreet and intelligent service.

Our advisory division is a separate, fee-based division, with no requirement for our clients to utilize any products or services developed by our investment operation. Our fees are based on an hourly charge for time spent on developing a plan and creating a data base for ongoing financial management.

We spend between 30 and 100 hours per plan, including client meetings, data gathering, reading and evaluating documents, coordinating with other advisers, creating a computerized data base, writing and debriefing the plan. Fees range between $3,000 and $10,000 to develop an accurate, high-quality plan.

The financial plan is the end of the beginning of a long-term client relationship that involves financial management of the client's assets to assure the attainment of his or her goals. A modest monthly retainer is charged for continuing data gathering; each client is provided with personal monthly communication, quarterly financial reporting, and a comprehensive annual strategy to reevaluate the efficacy of the plan.

To facilitate the implementation of plans and strategies required by the client's financial plan, our Product Division provides corporate finance and due diligence services on a continuous basis, with independence afforded through ownership of our own broker-dealer. This allows Balanced Financial to respond when and where needed to the special needs and preferences of our clientele.

I serve as president of Balanced Financial and am involved in the direction of the firm's investment management services; I am also dedicated to the financial planning industry. I serve on the national board of the Institute of Certified Financial Planners and am founder and currently president of the Dallas society of the ICFP.

Profile of Stephen P. Donaldson

I graduated from Wayne State University in Detroit in 1967, following a five-year study for the priesthood. On the advice of a counselor, I entered the life insurance business. He suggested it would give me an opportunity to "help people with a missionary zeal." That was true, and I enjoyed some success, opening my own agency in East Lansing in 1969.

After several years, I concluded that although working with clients was enjoyable, two things made my career less than perfect. First of all, I didn't like the reaction my chosen profession drew from most people, including my prospective clients. Secondly, I felt I had done the most difficult part of my job in locating a prospect and motivating him or her to become a client. Since I certainly couldn't make a case for selling him or her insurance every few months, I sought out other related products to present.

My first foray was into the mutual funds arena in the early 1970s. I subsequently expanded into real estate, property and casualty insurance, accounting, and computer services. I incorporated under the name of First Financial Group, Inc., and its related subsidiaries: First Financial Realty, First Financial Insurance, First Financial Planning Services, and First Financial Computer Services. I also hired a tax attorney with investment experience to put together financial plans for wealthy clients.

I found there were not enough wealthy clients and not enough ways to solve the problems of the clients I had. I realized I had insufficient knowledge to build the company I had envisioned. Although the business grew substantially and there were offices in three cities, I concluded that I had gone as far as I could by trial and error.

Leaving the firm, I accepted an executive position in New York for one year, followed by 18 months as co-manager of one of the largest insurance agencies in the U.S. It was absolutely essential for me to work with some experienced executives to develop certain attitudes, techniques and contacts needed for my growth. You not only have to know where you want to go, you must also know how to get there.

After my arrival in Greensboro two years ago, it was ultimately very easy to make substantial, rapid progress. I had an experienced sales force with a real interest in expansion into financial planning. Bill O'Neil, our Sales Manager, became our registered principal. Don Beaty, a CPA with extensive financial planning experience, agreed to head our planning operation.

We then incorporated as The Financial Group, Inc. and began to implement our business plan. The objective? To perform fee-based financial planning for business and professional people with incomes between $40,000 and $200,000.

Our operating strategy? To develop plans that really worked—with significant tax savings and high returns from quality investments. We felt if our work was really excellent, clients would be generous with referrals. We also talked with hundreds of CPAs, showed them actual results, and made them feel comfortable with our work.

Fortunately, this strategy has worked to our expectations. Not only has our insurance production doubled, our fee and investment income now exceeds our insurance income by a wide margin. We have also been retained by a major insurance company to support its agencies in developing financial plans for clients in more than 50 cities. Our difficulty in finding quality tax sheltered investments led us to form a partnership with an experienced syndicator. We have been general partners on four real estate and two cable TV limited partnerships. We expect to raise as much as $50 million in equity in the next 12 months. We also expect that proposals made to banks will result in a joint venture to develop plans for their clients.

I'm proud of my involvement with the Financial Group, a firm committed to excellence in financial planning. Working with our broker-dealer, Sentra Securities Corp.; our insurance company, Home Life of New York; and our syndicator, United First Investors, we are able to provide superior products and get the best results for our clients. We have all the elements necessary to become a major financial planning firm. Hopefully, we will live up to our potential.

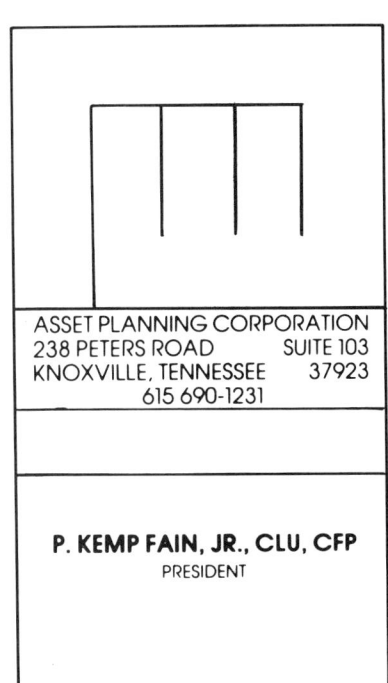

Profile of P. Kemp Fain, Jr., PhD, CFP, CLU, GRI

Before becoming a financial planner, my career was technically oriented. After graduating in 1962 from Georgia Institute of Technology with a degree in mechanical engineering, I took a technical sales job with Eastman Kodak Company. While still in college, I decided to concentrate on the marketing and managerial side of business, instead of the technical side. The "Eastman philosophy" had a very strong influence on my business career; they taught me the value of conservatism and fiscal responsibility. While with Eastman, I was able to pursue a master's degree in management at the University of Tennessee, which I received in 1970.

Early in my career, I got involved in several civic activities, one of which was a local Toastmasters Club. Through Toastmasters, I met the local manager for a regional stock brokerage firm. We became good friends, and I ultimately joined his firm as a trainee.

The stock brokerage business was rewarding to me financially, but I felt that something was missing. Instead of pushing securities, I really wanted to be a total financial adviser to my clients. I began moving toward that goal when I was recruited by Financial Service Corporation, a major financial planning firm, headquartered in Atlanta. I had heard of financial planning, but it took attendance at a seminar in Cincinnati, Ohio, to give me the courage to make a move. At that seminar, I met Loren Dunton and many other pioneers of the financial planning movement.

In fact, I was so excited that I ultimately became the very first person to enroll in the Certified Financial Planner program. Later, I helped form the first local chapter of the IAFP. Little did I realize how important these early efforts were. They helped start a major national industry. Upon receiving the CFP designation in 1973, I joined the other members of the first CFP graduating class in forming the Institute of Certified Financial Planners.

For seven years, I prospered and advanced through various sales and management positions with Financial Service Corporation. I learned much of what I know from them. But, hard times came and that company nearly folded. Because of the traumatic times we went through, I vowed to someday have my own company.

In April 1975, I founded Asset Planning Corporation (APC), which has been the vehicle for providing my style of personal financial planning and investment management to the public. With our 10-person staff, we are serving almost 500 individual, family, and company clients.

At APC, we charge fees for professional services, such as personal financial planning and investment management. For the implementation of plans, we charge fees or brokerage commissions, at the option of our clients. We always prefer to do a full-blown, written financial plan for a new client. Then, we use an elaborate, computer-assisted system to help us review and monitor our client's situation. Most of our clients are executives and professionals, but we impose no minimum income or net worth requirements. Our clients come to us from referrals, from speaking engagements, and from the University of Tennessee classes that I teach.

While building APC, I have continued to educate myself. More recently, I have also been active in my professional association, the ICFP. My service to the ICFP culminated with the chairmanship in 1984–85. I also acquired the Chartered Life Underwriter (CLU) designation, the Graduate, Realtors Institute (GRI) designation, and a PhD in business administration. In this business, one must never stop learning.

I feel very fortunate to have found the profession of financial planning. I want very much to give back to the profession a portion of all that it has given me.

DIVERSIFIED INVESTMENT ADVISORS, INC.

ROBERT W. P. HOLSTROM
PRESIDENT

SUITE 862
235 MONTGOMERY STREET
SAN FRANCISCO, CA 94104
(415) 433-5900

Profile of Robert W. P. Holstrom, JD, CLU, CFP

When I began my career as a financial analyst and planner over 20 years ago, it was not a clearly established profession as it is today. There were no educational programs, no academic guidelines, and few opportunities to exchange techniques and tactics with others in the field. To establish a career, my self-designed approach was based, of necessity, on combining my educational background with my work experience.

As an undergraduate in college, I had studied business and industrial engineering and had gone on to graduate school for a law degree. I was preparing myself for a future in law when military service changed the direction my career was headed. Immediately after receiving my Doctorate in Jurisprudence, I was called to active Naval Air Intelligence duty. After the Korean War, I further served as a legislative and legal liaison officer in the Office of the Chief of Naval Operations in Washington, D.C. It was through this broad-based, high-level military exposure that I first began to see opportunities opening up in the dramatically new financial planning profession.

When I resumed civilian life, I quickly established myself in a Washington, D.C., firm specializing in accounting and tax consulting for small businesses. There I developed contacts and a clientele that could participate with me in this new endeavor.

Soon after, I was fortunate to join a large financial analysis firm in San Francisco, which later became known as one of the pioneers of the financial planning profession. My eight-year association with this firm helped to hone my investment skills. I supplemented their excellent training program with numerous courses in finance, securities, and retirement and estate planning.

To round out my academic background, I completed the Chartered Life Underwriter (CLU) program and later acquired a Certified Financial Planner (CFP) designation. I also obtained a California real estate broker's license. During this busy period, I authored a series of six lectures on Investment Analysis and Planning for the University of California Extension Program, which I presented semi-annually for several years.

In 1970 I put my educational background and the financial skills and expertise I had acquired to work for me in my own firm, now called Diversified Investment Advisers, Inc., which specializes in in-depth financial analysis and planning. As in all investment programs, the success of the planning directly relates to the wisdom of the investments. The various investment recommendations we make are implemented through our own broker-dealer affiliate, Managed Securities Corporation.

Diversified Investment Advisers, Inc., does not charge for an initial consultation. Our fee is based on a percentage of the net assets, with a $1,500 minimum cost. Managed Securities Corporation charges the customary brokerage fees.

As president of these corporations, I personally meet with new clients, help them gather and organize their financial data, and formulate an investment plan for them based on the financial goals and objectives. With my planning department, we search out diversified investment opportunities for our clients. We have been very successful in arriving at innovative solutions to their special financial challenges.

Over the years, my leadership roles in various civic and charitable causes have often put me in contact with new prospective clients. However, most of our clients are referred to us by other clients or by other professionals. Typical clients generally have an approximate net worth of a million dollars and incomes often in excess of $100,000 per year. Our clients include leaders of business, top professionals, and distinguished academic scholars, as well as widows and retirees.

In my opinion, there is no "quick fix" or secret to wealth. Wealth is available to those patient enough to plan and implement. The benefits of a thorough financial analysis, together with wise plan implementation, can be enjoyed sooner than most expect.

Profile of Charles G. Hughes, Jr., MA CFP

Eight people are coming for dinner next Friday evening; it's an important occasion for social, career or family reasons. We wouldn't think of waiting until Friday morning to check the freezer; or begin flipping through the recipe book over coffee at lunch that afternoon; or look in the spice rack at 6:30 P.M., only to find we're out of a critical ingredient.

If it's important, we plan. We plan vacations and long weekends. We plan the shrubs surrounding our house and the furniture in the house. And we don't wait until Friday afternoon to visit the supermarket and the butcher for an important Friday evening dinner.

Financial planning is nothing more than an application of these same principles of organization, knowledge and discipline for the purpose of achieving specific personal/financial objectives. These goals are attained by arranging either income or assets so that they are used more efficiently and effectively. A good meal is the proper blending of ingredients. A comfortable room is the effective arrangement of furniture, color and light. And an enjoyable vacation begins by arranging time to reach the airport before the plane departs.

Why is there such an interest in personal financial planning? Our educational and capital system motivates and prepares us to earn, but not to manage once we've become successful earners. The wealthy have been known to receive financial advice for years. Business obviously employs financial planning techniques. In fact, if business doesn't plan, its chances for profit and success are greatly diminished. With planning, individuals and businesses alike create the most favorable circumstances for success. Because our financial lives have grown more complex and less certain in recent years, seeking financial planning advice is no longer a need arising from wealth, but rather a necessity in order to accumulate wealth. And, wealth is nothing more than financial independence and security.

These attitudes about the concept of financial planning and its value to individuals have influenced the type and variety of financial planning services offered to clients by the C. G. Hughes Company. I believe virtually everyone needs and will benefit from some form of personal financial planning. And because of the complexity of the issues and circumstances today, an individual probably needs a professional adviser.

The C. G. Hughes Company offers three types of financial services: personal financial planning advice and reports, personal financial counseling, and specific financial management services. Personal financial planning advice is in the form of a written report, which is either a comprehensive financial plan or a financial focus report. A comprehensive plan treats every component of a client's financial profile in detail, with specific observations, recommendations, and plan of action. On the other hand, a financial focus report addresses a limited number of issues, such as financial statements, cash management, investment management, tax planning, capital needs preparation for a child's education, or retirement. There is no minimum income or estate/asset requirement for a focus report. However, there is a minimum income requirement of $100,000 or estate/asset value of $500,000 for an individual—$1 million—for a family, for a comprehensive plan. The fee for these services is based upon the types of service, the amount of time needed to provide the service, and the amount of income or assets involved in the planning.

A financial planning client receives the following services:

- confidential personal information-gathering interview;
- analysis of personal and financial data, objectives and goals;
- preparation of written report;
- presentation of report;
- presentation of follow-up consultation;
- semi-annual update; and
- annual written financial review.

Some clients may not require the details of either financial planning report. Certain events or circumstances may dictate a series of financial counseling sessions instead. This is often the case when a particular event has or will occur, such as pre- or post-retirement, a death or divorce, the distribution of a sizable estate, the need to review various insurance coverages, or tax planning strategies and alternatives. This counseling is provided on a fee-for-service basis at an hourly rate with any advice summarized in writing.

The financial management services that are available to clients deal with two specific programs: a monthly expense/cash accounting system, MECA, which is a computerized cash management program; and a monthly consolidated asset statement, CAST, which monitors the investment results of a diverse portfolio of assets on a monthly basis. The fee for these services is established on a project-by-project basis.

Financial planning and counseling advice customarily involve specific recommendations that require the assistance of other professional advisers. Depending upon the nature of the client's circumstances and needs and the recommendations, these professionals may include attorneys, accountants, risk managers and underwriters, pension consultants and actuaries, and licensed investment representatives or real estate brokers. C. G. Hughes Company is not prepared to provide professional advice in all of these areas, especially those requiring particular expertise, education and licenses. However, as a licensed securities representative and insurance agent, I am capable of assisting a client in certain securities and insurance-related transactions. The use of these services is entirely at the discretion of a client.

I have been involved in the financial services industry since 1971, after serving as both a teacher and administrator in higher education. My formal education led to a bachelors and two masters degrees, while my professional education includes the Certified Financial Planner designation conferred by the College for Financial Planning. After spending almost 10 years with the Oppenheimer investment firm, I left to start the C. G. Hughes Company in 1981.

The design of these financial planning services is, on the one hand, the result of the types of clients C. G. Hughes Company serves, which include small-business owners, professionals, and career individuals as well as a growing number of pre- and post-retirement clients and widows or widowers. On the other hand, my experience as an educator before entering the financial services industry has influenced the structure of these services so that they are simple, presented in an easily understood format, and designed around the needs of the client with the objective that the client becomes increasingly self-sufficient.

The majority of clients now engaging C. G. Hughes Company for some form of financial planning or counseling have come to us through referrals from existing clients or other professionals, such as attorneys, accountants or bankers. This network is growing because of my professional involvement. I have served on the faculties of New York University, College of Mt. St. Vincent, the College for Financial Planning and the Center for Financial Studies. Serving as an officer on the board of the Institute of Certified Financial Planners has enabled me to address other professional associations, such as the National Council of Savings Institutions, California Credit Union League, American Association of University Professors, as well as to write for such publications as *American Banker* and *Bottomline*. Quotes on financial planning have been featured in *Money Magazine,* and *New York Times, Physicians Financial News,* and *Medica Magazine;* I've also appeared on network and cable television. My financial-related involvement extends to a politically appointed position as treasurer of the Incorporated Village of Brightwaters, New York. I have been honored with inclusion in *Who's Who in Finance and Industry* and *Who's Who in the East.*

I believe the client is the ultimate beneficiary of a professional who is involved, since the involvement exposes the professional planner to new and growing trends in the practice of financial planning and broadens the planner's base of knowledge and experience.

The achievement of well-defined personal financial goals is made possible because the planner, client and client's other advisers work in tandem for this purpose. The planner must be knowledgeable and competent; the client must be informed. Therefore, any effort to educate the public increases the possibilities of success.

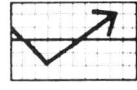

312 • 323-3143
312 • 773-1510

H. W. KASEY JONES
PRESIDENT

Re-Direct Services Inc.
414 Plaza Dr. • Suite 301 • Westmont, IL 60559
810 Arlington Heights Road • Itasca, IL 60143

Profile of H. W. Kasey Jones

I founded Re-Direct Services on the principle that average American consumers do not get proper information about the impact of financial management on their lives. Most people are surrounded by the "traditional" financial services: bank, thrift and/or insurance companies. Most often they are strongly influenced by the usually poor advice that they get from these areas when investing or controlling their money. Old sayings like, "It takes money to make money" keep the masses in line doing precisely the wrong thing during their early years with their few discretionary dollars. During the middle years, home, business and family eat up all of our time and most of our money. Suddenly at 45 or 60, Mr. and Mrs. Middle America come out of the ether, make poor investments looking for large returns, put away "something," hoping that it will be enough, or throw up their hands in frustration and do the same thing they've always done: nothing! We felt education was necessary, as well as someone who would push the consumer to make the most important step—the start.

    We needed a target, something that could cause the consumer enough emotion to overcome inertia. We selected life insurance that had been sold with little or no planning. We find old products still in force with outdated interest assumptions and mortality tables, a general lack of understanding on the part of the consumer, and greed as the apparent motivator for the agent and company.

Even with the restrictive and ridiculous replacement laws, we found that the market was tremendous, but we couldn't hire experienced agents. They knew our business wouldn't work; they wanted more income per sale and were really brianwashed on "permanent" insurance, so we created agents. We have developed classroom and field training, sales meetings, and award programs. We also developed a multicontract commission system, so they could see rapid progress. We allow every agent to recruit and earn overrides on people that they train to build a business within the business.

Has it worked? In 1980, we had a handful of part-time agents and produced 150 contracts. In 1984, we are operating two offices with three more on the drawing board. Thirty of our 80 agents are full time. We will write in excess of 2,000 life contracts this year. And we're not happy, because we could be doing more.

For the planning side of our programs, we use annuities. They are simple, secure and safe for our clients. Our staff also can be easily trained as to proper application for our troops. Each initial interview with a prospective client ends with a proposal information sheet that is returned to the office. That sheet is reviewed with a manager before any illustrations or proposals are ordered. Many people we call on have money in low-interest passbook savings accounts or NOW accounts. Others have cash values in their insurance that can utilized more effectively. We represent a variety of products from several companies and attempt to match the products to the clients' needs. As an example, we produced over $5 million in annuity premiums in 1984.

As Re-Direct and the consumer are both maturing, we realize that our product mix and our service will be changing in the future. The industry is responding to the consumer's needs; consumers are slowly getting the proper information about money management. Without some people like us to get them started, a number of consumers will never need or be able to afford a full financial planner. We are very excited about the benefits of our services to our clients.

Education is the key. That young person in school or at least in the late teens or early 20s can do dramatic things over a period of years. We need to continue to find ways to help them. The people who begin in any business are taking their first steps toward becoming financial planners. I'm sure some of my people will grow to become leaders in the profession.

DAVID M. KING AND ASSOCIATES, LTD.
INDIVIDUAL AND BUSINESS FINANCIAL PLANNING

DAVID M. KING, CFP
(913) 625-7393

KING FINANCIAL CENTER
103 W. 13TH ST.
HAYS, KANSAS 67601

Profile of David M. King, CFP

I guess you could say I'm one of the "old timers" in the financial services industry. I started out in 1950, after graduating from Emporia State University of Emporia, Kansas, with a bachelor of science degree in commerce. At that time, I went into a management training program with one of the major life insurance companies. I soon discovered that the life insurance industry, back then, gave no credibility to any other form of investment.

Soon, Uncle Sam decided I should go on active duty with the U.S. Marine Corps. After my discharge, I returned to the insurance business, stayed 2½ years, and then resigned.

Like many other people, I tried my hand in a couple of business ventures. In 1957, I learned about mutual funds and joined one of the major mutual fund distributors. It wasn't long before I realized that my clients had insurance as well as investment needs. In 1959, I became dually licensed for both investment and insurance products and wrote my first financial plan that year, which dealt with investments, insurance, and estate planning. Going back now and looking at those plans (yes, I still have copies in my files), I see how *very* basic they were and how little they resemble the plans we do today.

As far back as the 1960s, some of my acquaintances began talking about the need for financial planning. It's a great pleasure to see the movement grow to its recognizable importance today. My early commitment to the financial planning concept led me to be actively involved on the national level for many years. I am a past president and chairman of the board of the Institute of Certified Financial Planners. Currently, I am serving a two-year term as chairman of the board of regents of the College for Financial Planning. I completed my CFP work in 1974 and was in the second class to receive this professional designation from the college.

Today, David M. King and Associates is a small firm with three CFPs, two planners in training, a para-planner, and a support staff of six, with in-house computer support as well. Our goal is to help our clients achieve their financial objectives. We currently serve more than 300 active clients throughout the Midwest. Our associates are also fully licensed in both investments and insurance. Our investment broker is Investment Management & Research, Inc., a wholly owned subsidiary of R.J. Financial Corporation of St. Petersburg, Florida. This gives our associates the ability to implement any investment decision desired by the client.

My professional clientele is primarily made up of educators and business and professional people in the mid- to high-income levels. Our firm has clients ranging from the young career person just starting out to the senior citizen, who needs estate planning, income planning, and solutions to a wide range of other planning problems.

Many of our clients come to us through referrals from satisfied clients or from attorneys and accountants with whom we have worked.

Our compensation structure is based on a fee schedule and a fully disclosed commission arrangement. During the past 12 months, our fees for financial plans have ranged from a low of $400 to a high of $3,600 per plan.

In our firm, we specialize in giving highly personalized, efficient service to each and every client.

Lawrence A. Krause, CFP
Chairman of the Board

Profile of Lawrence A. Krause, CFP

In the early days, financial planning knowledge was acquired only through experience. That is, there was no formal training—one learned by doing.

My financial planning "doing" and career was essentially inaugurated in 1962, one year following graduation from the University of Iowa. At that time, I formed and headed Inventory and Business controls, Inc., a business consulting firm, in Waukegan, Illinois. From there, and for the next five years, I was a real estate broker in Rockford, Illinois, concentrating primarily on investment and commercial properties. But then the lure of the stock market called, and in 1968 I became an Account Executive with a national member firm of the New York Stock Exchange. It was while I was there that my education became strengthened in areas of tax and estate planning. The firm had enrolled me in special training courses locally and even sent me around the United States to attend various tax classes. While traveling, I met San Francisco—and left my heart. Thus, in 1970 I moved to the city, and while still with a brokerage firm, commenced applying my knowledge in areas beyond the stock market.

I really wasn't a very good stock picker. But that was okay, for I preferred to work with clients conceptually. A yellow tablet was my drawing board, and upon it I would demonstrate to clients the benefits of coordinating and integrating their entire investment picture with their personal financial goals. I was successful in helping my clients, and my clientele grew. In

1974 the oldest regional brokerage firm west of the Mississippi, Sutro & Co. (now 127 years old) hired me and provided the opportunity to formalize what I had been doing informally. I created and ran the Coordinated Financial Planning Department to provide financial planning for the clients of some 200 Sutro brokers. That department was considered to be one of the first comprehensive financial planning departments in a member of the New York Stock Exchange.

While at Sutro, I conceived the firm that I now head. In 1979 I founded Lawrence A. Krause & Associates, Inc., to provide financial planning and advice primarily for upscale clients. When I formed my company, Carol A. Wright, whom I hired at Sutro, joined me. She was, and is, one of the best financial planners I know.

Carol's and my goal was then, as it is today, to intelligently preserve our clients' asset purchasing power and opportunities to reduce their tax liability. Since our planning is highly tailored to the individual, we spend an inordinate amount of time attempting to gain personal insights into his or her special needs. For example, during our data discussion session, there will typically be two members of the firm present, yet we charge only for one person's time. We place great value on client relationships, believing if we provide a genuine service, our clients will remain with us "forever." However, because we charge an hourly fee, we state in writing that if a client does not feel that he or she has received value (and we make no attempt to define "value"), then that person owes us nothing. If we can't provide value, there surely won't be a long-term relationship—so we back what we stand for.

All of us at Lawrence A. Krause & Associates, Inc., have that same commitment. The firm is a San Francisco–based firm comprising four professionals (with MBAs, masters degrees in taxation, CPAs, CFPs...and more), a para-professional, and a staff of five. LAK is a firm concerned about people and their assets.

I have always found it stimulating, helpful and satisfying to engage in outside activities that are at least indirectly related to some aspect of the financial services industry. After I became a Certified Financial Planner in 1978 and became a member of the Institute of Certified Financial Planners, I joined the San Francisco chapter of the IAFP. In 1979, I assumed the presidency and was reelected to that position for a second year. Following that tenure, I became chairman of the board.

In 1982 I was voted by my peers the Financial Planner of the Year, an honor I still highly cherish. And in 1983, I was among the first individuals in the United States who successfully met the qualifications for admission to the Registry of Financial Planning Practitioners. Since that time, I have become a faculty member, an adjunct professor, and am on the advisory committee at three separate universities. I still maintain all three positions. In addition, I am on the advisory board for two separate financial publications and am a contributing editor for a third.

In 1982, I helped found and still serve on the Board of Directors of the National Center for Financial Education and also joined the board of directors of the American Cancer Society in San Francisco.

While the firm and my practice have continued to grow, I still find time to remain happily married to my wife, Donna, and be a doting daddy to my two little princesses, Alexis and Danielle. I also find time to lecture throughout the United States and to write. My book, *The Money-Go-Round,* was published and nationally released by Simon & Schuster in September 1985. I also co-authored a second book on how financial planners can better market their services, which will be released in 1986. In addition, I write a monthly column entitled, "Krause on Financial Planning" for *California Business* magazine, America's largest regional business magazine.

I find that writing is a give-and-take process. I enjoy providing knowledge to benefit others, but writing also forces *me* to keep abreast of the latest financial information and planning techniques. I have no regrets. The seven years of writing these columns is but another step to my learning by doing.

Vincent A. Lazara, Ph.D.
Certified Financial Planner

Prudential-Bache Securities

Prudential-Bache Securities Inc.
3420 East Broadway, Tucson, AZ 85716
602 327-7311

Profile of Vincent A. Lazara, PhD, CFP

My own approach to the financial counseling profession is twofold: educational and practical.

Let me first explain the educational side. My efforts in this regard are both formal and informal. In the area of formal education, I attempt to do my best to promote the CFP program, since it embodies the ethical and educational standards that I believe are the prime prerequisites for doing professional financial planning. By acting as CFP program coordinator for my IAFP chapter, I recruit qualified faculty and help ensure that the scheduling and curriculum information is disseminated both locally and to the College for Financial Planning. I also teach courses in the CFP program as an adjunct faculty member of the college. Over the last few years I have taught CFP I: Introduction to Financial Planning; CFP II: Insurance Planning; and CPF III: Investment Planning. I try to find time to teach at least one course per year.

In the area of informal education, I have been giving talks on financial planning for several years to local associations, including corporations, the CLU Association, CPA groups, and the Bar Association, as well as conducting public seminars on financial planning for the brokerage firms at which I have been employed. These talks have been designed to provide those who might seek financial counseling with some background about true financial planning and how to go about obtaining it.

On the practical side, my financial planning practice works on a commission-only basis with a major brokerage firm (Prudential-Bache Securities, since November of 1982). At the educational public seminars that I conduct for my firm, I offer one free hour for a financial consultation to determine if I can be of service to a potential client. Any interested parties are given a thorough questionnaire to be completed prior to our meeting, which details every aspect of their financial life in both quantitative terms (e.g., income, expenses, assets, liabilities, insurance, and tax return information) and qualitative terms (how property is titled, financial goals, etc.).

After interviewing prospective clients and reviewing this questionnaire, I determine whether or not I can assist them in the capacity of an investment planner in the context of *total* financial planning. If so, I offer to do detailed investment planning on a no-obligation basis. My planning covers all relevant financial concerns, such as IRAs, insurance, tax shelters, and educational funding. I work where appropriate with the client's attorney, accountant or insurance agent, either directly or indirectly. In this regard, I provide a written plan, including all personal financial statements and relevant quantitative analysis.

I am compensated by commissions generated by any investments the client chooses to make through my firm. (This is why I work with a major firm like Prudential-Bache Securities. It affords a virtually unlimited variety of investments, from CDs and government securities to real estate, stocks and bonds, mutual funds, insurance and annuities, as well as gold coins, commodities, and options.) If I find that my services are not relevant to clients' needs, I try to steer them in the direction of other professionals whose services may be more appropriate, whether they be budget counselors, attorneys, accountants, insurance agents, or whatever.

In closing, I would like to discuss briefly my hopes and apprehensions regarding the future of the financial counseling profession. As I anticipated several years ago in light of the proliferation of financial products that had been gradually emerging over the years (such as varieties of limited partnerships, mutual funds, and life insurance programs, just to name a few categories), the idea of financial planning is being used increasingly often by those who market these products. My hope is that genuine *total* financial planning, practiced by honest, qualified planners, will become the predominant method by which an informed public will allocate their investment dollars. My fear is that the current trend toward paying lip-service only to financial planning, by using it as a mere catch-phrase to market products, will become a more predominant factor in duping people into thinking their financial needs have been truly satisfied. These, of course, are the reasons I have wholeheartedly lent my efforts to the NCFE programs.

IDS/American Express Inc.
IDS Life Insurance Company

MASTER MILLIONAIRE CLUB

JAMES E. MOSS, CFP
QUALIFIED CORRELATOR-FINANCIAL PLANNING

4444 RIVERSIDE DRIVE SUITE 101   BUS. 818-843-0622
BURBANK (TOLUCA LAKE), CALIFORNIA 91505
AN AMERICAN EXPRESS COMPANY

Profile of James E. Moss, CFP

Many people have asked what I did before I became a financial planner. Basically, I attended the University of Southern California with the objective of becoming a stock broker and therefore majored in economics with a minor in finance. After attaining my AB degree from the University of Southern California in 1949, I realized that I did not want to be a stock broker for several reasons. I did not want to be a telephone salesman and also felt that, even with my accredited education, I did not have the knowledge to recommend to my prospective clients what stocks to buy, when to buy them, and when to sell them. Therefore, I started investigating different investment management companies that had investment managers whose full-time job was to manage people's money and invest their money with the objective of attaining their financial goals. After extensive research, I applied to go to work for Investors Diversified Services, Inc. Fortunately, they hired me!

To develop a clientele and because of my age (30) at the time, I asked the people that I called on to refer me to their parents and/or the people they worked for, who were in an older age bracket. Because of my excellent referrals, I was able to begin financial planning for my clients with the objective of college education for their children, going into their own business, and if the aforementioned were accomplished, coming up with tax savings ideas to attain greater financial success in their retirement years. Eventually, IDS began using the same approach with a personal management brochure that I helped coordinate, which was released in 1974–75.

I did not charge for my services for financial planning but received my income based upon the investments my clients made with me and IDS/American Express, Inc. Today, the company does charge a fee for complete financial planning, which ranges from $250 to several thousand dollars based upon the net worth and total evaluation costs to complete the full financial plan.

The majority of my prospects are personal referrals from existing clients. Since I have been with the company, for 30 years, most of my clients are 55 to 90 years of age and were in a high income tax bracket before financial planning. Also, I work with corporations on pension and profit sharing plans, deferred compensation, and "key man" protection for the other employees of the company.

Looking back on my 30 years in the business, I reflect upon the financial problems that people faced then and realize that times have not changed, because people who today need financial planning face the same problems. When I began in this business I did not realize that I was trying, in an unprofessional manner, to do financial planning. I guess at that time I was a typical salesperson who tried to sell just a product. Therefore, in the beginning I would do most of the talking, instead of listening to the needs and desires of the prospective client. As more products became available, including life insurance with IDS/American Express, I found that I should start listening to the needs and desires of the prospect in order to show him or her the different ways to accomplish financial goals. To do this, I started using a financial inventory sheet and, rather than just calling on a person to sell a product, I found out his or her needs and then came back with recommendations of products to fulfill those needs. I now had truly realized that I had to do more listening and less talking!

To obtain credibility in my community, I found that I needed to join different community activities. I also found that it was wise to join professional groups such as the Life Underwriters and Sales and Marketing Executives to increase my sales ability and knowledge.

In the past 10 years, due to tax changes, etc., I realized that I should obtain more education in the overall financial field. It was for this reason that I attended the College for Financial Planning and obtained a CFP. I also have to constantly devote much time to reading the different financial publications I subscribe to in order to keep up to date on the ever-changing world of financial planning.

People are becoming more aware that in order to accomplish their financial goals they must have financial planning. Therefore, I believe this particular field will become one of the major industries in America as future years come upon us.

PENNINGTON/BASS COMPANIES

Lee D. Pennington, CFP
CERTIFIED FINANCIAL PLANNER

916 Main · Suite 706 · Lubbock, Texas 79401 · 806/765-7471

Profile of Lee D. Pennington, CFP

"Lee D. Pennington, born October 3, 1930, in Oklahoma City to Lee and Fannie Pennington, their only child." We were of a lower socioeconomic background with reasonably decent education opportunities. I graduated from high school, junior college, served three years in the Marine Corps, and had additional work at Oklahoma University and Southern Methodist University in finance and insurance.

    I began selling life insurance while a student at Oklahoma University. It was difficult and uncomfortable for me to make this transition from a background of physical work. It seemed almost dishonest to earn so much money by selling and not by "working." My father worked physically hard most of his life. He believed salespeople were glib con artists and not to be trusted. This made it extremely difficult for me, since my father's opinion was important to me. I continued to sell in spite of his feeling. I wanted to be a salesman. I wanted this badly. I had enough success in the early days to be considered a "real comer" in life insurance sales and was soon offered an opportunity to go into home office work for a major insurance company. During the next 13 years, I worked through all the chairs—salesperson, home office supervisor, home office recruiter, assistant training director, manager of an agency office, assistant director of agencies and regional vice president.

    In 1967, while attending the Life Insurance Agency Officers School in

Hartford, Connecticut, I began to feel some tremendous changes taking shape; I was not sure when or if the life insurance industry would ever be willing to change. During most of 1968, I struggled with the ideas of this change and where I might economically fit in the future.

In the summer of 1968, I visited the Financial Service Corporation headquarters at the insistence of my good friend and mentor, Bill Kingsbery. I was very impressed with the concept and the developed methodology of that time.

September 1, 1968, I became associated with FSC and started attempting to become a financial planner. From that time forward, this profile is no longer singular but mixed with many other people who have contributed in some significant way toward what success I have had. Most of those will not be mentioned, but some must be for the profile to be authentic. The most important person of all is my wife, Beth, who has allowed me to work the hours necessary and given me the freedom to do so without worry about what effect this would have on our relationship. Without this contribution, nothing else would have been possible.

In 1968, I began my financial planning career. After the first full year in financial planning, I had earned in take-home commissions the largest income of my working life—over $32,000. I had found my life's work. I worked hard and diligently learning this new and exciting method of solving people's economic problems. It was a joy to offer more than one solution to economic problems. I made some major errors in judgment, but had a great many successes as well.

In 1971, I had the great joy of having Mark Bass join me as a "gofer." This only lasted a short while until he became an assistant, an associate, and then a partner. Throughout the balance of the 1970s, Pennington/Bass as a team continued to study, grow, develop and attempt to be on the cutting edge of the expanding financial services industry for our clients.

The basic philosophy toward our clients is the Golden Rule. This is enacted by using certain methods which permeate all the Pennington/Bass companies. These methods are as follows:

1. *Never experiment on clients.* This means not implementing with products that are unproven in the marketplace.

2. *Learn the best and worst of a particular investment situation by first investing in it ourselves.*

3. *Realize people's economic assets are almost as important on a surface level as their family.*

4. *Be totally straight-forward with prospects and clients.* When mistakes are made, frankly admit them and never attempt a cover-up of any kind.

5. *Abide strictly by the law as we interpret it in the best interest of the client.*

6. *Never quit trying to do better.*

In the years 1968 to 1971, I didn't concentrate on anything but personal growth. My goal was to be the best financial planner I could be. I was thrilled when I could join the society, the forerunner to the IAFP. I was delighted with the formation of the College for Financial Planning. (I was in the 1974 graduating class.) When the Institute of Certified Financial Planners was founded, I felt at last we were on our way toward professional recognition and the establishment of ethical standards. The Registry was one more step toward full accreditation, and I am delighted to have become a member in 1984.

During the period from 1971 to 1978 while Mark Bass, CFP, CPA, completed his education, we worked at developing a client base in West Texas and in Houston. In March 1974, we founded Associated Financial Planners, Inc., which is a registered investment adviser and our first company. We utilized this company to charge fees for financial planning. In addition, this firm also does portfolio management for a great number of our clients. Our relationship with a bank was established in 1975. This was nothing more than a referral system by the major officers of the bank so that their clients might have what they felt was the best in financial planning available.

I did the contact work, the data gathering, the presentation, and implementation. Mark initially wrote the plans. He did this from a format similar to the one used at FSC. We had Mark, a secretary, and me in the office. In 1976–77 we added Sharon Goldston, CFP, to write cases and free Mark to start developing his own clients. Sharon wrote and developed cases for us for five years, and much of the format and methods we currently use are her creation. She is now a very successful Registered Representative in Pennington/Bass Companies. In 1975, Mark became a CFP, and in 1978 he became a CPA and a full-time professional financial planner.

In the past six years, the Pennington/Bass Companies have grown and developed in a way we never expected. Mark and I continue to be significant producers of all the financial planning services and products with the companies. We develop our basic management guidelines each year during a three- to four-day meeting in the Rocky Mountains. Either of us can make major management decisions as long as we stay within the guidelines. I have grown tremendously as a person, as a producer, and as a leader during these years. We have made some mistakes, but we have had mostly victories. Our firms have grown from just myself to 27 people in some capacity within the Pennington/Bass Companies. In 1984, we had the following companies doing various financial service functions:

- Associated Financial Planners, Inc. is our registered investment adviser firm, which does fee-only financial planning and portfolio management. This firm is self-sustaining and makes a small profit.

- Pennington/Bass Equities is our broker-dealer, and it performs a wholesaling and manufacturing function. It is also self-sustaining as well as profitable.
- Pennington, Bass & Associates is involved in insurance, annuities, tangibles and collectibles and is self-sustaining as well as profitable.
- AFP Insurance Agency, Inc. is an independent fire and casualty agency. It is growing and is self-sufficient and profitable.
- AFP Realty is a real estate brokerage firm.
- Soupbone Enterprises is an investment partnership between Mark and myself.

All the firms operated well and within a flexible budget. We have the state of the art in computer hardware and software for all phases of our business.

In 1984, our total firm income from all sources will be in excess of $2 million. Most of this will be distributed to the employees of the companies who have made such a fabulous contribution to our growth. We will end the year with seven CFPs, four CPAs, one tax attorney, three CLUs, and several more in the educational process as part of the developing Pennington/Bass Companies.

Lee D. Pennington, CFP in only a part of this very fine group of people who are together because we truly like and respect each other. Our standards are the same, our values very similar, and our goals well defined. Our objective is a quality company that provides quality goods and services for the wonderful people who are Pennington/Bass clients.

This profile could have been written about me and what I have done, but what *we* have done is far more important and hopefully more interesting.

Where do we go from here? We don't know precisely, but wherever that is, it will be done with great joy, excitement, integrity, and with the firm belief that excellence in financial planning can be achieved by a dedicated company in a small city in West Texas and all lands contiguous to us.

GARY L. PITTSFORD
PRESIDENT

G. L. Pittsford & Associates, Inc.

FINANCIAL CONSULTING & WEALTH MANAGEMENT

6081 EAST 82ND STREET, SUITE 11
INDIANAPOLIS, INDIANA 46250
317-849-9559

Profile of Gary Pittsford

After spending four years in the investment industry selling all the products that were available in the late 1960s and early 1970s, I decided to stay in the investment industry but operate differently. I did not want to sell investments and receive commissions because I could sense that clients did not totally trust me because I was about to receive a commission. Also, I wanted to help everyone with whom I came in contact with all of their financial affairs, not just the ones that I could get paid on.

The public needed help in handling their complicated financial affairs, and I knew that my highly trained clients had not been educated in all forms of finances. Therefore, I decided to help my clients with all of their financial decisions and provide that service for a fee rather than for a commission. I wanted to become a financial planning consultant rather than a stock broker. These decisions made me feel better about the way I dealt with my clients. Obviously, people wanted someone to talk to who was not selling something, and this would give me an excellent way to attract a lot of clients. In the early 1970s, this was an unheard of approach, but it was something that I was very comfortable with.

An additional problem that I had in the early 1970s was the lack of formal education in the technical financial planning consulting areas. Basically, I spent several years working with the most qualified people I could find and learning from everyone I could learn from, in all phases of this business.

Now, 11 years later, I realize that I have chosen an occupation that will require constant study in all financial areas. I find it hard to believe that, being a small-town farm boy, I would wind up in this complicated and fascinating profession. Nowadays, Purdue University and many other schools actually provide a college degree in financial planning. Our firm has already hired two college graduates in this area, and in the future we will undoubtedly hire more. This summer, for the first time, we even had our first intern working in our firm learning this profession from the inside out.

Today, our firm has 10 employees, and we work with more than 200 clients in 20 states and four foreign countries. Our clients come from all walks of life and have all sorts of professional backgrounds. About one third of our clients are corporate executives for Fortune 500 companies; another third of our clients are professionals, such as doctors, dentists, lawyers and architects; and the final third of our clients are owners of closely held businesses.

We work with our clients on a fee-only consulting basis and help them in all areas of their finances. Our job is very similar to that of our client's family doctor. We help our clients with all of their financial aches and pains year in and year out and meet with them constantly throughout the year. But, if a special problem comes up, we call in a specialist to solve that problem. Then we continue to monitor and work with that client in future years.

Our company receives two types of fees. We charge hourly consulting fees for working with our clients on their normal year-in and year-out financial questions. Each of the partners in our firm has different billing rates; they all are responsible for keeping track of their time. The second form of income that we have is from investment management fees. Many clients ask us to help manage their retirement plans or their personal portfolios. For this investment management service, we charge a percentage fee, which is very similar to the fees charged by most investment management firms in the country.

During the first four or five years, I worked with all types of clients, while trying to build my firm. After approximately five or six years, I found that my satisfied clients were bringing new clients to me at a rate faster than I could handle. Our firm started growing so fast that I had to move it to larger facilities and hire additional people rapidly.

Today, we do practically no prospecting at all and are very fortunate to have a steady stream of new clients wanting to work with our firm. At this time, in the financial planning industry, there are very few established firms providing our types of services, while there are a very large number of potential clients wanting someone to work with. This gives us a very large number of potential clients from which to choose. I realize and hope other people realize that in the future there will be more competition, and it will not be as easy attracting clients as it is today.

Another thing that has happened through the years is that we have constantly improved the quality of our client base. Over the last 11 years, we have constantly worked with increasingly higher-income individuals. Today we work with clients who have incomes of at least $100,000 or more a year and assets of $400,000 to $500,000 or more.

In the future, we plan to expand all phases of our business and concentrate our client base more in the Midwest. We will probably start opening branch offices in the near future in order to create a presence in the various cities in which we want to acquire more clients. We will continue to hire good, qualified college graduates; we will continue to perfect our in-house training program for upgrading those college graduates into assistant financial planners and, ultimately, senior financial consultants.

The type of person who enjoys working with complicated financial problems and being with and helping people should seriously consider this profession as a career. Because this is a complex profession, the frustrations are high, but the rewards in helping clients are even higher, making all the hard work and long hours worthwhile. It is especially gratifying to work with clients who not only pay us fees for our long hours, analysis and recommendations, but also say "thank you" after they have seen what we have developed.

This is a profession whose time has come, and I encourage people who are considering it to proceed with a commitment to it. I wish everyone who reads this book much success! What we receive from our clients is in direct proportion to how much we give them.

Profile of Robert Poage

At about the time Loren Dunton was forming the IAFP, I was making a major career change. In October of 1968, I resigned my career contract with a major Eastern life insurance company. This was a serious decision because it meant saying goodbye to a substantial renewal account built up over nine years of very hard work. I had to; I wanted to become a financial planner, but this life insurance company (as was true of most others at that time) would not permit me to hold a securities license. You will soon recognize the irony of this fact.

Thus, I launched my new career, and looking back, it seems so simple now. Tax shelters were running rampant, and the laws were very lenient compared to today. It was exciting and fun to plan and save a client thousands of dollars with sometimes no out-of-pocket expenses or even an actual gain in cash flow.

The part of the game that wasn't simple then, and it still isn't, is when is an investment a good investment?

Financial planning as a profession was just evolving. The IAFP came to the rescue. It was the only organization that would provide some guidance and direction to this exploding industry. I didn't join right away, even though the president of our local chapter had an office right across the hall. Somehow I just didn't seem to fit in. I was a "life insurance agent." Even though I was embracing the concepts of complete financial planning, I was still at odds with most who came out of the mutual funds industry. Most IAFP members were ex-mutual funds salespeople in the beginning and had fixed and unyielding views of life insurance.

What a change the past 16 years has brought! The IAFP membership now comprises stock brokers, life insurance agents, accountants, attorneys, wholesalers of products, university graduates with degrees in financial planning, and even those who are simply aspiring to financial planning.

The real shocker, though, is how the life insurance industry has suddenly embraced financial planning. Most of the major Eastern life insurance companies are even changing their names, taking life insurance out of them. When they answer the phone, you wonder if you dialed the wrong number—even at the same company that wouldn't permit me to have a securities license 16 years ago!

Well, so much for history. My practice is a non-fee, commission-only practice. Although I do sell tax shelters and other equity investments, I tend to operate as the motivator, investigator, planner, coordinator, etc. The term "captain of the estate planning team" has been used to describe the designed role of the life insurance agent in the process of estate planning and working with the attorney, accountant and trust officer. I play a similar role in financial planning. I want to conduct the fact-finding interview, determine the objectives, draft the plan, and then work with others in implementing the plan as required. I'm a specialist. I'm a life insurance agent and a doggone good one—one of the best—and I'm proud of it. I can never hope to be as knowledgeable and competent in all of the other areas of financial planning. Therefore, I need to draw on and utilize the strengths of others, and I attempt to do so. The ideal solution for me is one of teamwork.

It's been a great experience, and I'm even more excited about the future of *what will become a profession* in spite of all our problems and challenges today.

ANDREW M. RICH
CERTIFIED FINANCIAL PLANNER
MS - TAXATION

146 Manetto Hill Rd.
Plainview, N.Y. 11803   (516) 433-0828

Profile of Andrew Michael Rich, MS, CFP

There are few professions as rewarding as financial planning. One minute you are dealing with investments, the next with taxation, the next with insurance, and the next planning for a college education. I am, of course, very proud to be a financial planner.

At the end of 1980 I left a very safe and secure position as a senior U.S. Customs inspector at JFK Airport to start my own practice. However, the career switch was not that difficult, since I had built up a part-time tax practice while obtaining my masters degree in taxation. The day I opened my office I had 125 clients.

Four years later, things have certainly changed. My little one-person firm has grown to 16 employees, including full- and part-time associate planners. We stress intense quality and personal service, and we are aimed toward the heart of the middle-income market.

Today middle-income clients need financial planning. The key is to deliver high-quality services and products at a reasonable cost. This, of course, becomes difficult to achieve if you need to spend hours interviewing, analyzing, and writing plans. As a result, our firm offers a financial review: a one-on-one session or series of sessions designed to analyze a client's financial needs and implement solutions as soon as possible. Middle-income clients need hand holding and solutions, not an in-depth case analysis. We, in effect, try to balance between overkill (providing the client with too much planning for too much money) and underkill (not providing enough essential detail). Most financial reviews cost from $100 to $500. We offer also per-hour counseling at $75 an hour and full financial plans for $750 and up.

In order to service the middle-income market fully, each January to April we take off our financial planning hat and convert to a tax preparation firm. At present, the firm prepares about 400 tax returns.

Besides a masters degree in taxation from Long Island University, I hold a Bachelor of Arts degree in economics from Queens College of the City University of New York. I am also an adjunct assistant professor of financial planning at New York University. On the professional side, I have completed the Certified Financial Planner designation at the College for Financial Planning and am a member of that school's adjunct faculty.

I feel, however, that my most important achievement thus far has been writing a book. *How to Survive and Succeed in a Small Financial Planning Practice* was the first book written for the professional market on how to set up, run and be successful in a small financial planning practice. A financial planner must not only be involved within his or her own practice but should also serve the professional community toward building the image, quality and professionalism of financial planners.

J&R

Judy & Robinson
Securities, Inc.

1155 Crane Street
Menlo Park, CA 94025

(415) 321-4305

Gilman G. Robinson
Certified Financial Planner

Registered for Security Transactions with
Judy & Robinson Securities, Inc.

Profile of Gilman Robinson, MBA, CFP

In 1964, while employed as a senior research engineer, I completed my MBA degree and then decided to enter the investment business full time. A primary reason for this change was that the investment business offered the opportunity to determine my own working schedule and also to meet, share, and work with individuals from many different walks of life. On the other hand, I had felt that engineering provided a very restrictive environment for me. Meeting a variety of individuals provided a stimulating environment and the opportunity to share and work with many different individuals. In addition, the business offered the opportunity to work more or less than the standard 40-hour week, while at the same time being rewarded solely for my own efforts without the establishment of a salary by another individual.

In 1971, I joined R. LaVern Judy in a firm that subsequently became known as Judy & Robinson Securities, Inc. We were able to offer a broad line of investment products, and I was involved in counseling clients on all types of financial matters.

When first meeting Loren Dunton and hearing him speak in San Francisco concerning the formation of the IAFP, I was impressed with the logic of his discussion. I was overjoyed with the formation of an association of financial planners, since the financial planning approach was one that I had personally adopted. In 1971, four of us joined to form the first financial planning chapter in the San Francisco area— investment business was very difficult during those early years, and few people in the business were interested in hearing about a new organization with the idealistic concept of providing comprehensive financial planning. In those days, we were fortunate if eight members from the San Francisco Bay area were present at a meeting! Lou Jamieson of the Franklin Funds supported the local chapter with both time and money and also provided a meeting room for the San Francisco Association. It is indeed rewarding to see several hundred people in attendance at a Bay Area Regional Conference and several thousand individuals at a national conference.

The College for Financial Planning was also an outstanding concept. I was honored to teach what I have been told was the first formalized class for Part One of the CFP, and I was a graduate of the second CFP class. Currently, I am serving as a member of the Board of Regents of the College for Financial Planning, and as Chairman of the NASD District Conduct Committee for District 2N.

The firm of Judy & Robinson Securities, Inc. has prospered, and the majority of my activities involve the active management of the firm. However, in the early 1970s I began teaching a class in the adult school to be of service to individuals and also to obtain more exposure as a financial planner. Subsequently, the majority of my clients currently come from personal referrals and from people who attend the estate planning class I continue to teach.

Judy & Robinson Securities, Inc. is a registered investment advisor, and consequently is able to offer investment management services and financial planning services as well as securities transactions. We have installed two IBM XT computers and are currently utilizing the IFDS computerized program. This service, coupled with the use of quality investments to implement the financial plan, assures that our clients are well served.

It is indeed an honor to be part of the organization, the formation, and now the ongoing success of the financial planning movement.

Cardinal Financial Planning

M.G. SAHR, Ph.D., CFP
Admitted To The Registry Of Financial Planning Practitioners

10855 Lee Hwy · Suite 200 · Fairfax, VA 22030
(703) 385-8040

Profile of Morris G. Sahr, PhD, CFP

My entry into planning came via the financial products industry. The major problem with products themselves is that they are confusing. They are confusing to the buyer and, sometimes, they can also be confusing to the seller. The confusion comes from duplication and hundreds of changing elements within these products.

It was under this umbrella of confusion that I joined the little-known band of men and women who were becoming involved in the IAFP. At the time I started the Washington, D.C., chapter, I also opened a firm with a small association of professionals to bring order out of chaos for our clients. I knew that we had to be paid for our services and that it would not make sense to have a cadre of specialists sitting around waiting to assist someone with a problem. After 32 years in the nation's capital, I knew where to find the persons who could provide help for a client when it was needed. That is how Cardinal Financial Planning came into being. It evolved with a set of different names, but its purpose is simply to find a road map and the best route for the client in meeting his or her objectives and staying with that client for all related needs, including implementation. You can write the best plan in the world, have it well documented, and provide top experts in any given field, but if you don't sell the appropriate product for the intended objective, then you really haven't helped the client. Also, if you do not provide the tax planning and preparation of the client's tax returns, then you aren't really standing behind your client.

The commissions are generally regulated or are the prevailing ones in the community. Our fees are based upon the complexity of the work we are asked to perform. Most of our fees are really paid for by the tax reduction that is included in the plan.

Our clients come from a wide variety of economic backgrounds and professional accomplishments. For the Washington, D.C., area, they would be thought of as:

- two-income families;
- mostly in the 40- to 50-year-old age bracket;
- an average of two children in their teens;
- total income between $60,000 and $110,000; and
- average net worth of $250,000.

We seek three-year plans with all of our clients, that is, written plans that account for maximum growth within stated risk/reward ratios. Projections are for a period of three years from completion of the initial plan. Likewise, the tax planning comports to comply with the investment schedule. Annual monitoring is an integral part of the relationship. Our clients must see a beneficial relationship when they retain us. As a result, more than 90 percent of our clients remain with us. Most of those who do not remain either move totally from this area of the country or believe they are sufficiently able to absorb the functions that were being performed by Cardinal. Even then we feel we have succeeded, because they have learned to help themselves. The result is satisfaction and the personal referrals from this client; and this is how our business grows.

Profile of Edward H. Savant, MBA, CFP

Prior to entering the financial planning field, I had worked for our family business and also for 10 years at an electronics company. My first job at the electronics company was as a chemist, but soon the lab no longer was a challenge and I moved into sales. Due to the success of the company and my contribution to that success, I soon moved through the sales managerial positions and was transferred to the home office as general manager for its research sales division.

In all my previous endeavors, there seemed to be a missing link. That link was the knowledge of not only doing the best job for my company, but also how to best handle my personal finances. Even after completing my MBA at the University of Chicago, I felt I was not prepared to answer basic questions about my own personal finances. I had learned ways to improve my management style, my ability to understand and apply accounting concepts, to understand the marketing techniques to help a company improve its profit. But I was never told what to do with my own finances.

My search for an answer led me to accountants and attorneys who just didn't seem to understand my problems and who were unprepared to answer my questions. I was assuming they would know everything about finances. Now I realize they are specialists, and I was placing a responsibility on them that they were not prepared or trained to accept.

We all have some event that changes our direction in life, and when my father died in 1976, I realized that there had to be a more efficient way to manage our financial affairs than he and I had. I quickly turned my attention to handling our family's financial affairs, and the rapidly growing financial planning profession seemed to have the answers.

I attended an IAFP meeting in Chicago in 1979 and knew I had found a starting point for not only answering my questions but also for a new career—even though I hadn't been looking for a new career.

I plunged into a total immersion program to prepare me to help people with their financial plans. I completed all the necessary regulatory licensing and completed the CFP program in 1981. Since that time, through education and experience, I have learned not only how to handle my personal assets but have assisted a number of people (my clients) to improve their situations.

I hope also to complete the Chartered Financial Consultant and Chartered Life Underwriter programs next year. Because the world of information for the financial planner is vast, I am always striving to obtain new credentials and educational experience. Every year, I am required by several of the professional organizations to which I belong to acquire a minimum of 30 hours of continuing education. I have always exceeded that.

My credentials and experience qualify me as a member of the Registry of Financial Planning Practitioners and the Institute of Certified Financial Planners. I teach undergraduate courses in investments and accounting at Saint Xavier College and adult education classes at Purdue University. I will also be teaching classes for candidates seeking the CFP designation.

I obtain most of my clients by referrals from existing clients. I also conduct a number of seminars and classes on financial planning subjects, and people attending these often are looking for a planner. Many decide to use me as their financial planner.

Most of my income is derived from commissions on products that I use to help my clients solve their problems. In addition, our investment advisory company does financial planning for a fee. Our fees are based on the amount of time it takes for us to develop the plan. Typical fees currently run from $750 to $5,000. We offer prospective clients a two-hour interview, at no cost or obligation, during which we can evaluate their situations and determine if a plan needs to be done and, if so, what the costs and benefits would be. Of course, this gives the prospective client a chance to evaluate our services without having to make a commitment.

We try to help the client to understand that the value of a plan is not just the finished written product, but rather it is the process itself. The identification of goals, problems, solutions, final recommendations, and implementation provide an opportunity for organization and motivation that would not likely happen otherwise.

Because the financial planning profession is so new, a great deal of organization, education and guidance is needed to develop and maintain its integrity and status. Many people are working to see that this happens. The

IAFP is the moving force in the industry and is setting the standards for excellence that planners must adhere to. I am committed to my profession. Several years ago, I helped establish a local IAFP chapter and am currently serving as president of that chapter. Our goals are to provide an atmosphere where planners can grow professionally and be constantly reminded of their ethical, moral and legal responsibilities to their clients.

I have conducted my financial planning practice with the goal of helping as many people as possible and therefore concentrate on those individuals with incomes between $35,000 and $75,000. Of course, I have clients who are millionaires and some who are blue-collar workers. I try to serve each with regard to his or her needs. My goal is to help people significantly improve the probability of reaching their financial goals.

HARRY SCHEYER
CERTIFIED PUBLIC ACCOUNTANT
714 CRESTBROOK AVENUE
CHERRY HILL, NEW JERSEY 08003

609-424-3318

Harry Scheyer, CPA, CFP

Several years ago I recommended to the partners of a large local CPA firm where I was employed that we develop a special department to service a unique group of clients. I felt that these clients could be more effectively serviced if they were put under the professional management of a small group of individuals devoted to their special needs. I was given permission to develop and staff the professional services department of the firm. The department's basic philosophy was to service fully all types of professionals such as physicians, dentists, architects, attorneys, insurance agents, and their related firms.

In developing the services for this department, I wanted to be most effective in the areas where these clients were not getting the proper attention. One of the main areas where many professionals needed help was in personal financial planning, especially in the area of maximizing the professional practice and individual resources for the achievement of their goals. This need required a higher level of service from their CPA, other than accounting and tax compliance. It was in this context that I developed financial planning services for my clients.

As a CPA with 15 years of accounting and tax consulting experience, I realized that a successful financial planner required a certain expertise in many areas. Therefore, to be better informed and skilled in providing comprehensive financial planning services, I completed the CFP program. This educational background, coupled with an intense personal continuing education program, has provided me with the necessary skills and level of knowledge required to successfully perform the financial planning engagement.

A few years ago I started my own CPA firm. One of the important services it provides is comprehensive financial planning. This service is provided on a very personalized basis and tailored to the needs of the client. Since many of my clients have practices or businesses of their own, I have also introduced important business-related planning into the total financial planning process. I find that if this aspect is not carefully considered, then the personal planning may be developed on a poor foundation. I believe my CPA background provides a strong skill in this area.

Once a plan is prepared and agreed upon, then an implementation schedule is prepared. It is my responsibility to help the client follow through on the planning. As a fee-only planner I am bound by state law and professional ethics from selling any financial product. Therefore, if specific financial products are purchased, I generally use the licensed professional of the client's choice. Otherwise, we may use an individual or firm that I recommend.

Finally, I believe one of the important roles of a planner is that of quarterback—someone who is able to coordinate and work with other financial professionals for the client's welfare. In all my planning engagements I try to work with all the key professionals in the client's financial life. I consider them important resources in providing a successful financial plan.

Currently, most of my financial planning clients come from my existing accounting and tax practice. I am also beginning to receive individual referrals from outside my practice. Although most of my clients come from the professions, I do have small business owners and individual clients.

I take pride in working with clients in all stages of financial life. For example, I have helped physicians plan their retirement program and recently divorced women adjust to their new financial lifestyle. I am always involved with young professionals trying to adapt to the financial demands of a growing family. Every individual client provides a unique challenge and opportunity to be of important service.

I am a fee-only financial planner. Therefore, I am compensated for only my time in providing independent, objective financial planning services. My initial meeting with a prospective client is at no charge. After the meeting, if we mutually agree to proceed, I provide an engagement letter outlining my services requested with approximate time and cost. When the client approves and signs the letter, then my services begin. I also provide continuing financial plan updating at various intervals agreed upon. I believe the financial plan is just the beginning of an important long-term relationship.

As a practicing CPA, I recognized many years ago the importance of objective, comprehensive financial planning services for my clients. Today, this service is greatly needed and sought after by prudent individuals. I have therefore educated myself and organized my practice to help meet that demand.

UNDERWOOD FINANCIAL PLANNING, Inc.

Robert J. Underwood
Certified Financial Planner

400 Century Park South • Suite 218
Birmingham, Alabama 35226 • 205/823-1120

Profile of Robert J. Underwood, CFP

I was very fortunate in my early life to be raised in a World War II housing project where everyone had approximately the same income and standard of living. My second fortunate break was when I became a diabetic at age 25 and could no longer continue in my former occupation.

Our family insurance consultant (debit agent) informed me that I could no longer purchase life insurance without paying three to four times the normal costs because of my health impairment. I had to search for some way other than the cash surrender value of life insurance in which to build my fortune. I found that a contractual plan mutual fund would most likely serve my needs, or so I was told by the salesman who sold it to me. As was the norm for the time, I was hired by the manager to sell mutual funds. This was very interesting in that he was going to make a salesperson out of me when, five years prior, the Army was going to discharge me because of a speech impediment. But having sold me a contractual plan, it was easy for him to sell me on the idea of becoming a sales rep and passing a test to become a Registered Representative.

So, in September 1963, I started on my financial service or planning career, selling contractual mutual funds to anyone who would hold still for 15 to 20 minutes for me to make my presentation. In 1965, to diversify my product line further, I received my life insurance license. At that point I felt I knew everything there was to be known about financial planning. In July

1965 I was appointed district manager. How about that? Two months insurance licensed, and now a district manager.

In September 1967 I became a broker-dealer and life insurance holding company which also had tax incentive investments. With all these various and sundry products, I began to become increasingly concerned, because there were so many things I could do for a client that I did not get paid for; those things I did not receive compensation for had a tendency to be put on the back burner. If I made a healthy commission on something else, I would give clients the added value of transferring income of the family members and things of that nature.

So January 1, 1969, I restructured my practice to charge a fee for my analytical service and a commission for implementing the normal financial planning recommendations. In 1973, it appeared to me that more and more people were asking for objective advice and my recommendations. Since this often did not require an investment on which I would receive a brokerage or commission, I made the decision, in January 1974, to do fee-only planning.

In May 1974, I cancelled all my securities licenses, all my insurance licenses, real estate licenses, and any other licenses that would legally entitle me to receive a commission or brokerage. This was directly against the advice I received from all of my friends and associates, who of course were commission salespeople and Registered Representatives. The unanimous advice at that time was, "Do not go into the fee-only financial planning business, because you cannot make a living at it. No one has ever done it before, and clients don't care whether they pay a commission or a fee."

One of the first problems we faced in the fee-only business was the outrageous fees that general partners put in the programs for themselves and the high commissions paid the sales force. No one, at the time of structuring the investment, represented the investor. With absolutely no experience, I decided to negotiate on behalf of the individual investors with the general partners. I found that if I told the general partner I would raise all the funds among my investors, the general partner was glad to eliminate the 10 percent sales charge and another four to five percent out of his or her fees, because he or she did not have to work with the due diligence officers, do the branch office seminars, and what is known in the business as "wholesaling." So my investor who was going to put $10,000 in some real estate investment for example, now only needed $8,500 to get into the same venture. His or her income tax deductions were exactly the same as if he or she had put in $10,000 (because commissions are not deductible).

The next major impact on my practice was learning that the truly good real estate managers were normally not good fund raisers. If I could raise all the funds with my investors, obviously they could have more time to do what they did best, which is manage the real estate. In 1976 I structured for my investors the first totally no-load real estate investment that I had ever seen.

The general partner, for buying the property, assigning his or her contract to a limited partnership, received *zero* up front. This was a high-risk investment, but the general partner made absolutely nothing unless the investors made the following:

1. 100 percent of their money back, and
2. a seven percent per year preferential return.

From that point on, 75 percent would go to the investors and 25 percent to the general partner. So much for the creation of real estate investments. My clients, however, needed more than real estate, and how was I going to find the other investments and services they would need?

I had spent much time on volunteer committees, boards, associations, directorships, and was on the ICFP Board for three years and on the IAFP Board for six years. One of the associations that I am most proud of, being a co-founder, is the Society of Independent Financial Advisors, a group of fee-only financial planners who meet a minimum of three times a year just to share ideas and to help each other's growth. The foundation of this organization made the practices of fee-only financial planning so much easier. We do not have to rely just on our own expertise, but have a mastermind association of like-motivated planners in which to fill in the gaps in our educational background.

In our little group, we have a financial planner who only works with oil and gas entrepreneurs. He therefore screens all oil and gas investments. I have now found that you do not need to be an expert in every field, but as John Naisbitt said in *Megatrends,* "high touch, high tech is the only way for the future," just as fee-only financial planning is the way of the future, as *real* financial planners do not take commissions.

VENITA VANCASPEL, CFP
PRESIDENT

VANCASPEL & CO., INCORPORATED
FINANCIAL PLANNERS
STOCKBROKERS, MEMBER PSE

1300 POST OAK BLVD.
22ND FLOOR
HOUSTON, TEXAS 77056
(713) 621-9733

Profile of Venita Van Caspel

I started in 1961 at a large brokerage firm that was a member of the New York Stock Exchange. It was difficult for me to get into the business because no one wanted to hire a woman. I began as a clerk in order to get in, and I studied on my own. After I'd been with the firm for six months, I asked to take the securities exam and passed. They let me become a broker, but I didn't get a draw—just a desk.

However, I found myself frustrated because I felt that I was not doing enough for my clients. I found that brokers were trying to get all of their clients' money into securities, and insurance agents were recommending whole life insurance policies as the solution for all their clients' money problems. CPA's were only calculating how much their clients owed on April 15, when it was almost five months too late to do anything about reducing tax liabilities. Even those few who had an attorney might not have so much as a properly drawn will, to say nothing of provisions for the reduction of estate taxes. There seemed to be a great need for a person or a team that was competent and caring to pull these diverse and fragmented elements together into a coordinated, functioning whole. There was a need for someone to sit down with clients and help them analyze where they were and where they wanted to be at a certain period in their lives, and to provide the directional help to enable them to arrive at their desired destinations.

I became convinced that this was a calling worthy of my life and talents. So in 1968, at a very low spot in the stock market when nearly all of the small brokerage houses were merging with the large ones, I left a large house to start a small one. It was a very scary move. You have no idea of the mass of regulations that entangle a brokerage firm, and the regulatory agencies make it especially difficult for smaller firms. But the move has gone well over these past years, and I have the satisfaction of knowing that I have made a truly worthwhile contribution to the financial future of thousands.

Our company gets clients from the seminars that I conduct, from referrals, and from people who have read my books. Our attendance comes from running ads in the newspaper, and the seminars are free of charge. Anyone who attends one can fill out a data sheet and obtain an appointment in our offices without charge. Consequently, our clientele have wide ranges of income, and represent a wide range of people. Some have low assets and annual incomes; others are in the millionaire category. I used to be surprised that millionaires would come to a public seminar, but after thinking about it, I decided that I gave these people an opportunity to evaluate me objectively as a financial planner. After attending one of my seminars, they could decide if they thought that I knew what I was talking about. And fortunately, many of them apparently thought that I did, because they asked for an appointment and are now clients. Our seminars have grown in attendance, and so has the number of clients. I feel that we have done our bit to raise the level of financial independence in Houston and the surrounding cities.

Until recently, we had been commission-only brokers, and that had worked satisfactorily for our clients and ourselves. Now, we have started our registered investment advisory firm, Van Caspel Wealth Management Inc., and we are now offering in-depth written plans on a fee basis. We expanded in this direction because we felt that there was a need for it. I think that this change is going to enable us to offer more services and more in-depth planning. It seems to me that there is a trend in the industry to move in the direction of fee-based planning right now. Adding fee-based planning offers a little more flexibility. It enables us to be more thorough and to do the research that needs to be done on the different products.

The world of finance is getting more and more complex, and as our clients have more complicated financial affairs, they need us to monitor and track their investments. We will also be doing a more in-depth study of our clients' casualty, life and disability insurance, and will do estate planning, tax planning, and tax flow analysis. The investment advisory firm is of course completely separate from our brokerage firm. Once the written plan is delivered to the clients, they are free to implement it with whomever they choose.

Thus, our clients have a choice of using fee-based planning or commission-based planning. We don't have a minimum net worth or income requirement to do business with our broker-dealer division, Van Caspel & Co., Inc. To get the maximum benefit from Van Caspel Wealth Management, you probably would have to have an income of at least $150,000 and a net worth in excess of $500,000. If you are working on the broker-dealer side, we require you to fill out a data sheet, schedule an appointment, and come into our offices. We usually have a portfolio analysis done before you arrive, and we usually also analyze your life insurance policies. We set aside two to 2½ hours for every appointment, and generally, one or two appointments are all that will be necessary if we are working on a commission basis. For the investment advisory, it takes more time and more meetings to gather all the data.

As the years have gone by, our brokerage firm has grown, even though I have tried diligently to keep it small. In addition to our vice president and me, we now have 11 Registered Representatives, six of whom are on a commission basis and do financial planning. We do our own clearing, which is headed up by a registered principal. Our total staff consists of 25 people. Qualifications for the planners are that they have been in financial planning for a number of years and are dedicated, loving, caring people. We have a superb support staff; as a matter of fact, they are the real heart of our business.

In addition to my brokerage firm, I do some things that are just for fun. For example, I have a new PBS program, *Profiles of Success,* that has very little to do with financial planning, although it has a lot to do with success. It's produced in conjunction with the Horatio Alger Association and highlights people who have achieved a large measure of success under our free enterprise system. I enjoy doing this tremendously, and I think that some of my television work has helped to educate the general public about financial planning. My MoneyMakers series is in its fourth year on public television and is broadcast on about 170 stations nationwide. Right now, we are setting up the funding for Moneymakers V, to continue the series. I feel that I have a mission of letting everybody know about how important financial planning is, and that these programs, as well as my books, can help people be aware of how they can become financially independent.

I started writing the books at the request of Weldon Rackley, the executive editor at Reston Publishing, formerly editor, a subsidiary of Prentice-Hall. He had attended one of the three-session seminars that I conduct regularly in Houston. The next day, he wrote me a letter that said, "You have the ability to make a difficult subject simple. Have you ever considered writing a book?" I had indeed considered writing a book, but I probably never would have done so if he had not signed me up and kept after me until the book was finished.

After my first book, *Money Dynamics,* came out, a marvelous thing happened. Stock brokers and financial planners across the country began to recommend the book and give it to their clients. Colleges began using it in their classrooms, financial writers began to praise the book, and bookstores began to have brisk sales. The sales increased with my second book, *The*

New Money Dynamics, which became a top seller. After that, my third book, *Money Dynamics for the 1980s,* hit the *New York Times* Best Seller List, as did my fourth book, the *Power of Money Dynamics.* Altogether, the sales have reached over 800,000 in hardcover. This has been a gratifying experience for me, because I now feel that I've helped raise the level of financial independence across our nation and abroad. My fifth book, *Money Dynamics for the New Economy,* will be available in 1986. Because the world of money changes so rapidly, and Congress keeps changing our tax laws, I must keep writing to keep you current.

There are a number of reasons why I think my books have filled such a great need. First, most of the people in this country are financial illiterates. Even the rudiments of money management are not taught in our schools. We continue to spend millions of dollars teaching our youth how to earn a dollar, but not what to do with it once it has been earned. There is a real dearth of knowledge about money. Second, my books are written in lay language from experience, not theory. They are based on problems that I have seen during my daily counseling with clients in my office. I have been able to see what these clients need, and I have worked to coordinate their investments in order to match their needs to their tax brackets, the amount of money they have to work with, and the time they have to reach their goals. My books are how-to books; they are also motivational books that attempt to get readers to act on their newly acquired knowledge. After reading my books, someone might glowingly say, "I can be financially independent." But unless they act, I will have left them right where they started.

I think there is a growing awareness of financial planning. I can tell from the number of people who attend the seminars and the wide range of their income levels. There is more written in the press today about financial planning; IRAs are now available, and that gives people a choice as to how they will put their money to work. More women are working; they have more money to invest, and they are taking a more active role in managing family finances.

I don't think there is anything that I don't like about the profession. I find that my hardest job is to keep informed of all the different investments that are available. The financial planning industry is changing very rapidly as we enter the new economy so aptly described in *Megatrends* by John Naisbett. It should be an exciting new era in this profession, and I'm delighted to be a part of it.

FINANCIAL PLANNERS / INVESTMENT ADVISORS

Lewis J. Walker, CFP
404-452-7222

SUITE 608 • 4340 GEORGETOWN SQUARE • ATLANTA, GA 30338

Profile of Lewis J. Walker, MBA, CFP

In thinking about how I became a financial planner, the word *serendipity* comes to mind. Becoming a financial planner was an evolution of sorts—a process of experience combined with education.

Perhaps I was fortunate in being introduced to the concept of total financial planning in my mid-30s, after a wide variety of educational and work experiences. A broad frame of reference is useful in understanding the myriad backgrounds of clients and in empathizing with their goals, objectives, problems and aspirations.

My formal education was heavily salted with economic and business-related subjects: Bachelor of Science in Foreign Service (international business), Georgetown University, Washington, D.C., 1960; MBA, Marketing, Northwestern University, Chicago, 1971. Prior to entering the financial services field in 1972, full-time work experience consisted of $4^{1}/_{2}$ years as a military officer, U.S. Air Force, followed by six years in management with two major airlines.

Most financial planners of today did not start out with that end in mind. Whether they entered the investment field as a stock broker, insurance agent, or real estate agent, the objective was the same—find a customer and sell a product.

My case was no different. As a vice president of marketing for a local Atlanta real estate syndicator, my task was to find investors to buy properties offered by the company. My first reaction to the idea of financial planning back in 1972 was that it had to be a better way to sell.

Financial planning probably started with insurance agents, stock brokers, and others like myself, looking for a sales tool. But along the way, a more powerful concept developed. Don't start with a product looking for a customer, start with a *client*. (There is a difference between a customer and a client). Identify the goals and objectives of the client, solve problems, and create a plan: a financial road map. Once the plan is implemented, ongoing progress should be monitored with periodic updates, strategy sessions, and additional planning as required. This was a strong idea, the nexus for an emerging concept of total financial planning, and a departure from the traditional sales process.

A British friend of mine, in remarking on changes in the English financial services industry, said, "You cannot institutionalize the entrepreneur." Most successful financial planners today are entrepreneurs, men and women who saw the power in a client-oriented financial planning process, and who struck out on their own to make it work.

My firm started on that premise in 1976, as a partnership, and later incorporated as Walker, Cogswell & Co., Inc., in 1982. Walker, Cogswell & Co., Inc., is a registered investment adviser with the Securities and Exchange Commission and is our planning and investment advisory arm. The principals of the firm, Lewis J. Walker, MBA, CFP, and Austin C. Cogswell, MBA, CFP, as well as other planners with the firm, are registered representatives with Investment Management & Research, Inc., a securities broker-dealer with a range of full Wall Street services. This relationship creates unusual flexibility.

Planning is done on a fee basis with a fee schedule related to time, complexity, and the client's net worth. The client may elect to have planning only effected by Walker, Cogswell; he or she is under no obligation to obtain products through our brokerage sources. Most clients elect to do so, however, for reasons of convenience and efficiency. In dealing with securities, especially in tax incentive investments such as real estate, energy, equipment leasing, etc., products obtained from our sources are of known quality. Due diligence, a process of evaluating investment offerings, becomes easier when you deal with the same people over time. Financial data are obtained more easily, and tracking and reporting are simplified. A key point, relative to objectivity, lies in the fact that we are not employees of a Wall Street firm. We are free to pick and choose those products that precisely fit the client's goals. We are not compelled to sell or merchandise any particular product to a client and may reject those items that are counter to our own investment philosophies or those of the client.

In similar fashion, we are independent of any insurance company and free to shop on behalf of clients. We understand hard asset investments and "hard money" and have sources for client needs relative to gold, silver, other precious and strategic metals, numismatic coins, etc. International business and investment services are provided through affiliations with a top international financial planning firm in London, England.

As noted, clients are free to select any broker for implementation of specific recommendations in a financial plan. All brokers charge a commission for their services; should a client choose to execute corresponding transactions through Registered Representatives associated with the firm, planners may receive the usual and customary commissions or fees from such transactions in their capacity as licensed agents. Fees and commissions are disclosed as required by applicable federal and state regulations, and are competitive.

Clients of the firm generally have above-average income (total family income of $50,000 or more), with growing net worth. The firm works with a variety of clients, including two-income career couples, key executives, closely-held-business owners, professionals, pre-retirees, and retirees. Walker, Cogswell also advises a number of pension plans, including corporate plans, HR-10 plans for the self-employed, and holders of IRAs and IRA rollover accounts.

Clients come from referrals from existing clients and other professionals such as CPAs and attorneys, but also as a result of seminars, media publicity, and a company newsletter. A monthly (11 issues per year; July-August are combined) investment commentary and financial planning newsletter, *The Walker-Cogswell Commentary*, goes to more than 1,500 clients, potential clients, subscribers, and media representatives. Pass-on readership appears to be high, triggering inquiries about our services.

Media exposure has been helpful. Members of the firm have been interviewed by a number of local, regional, and national publications. Radio and television interviews have been frequent, also creating consumer awareness.

The firm conducts a variety of seminars for clients and the public at large, covering a range of financial topics. Seminars also are conducted on behalf of various universities as well as several corporations, largely dealing with pre-retirement financial planning.

All planners in the firm must have heavy academic backgrounds, and advanced degrees are common. All planners must be Certified Financial Planners (CFPs) or be enrolled in the College for Financial Planning. We must educate consumers to the wisdom of prudent planning and wise investing; our commitment to continuing education is high. All planners must attend various seminars and courses throughout the year and meet the continuing education requirements of the Institute of Certified Financial Planners.

Philosopher Ernest Renan once said, "The real people of the future are those whose roots are nurtured by a profound respect for the past." The history of the growth of true conceptual financial planning portends exciting future prospects for the investor, the professional financial planner, and the capital formation process in the United States.

(213) 557-200

LEWIS M. WALLENSKY
CERTIFIED FINANCIAL PLANNER

1901 AVENUE OF THE STARS / LOS ANGELES, CALIFORNIA 90067

Profile of Lewis M. Wallensky, CFP

I graduated with an honors diploma from Oakwood Collegiate Institute in Canada, continued my education at the University of California at Berkeley, and recieved my bachelor of science degree in 1961. My major area of study was industrial management and engineering, with emphasis in business economics and operations research.

After military service, I accepted a management position with Pacific Lighting Corporation in sales and marketing of its energy division, Southern California Gas Company.

In 1967, after developing a personal interest in investing, I became licensed in insurance and securities. At that time I was approached by a company doing financial planning for physicians and dentists. United Professional Planning was one of the pioneers in the soon-to-be-defined field of financial planning. They developed the financial clinic concept where the client's data were analyzed by specialists in law, insurance, securities, taxes and business, after which a formal report was presented to the client. They were quite successful and opened offices in several locations throughout the western United States. I was promoted to director of sales training for the new financial consultants hired and was forced to learn all aspects of financial planning.

In 1970, I realized my interests focused on working directly with clients, and soon thereafter I opened my office in Beverly Hills, sharing offices with a CPA and an attorney. The firm became Lewis Wallensky and Associates, and I hired an administrative assistant. We began to service clients from all walks of life, not just physicians and dentists, over the next several years. The client base expanded to include other professionals, executives, middle management, working women, and single parents. We still service many of these clients, including my first client, and in some cases the second and third generations of the same family.

In 1974 I learned about the IAFP and joined the Los Angeles Chapter. Desiring to contribute to the financial planning profession, I became president in 1975 of the L.A. Chapter. While I was president, the chapter grew from 80 members to 250. It was a rewarding experience and taught me that the more one contributed to his or her profession, the better job one can do for the clients. I was asked to serve on the national board of the IAFP and was elected for the consecutive terms 1978 through 1984.

During this tenure I served as chairman of a number of committees. In 1976 and 1977 while president of the Los Angeles Chapter, I initiated a study group for the CFP curriculum. The program from the College for Financial Planning is usually a minimum of 18 months, but our group completed the course in nine months, and those who finished received the CFP designation in June 1977.

Since we recommend the income continuation philosophy to our clients, I received the Registered Health Underwriter designation in 1980. In 1983, I was one of the first to be admitted to the Registry of Financial Planning Practitioners.

Each of these designations requires continuing education requirements, and I have met each of them, every year.

As a result of my activities and interest in financial planning, I have been consulted by many sectors of the media and have been invited to speak at various professional and consumer organizations. I have lectured at the University of California—Los Angeles Graduate School of Management, the University of Southern California Extension, and other colleges and universities over the years, including Loyola Marymount University. Audiences for other lectures have included the Stanford University Graduate Business School Alumni Association, San Diego Medical Symposium (10 years), Western Periodontal Society, American Commercial Lawyers, Certified Court Reporters Symposium, and Legal Administrators Society. I have also lectured on Making Marriage Work (financial aspects) and conducted the preretirement training for UCLA.

Some of my professional lectures have included being a featured speaker at the national convention of the IAFP for three years, lecturer at the conferment exercises for the College of Financial Planning, speaker on client service for three years, speaker at the Life Underwriters Society, and speaker at numerous IAFP chapters throughout the country.

For the past several years I have been on the advisory board of the University of California for the Professional Designation Curricula, where I also teach the last course on the curriculum—the Financial Planning Practicum.

For the past year I've served as chairman of the board for the California Association for Financial Planning and appeared before a state hearing testifying in favor of regulating financial planners.

Over the years my articles have appeared in many magazines and newspapers, some of which include *Money, L.A. Magazine, Los Angeles Times, Cosmopolitan,* and *Dynamics Years.* I have also made television appearances on the Dinah Shore Show and NBC Nightly News.

Having worked with clients over the years, we have seen that financial planning has helped them attain their goals. It has been gratifying to see our clients' children graduate from college, clients retire with their dignity preserved—all by our proper planning. Our company now includes two junior planners, administrative assistants, and college trainees, who all work together on the firm's clients. It has been our intention to have a long-term relationship with the clients and assist, not only in solving their current problems, but also in defining the other issues that will be important to the client. This is done by taking a client-oriented personal interest in the needs of the individual. Even as we have grown, we still care about our clients from all fields and income levels.

Newcastle Financial Group, Inc.
Securities through FPI Securities, Inc.

Henry L. Whiffen
President and
Chief Executive Officer

P.O. Box 2400, Provo, Utah 84603
Toll Free (800) 453-1466 In Utah (801) 224-9800

Profile of Henry L. Whiffen, MA, CFP, CLU, ChFC

My career in the financial planning services industry started 22 years ago after graduation from college. I started as an estate planning specialist dealing with a clientele consisting of business owners, professionals, and executives. From that I moved into covering seven specific areas of service: estate, income tax, investment, insurance, cash flow, business, and employee benefits planning. Until 1981 I was president of Whiffen, Kindschi & Associates, a financial planning firm in southern California. In 1981 I co-founded Newcastle Financial Group, which is now the largest comprehensive financial planning firm in the nation, with more than 85 employees and clients in every state of the nation plus several foreign countries.

The philosophy of Newcastle consists of several specific points. One, we believe in developing long-term relationships with our clients. This long-term relationship is built upon professionalism, integrity, a commitment to service, a genuine caring for each client, and recommendations that are truly in the client's best interest.

A second aspect of our philosophy is that while we deal with both economic strategies and investment products, we feel that the strategies should come first. Therefore, we attempt to help our client to rearrange his or her affairs in such a manner as to achieve the greatest tax savings and help obtain his or her financial objectives through these strategies, before looking to products that will help save taxes, i.e., tax advantaged investments. Too often, in our opinion, advisors look first to products as the best means of reducing taxes, when strategies might do an even better job.

The third part of our philosophy is that we believe in an approach that emphasizes economics rather than tax shelter. Too many people focus on lowering their taxes rather than building their net worth. As a consequence they end up as tax shelter "junkies," constantly keeping the tax down but never building their economic net worth. We feel that if the main emphasis is on building that net worth through strategies that make sense, the client is much better served in the long run.

A fourth aspect is that the financial services field is very diverse with many areas of specialty. No one person can be an expert in all of those areas, but many clients need expertise in several areas. Rather than taking the one-man band approach, we have developed an orchestra with specialists in many various areas, which enables us to provide a full-service financial clinic. Our group consists of several affiliated companies with specialists who address the many areas of planning strategies, plus others who thoroughly oversee and approve the many categories of investments, insurance and other products we provide to our clients.

Because of the uniqueness and size of our team, we also function in a supportive role for other financial planners who do not have our staffing resources. We provide planning services as well as investment products on a wholesale basis to the planner.

By way of credentials, I have a bachelor's degree with emphasis in accounting and business management and a master's degree in financial planning. Other qualifications include Certified Financial Planner (CFP), Chartered Life Underwriter (CLU), and Chartered Financial Consultant (ChFC). Licenses include registered investment advisor, registered general securities principal and registered financial and operations principal. These are with the Securities and Exchange Commission and National Association of Securities Dealers. Also held are licenses in real estate; life, health and disability insurance; property and casualty insurance; variable annuities; and commodities. Affiliations and activities include membership in the Institute of Certified Financial Planners, International Association for Financial Planning and the Ethics Committee of that organization, Estate Planning Council, head of the Financial Planning Program for the Million Dollar Roundtable, National Philanthropic Affiliates (a think-tank on charitable/estate/income tax planning strategies). I am also part-time instructor in financial planning at Brigham Young University, which was the first university in the nation to have an undergraduate major in financial planning.

Other activities have included many guest speaking engagements throughout the nation, conducting seminars in this country and several others, being a guest on TV talk shows and radio shows, and writing articles for national publications.

RESOURCE MANAGEMENT, INC.

A Financial Planning Corporation

JUDITH ZABALAOUI

CHIEF EXECUTIVE OFFICER

3510 CAUSEWAY BOULEVARD, SUITE 506 • METAIRIE, LOUISIANA 70002
504/833-5378

Profile of Judith Zabalaoui, MBA, CFP

These days I'm frequently introduced as a "pioneer in financial planning." It seems a bit exaggerated for someone in practice only 10 years, and yet it is an accurate description of anyone who has practiced financial planning 10 years or more.

Ten years ago when I began my practice, I didn't realize I was pioneering. The concept for financial planning seemed to me such a valuable service that I was sure the financial services industry and the public would immediately seize upon it. I was wrong.

The financial services industry was made up of insurance companies, banks and brokerage firms, and none was interested in this new kid on the block, "financial planning." The public hadn't yet learned about financial planning. Once they did, however, they loved it.

Such was the environment when I decided to go into private practice as a financial planner.

I had earned my MBA degree at Loyola University of the South, where I taught economics and finance for five years. Part of my teaching responsibilities included a noncredit course in financial planning for the adult education division. Teaching those courses made me determined to build a financial planning practice.

There were, however, no corporate career opportunities 10 years ago for financial planners.

One evening, tired of hearing me bemoan the fact that there simply were no openings, my husband, a wonderful man and my greatest booster, said, "Honey, if you're so convinced there is a demand for the service you've trained yourself to provide, rent an office, hang out a shingle, and go for it." That's how I got into the financial planning business.

After I had been in business for about three years, I made three significant decisions.

First, I decided to build a firm—not just a practice. I set out to build a firm of a few, highly trained, highly competent financial planners offering a high level of personal service.

Second, I decided to work with a small clientele of individuals who have annual income of at least $150,000, and/or investable assets of at least $100,000. Because of this decision, most (but not all) of our clients are entrepeneurs or self-employed professionals.

Third, I decided to write a book for the self-employed. That book is now a best seller called *How to Use Your Business or Profession as a Tax Shelter*.

I made these decisions for several reasons, all based on my personal philosophy of how financial planning should be practiced.

I believe financial planning should be a team effort. At Resource Management we believe that every client belongs to the firm. We assign a primary planner to every client who is responsible for the work done on behalf of the client, but the thinking, strategy and research are a team effort. Our clients get the benefit of all the talent our firm has to offer.

I also believe that clients want and deserve:

1. a high level of personal attention;
2. to have their tax bill monitored and controlled without resorting to whatever ridiculous tax shelter is available; and
3. to have their net worth grow each year.

These expectations should be addressed in the context of an individually designed written financial plan, and should be achievable with tax and investment strategies that are based on reasonable and moderate tax write-offs and yields.

My firm is fee only. We earn no commissions, nor do we accept "research fees" from companies whose investments we recommend to our clients. My professional staff is highly trained in tax and investment strategy. We are all college graduates (most of us hold masters degrees), and all are Certified Financial Planners. My partner, Randy Waesche, and I are in the IAFP Registry of Financial Planning Practitioners.

Delivering personalized financial planning by highly talented practitioners is costly and dictates that our service be offered to those individuals who need and can afford the service we offer. Experience has taught us that it takes about $150,000 or more of annual income and/or investable assets of at least $100,000 to justify our fees. Our fees are variable but normally average 2 percent to 2 1/2 percent of gross annual income, plus an 0.9 percent asset management fee on assets our clients ask us to manage.

We are completely committed to the multistep financial planning process. The process we employ is:

1. Data Gathering: To learn all factual information about the financial situation of a new client and to discuss the financial objectives, goals, concerns, and risk/reward tolerance level. We take time to learn enough about a client to design a plan that fits a client's needs.

2. Preliminary Plan Design: To form the conceptual design of the plan. Our financial planning professionals outline possible alternatives to addressing the client's needs.

3. Concept Session: To outline and explain the proposed conceptual approach to the financial plan and invite the client's response.

4. Final Plan Design: To prepare the written financial plan, which formalizes those concepts upon which the client and the financial planners have agreed.

5. Recommendation Session: To review the completed plan in detail—outlining what is to be done, why, the probable effects, when, how, by whom, and how funded.

6. Implementation: The financial planners work with the client and/or the client's CPA, attorney or other advisers to create and install documents and to select and purchase investments.

7. Monitoring: The primary financial planner meets with a client as necessary to update him or her on the results of the implementation of the financial plan, and to monitor ongoing needs.

By the way, my years of delivering financial planning to our clients has made me even more of a believer than I was 10 years ago. Financial planning can create a significant improvement in a client's financial life.

Some Final Notes

Not everyone who claims to be a "financial planner" is, unfortunately. Nevertheless, for the most part, financial planners are sincere and conscientious practitioners who enjoy a real satisfaction from preparing individual plans (often with the help of a computer) to assist people accumulate or conserve assets and achieve specific financial goals.

To all of them, a special and personal thanks. I may have founded this profession, but I surely couldn't have done so without their dedication and support.